Whitman East & West

THE IOWA WHITMAN SERIES

Ed Folsom, series editor

Whitman East & West

New Contexts for Reading Walt Whitman

EDITED BY ED FOLSOM

UNIVERSITY OF IOWA PRESS Ψ IOWA CITY

University of Iowa Press, Iowa City 52242
Copyright © 2002 by the University of Iowa Press
All rights reserved
Printed in the United States of America
http://www.uiowa.edu/uiowapress

The publication of this book was generously supported
by the University of Iowa Foundation.

Printed on acid-free paper

Library of Congress
Cataloging-in-Publication Data
Whitman East and West: new contexts for reading
Walt Whitman /edited by Ed Folsom.
p. cm.—(The Iowa Whitman series)
Includes bibliographical references and index.
ISBN 0-87745-821-9 (cloth)
1. Whitman, Walt, 1819–1892—Criticism and
interpretation. 2. Whitman, Walt, 1819–1892—
Appreciation—Asia. 3. Whitman, Walt, 1819–1892—
Knowledge—Asia. 4. Books and reading—Asia.
5. Asia—In literature. I. Folsom, Ed, 1947–. II. Series.
PS3238 .W46 2002
811'.3—dc21   2002021133

02 03 04 05 06 C 5 4 3 2 1

FOR ROBERT STRASSBURG,

who has put Whitman's words to work in his music,

his teaching, and his life. His performance of his

Whitman compositions in Beijing literally set the tone

for the "Whitman 2000" conference.

Contents

Preface

Whitman East and West is the result of a remarkable collaboration between Peking University and the University of Iowa and among scholars from Asia, Europe, and North America — an international collaboration that led first to a major conference on Walt Whitman held in Beijing in October of 2000 and then to the publication of this book of essays that grew out of the conference. The working premise of the project was that scholars from different parts of the world working on the same author had a lot to teach each other, and this proved to be even more true than we had initially imagined.

While the book grows out of a Whitman conference in China that brought together scholars from the East and the West, not all of the essays focus on Whitman's Chinese connections. When Whitman and China do get discussed in these essays, the topic is not so much what Whitman thought of China (though that topic does get addressed in a couple of the contributions) but more what China thinks of Whitman and, beyond that, how China has over the years thought *with* Whitman, engaging him on political, poetic, and philosophical levels and melding his work with Chinese traditions. Encountering a Walt Whitman absorbed into Chinese poetic traditions will be surprising and revealing for most Western readers. The essays in this volume that do not focus on Whitman and China deal with him in equally striking new contexts. The fact that the participants were presenting papers to scholars who usually are half a world away led everyone to imagine Whitman in unfamiliar contexts, and so this collection of essays reconfigures Whitman's work in multiple new ways.

Whitman himself did not have a lot to say about China, but in 1891, a little over a year before he died, in a conversation with the Philadelphia playwright Francis Howard Williams, he did speak of China. In this unpublished interview now housed in the Library of Congress, Whitman contrasted China with the United States in a potentially illuminating fashion. Here are Whitman's words as transcribed by Williams:

> The Chinese don't progress. They can originate but can't apply. We Americans apply too fast. We're too damnably smart and if we don't

look out it'll be the ruin of us. We cultivate intellect unduly. All things in moderation. My motto is: Be Bold! Be bold! But don't be too damned bold! We are refining the intellect so fast that we are emasculating our raw material. What's the use of a highly finished work of art if it's got no guts? Culture is well enough, but we mustn't forget the guts. If we don't look out we'll become the damnedest, sneakingest, hoggishest, selfishest people under the sun.

From one perspective, Whitman's comments sound like cultural stereotyping in his contrasting of the two cultures, but it is important to notice that his analysis characteristically assigns negative qualities to both the Chinese and American cultures. Unlike some of Whitman's comments on race and culture where he subscribes to then-popular notions of racial and cultural hierarchies, here Whitman bemoans the loss of a wholeness of identity that might emerge if China and America were to form a new hybrid, a union of divergent beliefs and discrete talents. It's vital to be able to originate and conceive, and it's also vital to be able to apply and develop, but to focus only on "finish" is to end up repressing the liberatory originating impulse, and Whitman was afraid that's what he saw happening in late nineteenth-century America. Originating and applying can occur only if cultures blend, learn from one another, recognize both what they have to offer and what they have to learn from others. *Whitman East and West* sets out to create a new mix of critical insights from the West and the East, to originate new ideas about Whitman and apply those ideas to a fresh understanding of the poet as we read his work again in a new century, a century of expanding international awareness.

There were a number of excellent papers at the "Whitman 2000" conference that we were not able to include in this collection. Hongkyu A. Choe (Chung Ang University in Seoul, Republic of Korea) spoke on Whitman studies in Korea and examined the Korean view of Whitman's concept of God; Duan Jingwen (Sichuan International Studies University, China) offered a comparative study of Whitman and the Chinese poet Xin Qiji (1140–1207); Tom Greer (Ouachita Baptist University, United States) examined the "priestly role" of the poet in "Song of Myself"; Huang Zongying (Peking University, China) discussed the "I" and "you" in "Song of Myself"; Ronald R. Janssen (Hofstra University, United States) looked at the legacy of Whitman in the era of globalization; Lin Fengmin (Peking University) compared Whitman and the Arabic poet Gibran Khalil Gibran

(1883–1931); and Tim McGee and Ellie Gebarowski-Shafer (Worland High School and North West Community College, Wyoming) explored Whitman's pedagogy and global education in the new millennium.

There are many people and organizations to thank for their support in making this international collaboration possible. At Peking University, the Department of Scientific Research and the College of Foreign Languages made major financial contributions, and Hu Jialuan, dean of the College of Foreign Languages, was involved in the planning of the conference and offered invaluable advice. Liu Shusen of the Department of English served as associate director of the conference and handled all the arrangements in Beijing. At the University of Iowa, sponsors of the conference included the Arts & Humanities Initiative, the College of Liberal Arts and Sciences, the Department of English, the *Walt Whitman Quarterly Review*, and the Center for Asian and Pacific Studies. Special thanks to David Skorton, Iowa's vice president for Research; Linda Maxson, dean of the College of Liberal Arts and Sciences; and Jay Semel, director of the Obermann Center for Advanced Studies, for their support and advice. And thanks, too, to Kevin Wyne, my research assistant, for help in the initial editing and formatting of the essays.

Introduction

Whitman East and West

ED FOLSOM

When I was in Beijing for the first time, in October 1997, my taxi went by a kind of graveyard for Mao statues. There, in a vast field, were stacks of dismembered statues of the former chairman, decapitated heads lying in a long row and concrete torsos piled up like logs. I had heard of monument cemeteries all through Eastern Europe and had seen news reports about the wholesale dismantling of Lenin statues in the former Soviet Union. But China was still very much under the control of the Communist Party, and Mao Zedong remained very much a presence in Beijing, with his preserved body still on display in the very heart of the capital city. His giant portrait still towered over Tiananmen Square, looking down from the wall of the gate leading into the Forbidden City.

It was clear, however, that a significant change was under way, not as sudden as in Russia and Eastern Europe but every bit as inexorable: fewer and fewer statues, a gradually decreasing presence of the Maoist past. Now, throughout Beijing, there were new statues, life-sized sculptures of Colonel Sanders — looking suspiciously Mao-like, almost as if they might have been recycled from the statue cemetery — in front of each of the numerous Kentucky Fried Chicken outlets that now dotted the Chinese urban landscape. When I saw these multiple Colonel Sanders standing there with one arm raised as if to inspire the masses, I knew for certain that this vast nation was undergoing another of its periodic great changes. One of my cab drivers told me he had counted fifty-two McDonalds restaurants in Beijing. When I asked my Chinese hosts how they felt about the invasion of corporate America in the form of fast-food chains, many of them countered my derision by insisting that they loved McDonalds — safe and clean "foreign" food (no hepatitis there, one person told me) served in a comfortable environment and arranged according to Western notions of space (you could claim your own booth!).

As I lectured on Walt Whitman and American poetry at three universities in Beijing, I realized that, like Mao, Whitman, too, was being deconstructed and reconstructed in China. The world's most populous nation was in the process of inventing a new Whitman for a new era, an era of American fast food and English-language billboards and visits by Bill Clinton and Colin Powell, the era of the 2008 Olympics in Beijing, an event that no doubt will further accelerate the already frenzied remaking of that huge city into an urbanscape that will seem more familiar, less foreign, to Western visitors when they arrive there for the summer games.

Walt Whitman is already part of the blended cultural landscape in China. The American poet has had a Chinese existence for nearly a century, and during that time he has been variously cast as a force of modernism, an innovative influence in Chinese literature, a Western socialist poet, a celebrator of the laboring class, and, most recently, a conduit to contemporary American culture and democratic reform. Many Americans recall what appeared to be a model of the Statue of Liberty that Chinese students constructed during the Tiananmen Square demonstrations in 1989: there was a lot of debate then about whether that statue was actually inspired by America's symbol of freedom or whether it grew out of Chinese traditions and only looked like the Statue of Liberty to American eyes. What is less well known is that a new mass-market edition of Whitman's *Leaves of Grass*, translated into Chinese by Peking University professor Zhao Luorui, was due to be released just as the student demonstrations got under way; the Chinese government intervened and delayed publication because someone in the party leadership deemed it unwise to make the American poet of democracy suddenly available in a new translation just when prodemocracy student demonstrations were threatening to get out of hand. Whitman at that moment seemed like dangerous fuel on the fires of democratic reform.

When Zhao Luorui's masterful translation finally appeared in 1991, Whitman's entire *Leaves of Grass* became available for the first time in a unified version by a single translator, and, as China began a decade of opening itself to Western investment and of absorbing a kind of controlled capitalism into its socialist machinery, Whitman became a safe, amenable, and instructive foreign author for Chinese consumption. It was during this period that Zhao Luorui invited me to come to Beijing to lecture — she had been bringing Whitman scholars, including James E. Miller Jr. and Kenneth M. Price, to China for several years — and I was honored to have a turn. Professor Zhao was seriously ill by the time I arrived in China, however, and I spent a memorable afternoon with her in her triple-room at a Beijing hospital. She apologized for being unable to attend my lectures, and she expressed a strong desire — it turned out to be her dying wish — to gather a large group of Whitman scholars from around the world for a conference in Beijing. What better place, what better time, and what better poet, she said, than Whitman in China in 2000?

Less than three months later, Zhao Luorui died. She was eighty-five years old. Her former student Liu Shusen, who had become a faculty member in the Department of English at Peking University (where Professor Zhao had taught for many decades), joined me in pledging to make her dream of a Whitman conference in Beijing come true. Professor Liu and I worked for two years to put the conference together; raise funds; invite the top Whitman scholars from North America, Europe, and Asia; and make preparations for "Whitman 2000," the first major conference on an American poet to be held in China. "Whitman 2000" took place in October 2000 at Peking University and was dedicated to the memory of Zhao Luorui, known in the United States (where she received her Ph.D. at the University of Chicago in 1948) as Lucy Chen.

Such a conference, we decided, would send just the right message about how American literature, like so many other parts of American culture, was undergoing a significant change as it became a global commodity and was read in increasingly unfamiliar contexts. American studies has in recent years begun to shed its provinciality, to realize, for example, that American writing itself comes in more than one language (among the unstudied vast archives of American literature are the countless poems, novels, stories, and memoirs written by immigrants in a variety of languages) and to realize that American writers now exist in more than one culture. Walt Whitman has many cultural lives and resides in many languages: he exists not just in American contexts but in German ones, and French ones, and Indian ones, and Chinese ones. As he once said when referring to his photographs, there are "new Walt Whitmans every day," and one of the exciting prospects in American studies today is the search for the variety of figures and forces Whitman has become as he has been absorbed into other cultures and translated into other languages. What cultural work does Whitman do in China, and how, and in what ways does it relate to the cultural work he is doing in the United States or in South American nations or in African cultures? The conference in Beijing and this volume of essays emerging from that conference confirm that, as the twenty-first century begins, American studies has gone international. The essays in *Whitman East and West* contribute to the emerging realization that American culture is never simply an export but rather always a hybrid. The challenge in more and more cultures is to define the *mix* instead of the separate ingredients.

M. Wynn Thomas suggests in his essay in this volume that, as American literature goes global, multiple Whitmans are appearing, and we are now entering the era in which we need to study both "Whitman" and "whitman": "Whitman," the historical figure embedded in nineteenth-century American culture, the "American poet," and "whitman," the "world poet" who has been radically realigned as various cultures have adopted him into their own literary traditions and have read his works in defamiliarizing contexts, so that "whitman" does different cultural work in, say, China than "Whitman" does in the United States. The terms "Whitman" and "whitman," Thomas notes, parallel the postcolonialist distinction between English (the language of England) and english (the variety of versions and dialects spoken around the world): Whitman and whitman, like English and english, are related, but they are often, at least initially, unrecognizable to each other. Tracking the ways that Whitman becomes whitman contributes to the globalization of American studies.

The essays in this volume, then, set out to read Whitman in unconventional and defamiliarizing ways. M. Jimmie Killingsworth examines Whitman in the light of recent work in ecocriticism, a kind of literary analysis that intervenes in the ecological challenges facing the world today and that investigates the ways the natural world is portrayed in language and the ways that language shapes (and even creates) the world. Killingsworth proposes that Whitman offers both negative and positive examples for ecocritics, and he makes the provocative claim that "the discursive counterpart of using good judgment in protecting the environment may well be the act of keeping the personifying impulse in check, refusing to allow the demons of human imagination to fully possess the earth and reduce it to a mere reflection of self-serving desires." The metaphors we use to talk about the world have serious ecological implications, and Whitman's figurative language — particularly his personifications of nature — becomes the focus of Killingsworth's incisive reading of Whitman's "Song of the Redwood-Tree," "Passage to India," and "This Compost."

Walter Grünzweig places Whitman in the emerging new field of "normality studies," the exploration of how in democratic cultures the "average" comes to be the new norm of behavior, replacing the old stable and unchanging religious, philosophical, and political tenets and rules of behavior. As norms get defined through such tools as polling and behavioral studies, we become increasingly aware that separating the "normal" from the "abnormal" is always a judgment call, contingent on how wide a range of behavior we agree to include in the "normal" category. Normality therefore becomes a fluid concept in a democratic society, one that allows for the expansion of norms (including norms of sexuality). Grünzweig argues convincingly for reading Whitman as the inventor of the "divine average" concept of evolving democratic expanding norms: "The chief American bard of democracy," says Grünzweig, "is indeed one of the earliest voices of normalism."

Kenneth M. Price examines Whitman in yet another context, that of film studies, as he tracks the nearly century-long use of Whitman in movies. Starting with an examination of Whitman's own protocinematic poetics, Price looks at the way filmmakers from D. W. Griffith through Paul Strand and Charles Sheeler and on up to contemporary directors like Peter Weir, Jim Jarmusch, Richard Kwietniowski, and Maria Meggenti have appropriated Whitman and used him as a kind of shorthand for a variety of cultural meanings — including, recently, unconventional sexual relationships revealed in what Price shows to be an intriguing cinematic series of Whitman-inflected love triangles. Joel Myerson develops another visual context for understanding Whitman by entering the field of children's literature and looking at how children's books have packaged Whitman's poetry, especially the poetry that conventional sensibilities might find inappropriate for young readers. Myerson analyzes how children's book illustrators often create a visual context for encountering Whitman's poetry that encourages readers not to imagine too vividly what Whitman's poetry is portraying. In making Whitman safe for kids, Myerson argues, illustrators of children's books often create a picture-substitute for the poetry that serves to interpret the poem before the reader has a chance to interact with Whitman's actual words. Price and Myerson remind us that many people first encounter Whitman mediated by someone else — a filmmaker or illustrator who has a particular angle on the poet and who frames our understanding of Whitman in that way. Many more people encounter Whitman in popular films like *Dead Poets Society* or *Bull Durham* than in actually reading *Leaves of Grass*, and young people who become serious adult readers of Whitman may have their views of the poet shaped by versions of the poems that they encountered in children's books at a particularly impressionable age.

Robert K. Martin turns to another kind of mediation of Whitman, this time Mark Merlis's novel called *American Studies*, a book that offers a fictionalized account of critic F. O. Matthiessen's life and the ways American culture forced him to silence and disguise his sexual identity in the witch-hunt atmosphere of the United States in the 1940s. Matthiessen's conflicted attitudes toward Walt Whitman, complicated by his own identification with the poet's sexuality, are recorded in his classic study *American Renaissance* (1941), where, Martin says, Matthiessen camouflages his true feelings toward the poet's homosexuality and does so with tragic consequences: "Matthiessen produces not a democratic canon but a white male New England canon. Whitman is the only exception — as a working-class man from Brooklyn. But Whitman was canonized by being washed clean, his rough edges filed down. Whitman could not be eliminated, but he could be straightened up." The ironies and paradoxes of Matthiessen's life abound and are the subject of Merlis's powerful and evocative novel. Martin captures the hope, the failures, and the tragedies of Matthiessen's relationship to Whitman. He also captures the complexity of Merlis's suggestions of what was at stake personally and culturally in Matthiessen's relationship to Whitman: "Is there a danger in taking Whitman's idealism too seriously? Surely less danger than in having no dream at all."

Sherry Ceniza takes up the issue of Whitman's sexuality and proposes that it is time to go beyond reading Whitman as simply or essentially a gay poet. Now that we've reached consensus about his homosexuality, Ceniza argues, it is important for us to underscore the fluidity and absorptiveness of his sexual imagery, an imagery that does not exclude heterosexuals but that calls for an open accessibility for all readers. "Finally, it's the ties between people, not the difference, that Whitman's poetry enacts," Ceniza reminds us, and so exclusionary biographical readings of the poetry on any basis undermine the very democratizing foundation of Whitman's work. It is that democratizing foundation of Whitman's work that Betsy Erkkila probes in her essay on Whitman and "public love." Erkkila, too, argues for going beyond narrow sexual readings of Whitman's poetry, but without giving up the radical, marginalizing, and erotic aspects of what she has elsewhere called Whitman's "homosexual republic." Grounding her study in Jürgen Habermas's notions of the "public sphere" as a place where officially repressed behaviors can be openly discussed, Erkkila reads Whitman's poetry as an enactment of the making public of private emotion, the space where the personal becomes the political. The U.S. Constitution, Erkkila observes, "left unresolved when it did not overtly repress or privatize the role that passion, eroticism, sympathy, and love might play in bringing about what Whitman would later call democracy as 'a living union' among people," and she goes on to explore "the relations among public emotion, homoeroticism, political union, and democratic theory" that form the most radical elements of Whitman's work.

M. Wynn Thomas comes at Whitman's radical elements from a different angle, arguing that the poet exhibits two often-contradictory attitudes — a localized and usually contemptuous response to the democracy he saw operating around him and a more universalizing and millenarian imagination of what a future perfected democracy would look like. Depending on which version of America Whitman was dealing with at any particular time — the degraded present or the transformed future — his tone changed from anger to hope, from confrontation to conciliation, from revolutionist to representative. Whitman as "revolutionary representative" is Thomas's subject, and he examines Whitman's "rich, volatile mix of feelings about contemporary democratic America" that leads to the poet's "unpredictable switches of mood, sudden changes of direction, and baffling somersaults of opinion." Thomas's examination of this tension — between Whitman's gradualist evolutionary faith in a historical progression toward democracy and his edgy, impatient revolutionary urge to bring democracy into being through confrontation — leads him to speculate about how we might connect a thickly historicized Whitman with a more diffuse global "whitman," how "Whitman, the 'local' New York poet, became (and continues to become) whitman, a poet of the world."

Thomas's test case — Whitman's reactions to New York mayor Fernando Wood and Wood's factional politics based on pitting immigrant groups against each other — relates nicely to Guiyou Huang's essay, which offers an overview of Whitman's attitudes toward immigration. Like Thomas,

Huang grounds Whitman's work in the specific historical period when America became the nation of immigrants. Huang analyzes Whitman's poems focusing on Asia and Asian immigrants and finds them keys to the understanding of "Whitman's evolving definition of America as a new nation and new race." Huang identifies another contradictory but finally reconcilable tension in Whitman, who, as he "remaps the composition of America, acknowledging its changing demographics and anticipating the birth of a new people by embracing and intermingling all world races," becomes "both an Ameri-centric and internationalist poet."

Huang wrote the long essay "Whitman in China," in *Walt Whitman and the World* (Iowa City: University of Iowa Press, 1995), an essay that offers an invaluable summary of the century-long absorption of Whitman in Chinese culture, and he also has written a book-length study, *Whitmanism, Imagism, and Modernism in China and America* (Selinsgrove: Susquehanna University Press, 1997), which develops his analysis of Whitman's influence on Chinese poets. Among the important observations that Huang makes is that Whitman has been viewed in China as an "import," as a writer the Chinese "picked up . . . of their own accord" (*Whitmanism* 57) — unlike, say, Shakespeare, who was viewed as a British export, imposed on China by British missionaries — and thus a writer who was readily absorbed into modern Chinese literature. Huang also claims that "Whitman's aficionados have included the supreme leader of modern China, Mao Zedong" (55). Huang's evidence for this claim is largely circumstantial: the poet Guo Moruo, who (as several essays in this volume demonstrate) was clearly influenced by Whitman before 1920, and the writer Lu Xun, who read Whitman in the late 1920s, both were "Mao's friends and political allies and the top literary figures in the nation" (71). Thus, Huang argues, we might conclude that Mao — a poet himself and a writer about vernacular poetry — was made aware of Whitman and approved of his work. Huang's claim initiated some heated debate at the "Whitman 2000" conference, where some Chinese scholars denied that Mao knew about Whitman or that, if he did, it was in any way significant. The debate was illuminating, because it seemed to reflect a desire by some Chinese scholars today to distance Whitman from the Maoist past (when he was read as a kind of Western socialist) and reclaim him as a modernist literary pioneer, more important for his formal innovations and his pantheistic philosophy than for his political ideas.

As we turn to the Chinese contributions to this volume, Western readers will find Whitman cast in even more unfamiliar and disorienting contexts. Names familiar to most Chinese readers — Chuang-tzu, Wang Yangming, Guo Moruo, Hu Shi, Zong Baihua, Tian Han, Xu Zhimo, Wen Yiduo, Liu Bannong, Ai Qing, Gu Cheng — will be new to many Western readers, and yet, in the Chinese context, these are the names most often invoked to describe Whitman's influence and impact. Western scholars are accustomed to hearing about historical events like the Fugitive Slave Law, the Civil War, Emancipation, Reconstruction, or the Gilded Age when they talk about Whitman, so it is surprising to find Whitman invoked in relation to a whole new series of events out of a whole different history — the May 4th period, the New Culture Movement, the Cultural Revolution. While many of the names and allusions in these essays are disconcerting to Western readers, perhaps even more surprising is what is *not* mentioned: Whitman's sexuality, for example, a key component of almost all the essays by Western scholars in this volume, goes virtually unmentioned by the Chinese scholars. Such divergent interests allow us to begin to discern the different kinds of cultural work Whitman does in the East and the West.

The major Chinese poet most clearly and directly influenced by Whitman is Guo Moruo, and he is the subject of three of the essays in this book — those by Liu Rongqiang, Ou Hong, and Wang Ning. Liu Rongqiang offers a detailed examination of Guo Moruo's career, including Guo's introduction to Whitman's work while he was living in Japan in the years just before the May 4th Movement in 1919. This phase of Chinese history was initiated by demonstrations that took place across the nation in protest of the pro-Japanese Treaty of Versailles. Beginning as a student demonstration in Beijing, the May 4th protests spread to workers, and a cultural and intellectual revolution was suddenly under way, influenced by Marxist ideas and leading to the New Culture Movement. Out of this movement emerged the Chinese Communist Party, as well as leaders of both sides of the Chinese Civil War. (The continuing importance in Chinese culture of the May 4th Movement was seen when the Tiananmen Square student prodemocracy demonstrations in 1989 began on May 4th, exactly seventy years after the original demonstrations.) In 1939 Mao Zedong called the May 4th Movement "a new stage in China's bourgeois-democratic revolution against imperialism and feudalism," leading to a revolutionary coalition of "the working class, the student masses, and the new national bourgeoisie" (*Selected Works of Mao Tse-tung* [Beijing: Foreign Languages Press, 1967], 2:237).

Whitman's introduction into Chinese culture at this key historical moment is therefore a remarkable occurrence, and Liu Rongqiang tracks the biographical, historical, and aesthetic reasons for Guo Moruo's embrace of the American poet, which helped Guo become one of the most powerful voices of the New Culture Movement. Liu Rongqiang concludes that "if Guo Moruo had had no access to Whitman's poetry in the years before 1920, he would probably not have become so successful a poet, and he certainly would have become a very different poet." Ou Hong takes a different approach in analyzing Whitman's influence on Guo Moruo, arguing that Whitman served as an intermediary who reattached Guo to his Taoist roots in the ancient texts of Lao-Tzu and Chuang-Tzu. One aspect of Whitman that rarely gets discussed anymore in Western scholarship is pantheism, but all of the Chinese critics in this volume look to Whitman's pantheism as an important aspect of his poetic program. This is because pantheism's many forms share key ideas with Taoism and some Confucianism, and Ou Hong makes the case that Whitman influenced Guo Moruo via Guo's love of Chuang-tzu, the fourth-century B.C. Chinese philosopher who wrote the most important early book of Taoism. Guo's reading of Whitman in the years before the May 4th Movement stirred his childhood memories of Chuang-tzu's philosophy, and Whitman's pantheism returned Guo to Taoism. It is as if the American intervention of Whitman reattached Guo to the origins of Chinese Taoist thought (a circuitous international influence reminiscent of the way Thoreau's "Civil Disobedience" was exported to India by Gandhi, only to be reimported to the United States by Martin Luther King Jr. — U.S. civil rights protesters thus looked back to Thoreau via Gandhi).

Wang Ning adds to the story of Whitman's impact on Guo Moruo but also broadens the discussion of Whitman's influence to other modernist Chinese writers and discusses Whitman in terms of "the unique role he played in the process of China's political and cultural modernity as well as in the Chinese literary modernist movement." Wang Ning argues that Whitman's influence "has actually helped rewrite modern Chinese literary history, especially in terms of poetry," and notes that "Whitman was one of the very few Western writers who became regarded as Chinese cultural intellectual idols." Finally, Liu Shusen looks at Whitman's influence on the contemporary Chinese poet Gu Cheng, who, Liu argues, is "the poet whose indebtedness to Whitman is the greatest among his Chinese peers." Gu Cheng began reading Whitman in the 1960s and returned to him in the early 1980s; Whitman inspired the Chinese poet "in ways that demanded him to restructure the political, economic, and cultural contexts within which he worked." Liu offers a moving portrait of Gu Cheng's tragic life and his illuminating encounter with Whitman.

At the 1992 Whitman Centennial Conference in Iowa City, four senior Whitman scholars were honored as "Centennial Scholars"— Gay Wilson Allen, Roger Asselineau, James E. Miller Jr., and C. Carroll Hollis, all of whom had at the time been publishing on Whitman for at least forty years (in Allen's case, sixty years). In the eight years between that international Whitman conference and the "Whitman 2000" conference, Gay Allen and Carroll Hollis died, Allen just before *Walt Whitman and the World*, the book he and I were editing together, appeared. But Jim Miller and Roger Asselineau, now the senior figures in the field and two of the most respected names in American literary studies, both made the trip to China. Asselineau's first essay on Whitman was published in 1948 (not long after he had narrowly escaped a Second World War death sentence imposed by the Nazis for his aiding Allied airmen who had been shot down over France), and Miller's first essay on Whitman was published in 1955. Together, they have published a century's worth of illuminating commentary on Whitman, and they were honored at "Whitman 2000" as "Millennial Scholars." It was appropriate that they presented the first two papers at this conference, since Chinese society has always had a keen reverence for its honored senior members, and Miller and Asselineau demonstrated how energetic and vital their leadership of the field still is. Their essays serve as a frame for this volume, which begins with Miller's evocative tribute to Zhao Luorui, with whom Miller worked on her translation of *Leaves of Grass*. Zhao also shared with Miller the same surprising career-long fascination with Whitman and T. S. Eliot, two figures not often juxtaposed. Miller's recollections of Zhao set the tone for the essays that follow, initiating the dialogue between East and West, modeling the developing friendships between Chinese scholars and Western scholars, and honoring those from East and West who devoted major parts of distinguished careers to the understanding of Whitman. Asselineau's essay offers a fitting close to the book: after all the surprising contexts for understanding Whitman — from ecocrticism to public love to normalism to film to Taoism — Asselineau brings us back to the simple fact that Whitman's poetry is imagery and that whatever subjects we discover that illuminate this work, the one subject we can never forget is the resonance of the imagery, its fluidity and solidity, Whitman's ever-present water and his leaves of grass.

Introduction

Abbreviations

Quotations from Whitman's works are
cited parenthetically in the essays by abbreviations and refer
to the following texts:

LG
Walt Whitman, *Leaves of Grass*, Comprehensive Readers Edition,
ed. Harold W. Blodgett and Sculley Bradley
(New York: New York University Press, 1965).

LGV
Walt Whitman, *Leaves of Grass: A Textual Variorum of the Printed Poems*,
ed. Sculley Bradley, Harold W. Blodgett, Arthur Golden, and
William White, 3 vols. (New York: New York University Press, 1980).

NUPM
Walt Whitman, *Notebooks and Unpublished Prose Manuscripts*,
ed. Edward F. Grier, 6 vols. (New York: New York University
Press, 1984).

PW
Walt Whitman, *Prose Works 1892*, ed. Floyd Stovall, 2 vols.
(New York: New York University Press, 1963–1964).

WPP
Walt Whitman, *Complete Poetry and Collected Prose*, ed. Justin Kaplan
(New York: Library of America, 1982).

WWC
Horace Traubel, *With Walt Whitman in Camden*, 9 vols.
(Various publishers, 1906–1996).

Whitman East & West

"Poets to Come . . . Leaving It to You to Prove and Define It"

Lucy Chen, Whitman, T. S. Eliot, and Poets Unknown

JAMES E. MILLER JR.

The words of my title come from a short poem in the opening section of Whitman's *Leaves of Grass*, "Inscriptions," which reads in whole:

> Poets to come! orators, singers, musicians to come!
> Not to-day is to justify me and answer what I am for,
> But you, a new brood, native, athletic, continental, greater than
>   before known,
> Arouse! for you must justify me.
>
> I myself but write one or two indicative words for the future,
> I but advance a moment only to wheel and hurry back in the
>   darkness.
>
> I am a man who, sauntering along without fully stopping, turns a
>   casual look upon you and then averts his face,
> Leaving it to you to prove and define it,
> Expecting the main things from you. (*LG* 14)

I am aware, of course, that Robert K. Martin used this poem as an epigraph to his "Introduction" to the 1992 volume he edited, entitled *The Continuing Presence of Walt Whitman: The Life after the Life*, a pioneer volume in treating Whitman's sexual themes in the most open possible way, in both their frankness and complexity, opening new paths for Whitman readers and critics to explore. I place Martin's book alongside Gay Wilson Allen and Ed Folsom's 1995 collection of essays, *Walt Whitman and the World*, as two of the important works to appear on the Good Gray (or Good Gay) Poet in the

1990s. I mention these two works primarily to affirm that I follow their lead in exploring key aspects of Whitman's shaping influence.

The lines of Whitman's "Poets to Come" seem to come from a self-assured national poet and represent only one example of the many in Whitman's epic *Leaves of Grass* in which he confidently addressed the poets of the future. It should be noted, however, that he presents an expansive definition of "poets"— they are "orators, singers, musicians." And I would suggest that, by implication, Whitman is indicating that it would be these "poets to come" who could best literally translate him, or re-create him, for foreign readers. Many critics have affirmed that poetry simply cannot be translated, but I have always thought that if anyone sets out to attempt that impossible task of translation, it should not be scholars or critics but those who are poets in their own right. I would argue, in addition, that Whitman in "Poets to Come" was addressing, in his inclusiveness, the Chinese scholar/critic/translator/poet Zhao Luorui, known in America as Lucy Chen.

As you will see, I have composed this essay not only by looking over selected literary materials but also by searching through my half-faded memories of the past. Two of my Ph.D. students who wrote dissertations on Whitman came to Peking University to lecture, met Lucy, and wrote about her in the *Walt Whitman Quarterly Review*. David Kuebrich, a Fulbright Professor of American Literature in 1982–1983, published his piece entitled "Whitman in China" in the September 1983 issue.[1] Kenneth M. Price, some ten years later, lectured at Peking University and recorded an interview with Lucy in the summer/fall 1995 double issue, "Whitman in Translation." From Price's interview we learn that during the Cultural Revolution in China (1966–1976), which disrupted and uprooted many Chinese people, especially intellectuals, Lucy's home was ransacked, and books and manuscripts, as well as her Ming-dynasty furniture, disappeared. Although later many items were returned, one volume never reappeared: her "own book of manuscript poems."[2] In this essay, I shall discuss first Lucy Chen as I came to know her personally, and then I shall turn to the relationship of the two American authors she translated, T. S. Eliot and Walt Whitman. Her Chinese versions of Eliot's *The Waste Land* appeared in 1937 and of Walt Whitman's complete *Leaves of Grass* in 1991. She expressed her feelings to me about both of these American poets in our correspondence.

James E. Miller Jr.

My life has been intertwined with the life of Zhao Luorui. She took a Ph.D. at the University of Chicago in 1948 with a dissertation on Henry James. There she became known as Lucy Chen. I came to the University of Chicago in 1946 after four years' service in the army during World War II. I was in a hurry to finish my graduate work and took courses year-round, easy to do then because the University of Chicago was on the quarter system, with full offerings four quarters a year. I took my M.A. in 1947 and my Ph.D. in 1949, the year after Lucy took hers. I am surprised that I did not come to know her then, but I am sure that I had many of the same professors who taught her.

She herself has named some of her teachers in her introduction to her book of essays published in China in 1996 (perhaps one of *her* students will bring out an English translation in the future). Among those she named are E. K. Brown, Morton D. Zabel, James Hulbert, and Napier Wilt. I had courses with all these professors, and the classrooms were filled with the influx of veterans going to college on the GI Bill. It is even possible that I sat in one or more of the classrooms in which Lucy sat, but in any event I did not get to know her then. Napier Wilt was an Americanist with specialties in Henry James and Walt Whitman. He taught courses devoted to each of these major authors. In the course on Walt Whitman, students read the whole of *Leaves of Grass*, along with Whitman's prefaces and essays. I took this course, as did Lucy (see Price 60).

I came to know Lucy only in the latter half of her career when on occasion she returned to the University of Chicago to see her old professors and talk with them about her then-current enterprise, the translation of Whitman. It was 1981. If I remember right, the first time I met her was at a Department of English "barbecue" in a park outside Chicago, with many of her (and my) old professors in attendance. And I believe that it was the Americanist Walter Blair who introduced us. At one point in time, she sat in on a few sessions of my class devoted to Emerson, Whitman, and Dickinson. I can remember her presence in a full classroom quite vividly — poised, unassuming, taking notes occasionally. In the same class was Jean Tsien (Qian Qing), who had come from her post at Beijing Foreign Studies University to take a Ph.D. in English at the University of Chicago (which she subsequently took, writing a distinguished dissertation on Willa Cather).

In any event, in subsequent years Lucy and I corresponded, usually about some problem she was having in translating Whitman. As I have tended to save everything that crosses my path, I have saved our correspondence. I would like to share with you some passages from her letters to me that touched on her translations. The letters were written in small, if not tiny, script on very thin white paper, and she always signed her American name, Lucy Chen.

In the first letter I received from her, dated April 29, 1982, she summed up the state of her translation of Whitman's *Leaves of Grass*:

> I am still working on six poems from "Drum-Taps," going over them again and again. Of course I will do "Song of Myself"; it's almost done, but I must leave revisions to a much later date. The fact that Whitman is a genius, a great writer, but not a learned man makes for the difficulty. It is a discipline for me, very valuable, because in the past I had spent too much time on meticulous writers who were clotted with erudition. They were, however, much easier to do than Whitman. There is so much spontaneity and originality in him that one really must enter into his whole personality to do him at all competently.

This passage suggests the brilliance of her insights into the authors she has translated. Those writers "clotted with erudition"— obviously she meant T. S. Eliot —were easier to translate than the "genius" who was not a "learned man." Lucy found in Whitman the challenge of translating a "whole personality" containing "multitudes," one who exclaimed "I too am not a bit tamed, I too am untranslatable, / I sound my barbaric yawp over the roofs of the world" (*LG* 89).

After this summary, Lucy then added this illuminating comment about her then-recent past: "I shall never forget your kindness when I was in Chicago. Here in China we are trying to get used to the good fortune of being allowed to work again. I am glad I am in pretty good health so that the last years of my life need not be wasted." These lines reveal the importance to Lucy Chen personally of her all-consuming task of translating the whole of *Leaves of Grass*. After the horrors of the decade of the Cultural Revolution, she was back at what she had started out to do before that terrible time had cut her off from it. Offering insight into the seriousness with which she took her task of translation, Lucy said: "I am striving to evolve a style that will approximate his style; it won't be easy. The best poems can not be equalled and the worst tempt the translator to improve them a very little." Lucy closed the letter with a single one-line paragraph: "I can never forget the education I received at Chicago."

In the fall of 1982, David Kuebrich, along with his wife, arrived in Beijing on a Fulbright to teach at Peking University and thus became a colleague of Lucy Chen during the academic year of 1982–1983. In letters during this period, she told me over and over again how helpful she had found the Kuebrichs. In a letter of October 27, 1982, Lucy wrote:

> I did the Lincoln poems these last months and now I am continuing the translation of "Song of Myself." I started the translation some twenty years ago when the cultural revolution broke out and ruled out the possibility of doing any such work. Right now I am in the middle of the long catalogue of Section 33. The Kuebrichs have been a great help. So I finished working on the Lincoln poems with some assurance.

Near the end of this academic year, Lucy expressed her gratitude to David Kuebrich in a letter of April 8, 1993:

> I don't know where I would be without him around and he kindly told me that our cooperation should continue even after his return to the States. I have completed "Song of Myself" (more revisions will have to be done). The poems of Lincoln, "Song of the Open Road," "Song of the Broad-Axe" (again with your help from [your] "Critical Guide [to *Leaves of Grass*]"). . . . If everything goes on smoothly I shall do the songs closely following "Song of Myself," and perhaps a small volume entitled "The Twelve Songs of Whitman" will come out before the complete works. So far 4 groups of poems will appear in [a] magazine. It takes a long time for anything to get printed. When they do come out I shall send you copies.

On June 7, 1983, Lucy had the idea of publishing her translation in two volumes, the first to contain all the poems from "Inscriptions" through the "Songs" section, including the eleven songs from "Salut au Monde!" through "A Song of the Rolling Earth." She expressed some uncertainty about doing the "Annexes," and she was unsure as to whether she should include one, none, or all of the "Prefaces." On March 8, 1984, Lucy reported to me that her publisher had endorsed her idea of the two volumes, and she hoped to complete the first volume by the end of the year: "I work very slowly and I hope very carefully. But there'll bound to be inaccuracies and even mistakes."

But the immediate purpose of her letter was stated in the first paragraph: "I am in urgent need of help in understanding these lines from Whitman's 'Song of the Redwood-Tree': ll. 71–72: 'To duly fall, to aid, unreck'd at last, / To disappear, to serve.'" I stared at the lines in puzzlement for some time and then read the poem to see whether I could write anything to help her. They were lines that I had never explicated, and indeed I had never analyzed in its entirety the "Song of the Redwood-Tree." At first the lines seemed to present a series of contradictory elements. I reread Whitman's poem and wrote to Lucy (March 19, 1984): "The lines come from the song itself and thus are spoken or sung by the dying tree. They come from a visionary part of the poem in which the dying tree envisions the western man of the future, who is of a more self-reliant, self-fulfilled, grander, and heartier race than men of the past. But even he, this new man of the future, must (like the mighty redwood tree) die."

Lines 70–72 read:

Here heed himself, unfold himself, (not others' formulas heed,) here fill his time,
To duly fall, to aid, unreck'd at last,
To disappear, to serve.

I wrote: "The last two lines are filled with paradoxes. 'To duly fall' is to die (as the redwood tree fell) when the time comes to die. 'To aid' is to contribute to the destiny of the human race by fulfilling self on the grandest scale and thus *aid*ing the implicit or hidden cosmic scheme or plan. 'Unreck'd at last' indicates that his contribution is not that of the acknowledged but visible and recognized hero in the old-fashioned sense but rather the contribution of one of many similar self-fulfilled individuals; thus his 'aid' or contribution is 'unreck'd' or unreckoned, uncounted, untabulated, or uncelebrated (as Greek or Medieval heroes were 'reck'd' or celebrated by reciting their accomplishments). Note the similar use of *unreck'd* in line 28 of the poem."

So much for the first of the two lines Lucy asked me to explicate. I wrote on: "The last line ['To disappear, to serve'] appears to be a recapitulation. 'To disappear' is the physical dissolution of death. 'To serve' links with 'to aid': it indicates that the death, the disappearance or dissolution of death contributes because it completes the appointed cycle of the self-fulfilled new man, in accord with the concealed or implicit cosmic scheme." I added near the end of this letter: "I hope this is helpful. Reading it over, I find it a little repetitive, but maybe you'll be able to follow it." I add now, having again reread what I then wrote, that I find myself wondering what today's determined conservationists would think of Whitman's poem. The redwood trees of California have been an important part of that conservationist debate. I think it likely that teaching this poem in today's classroom would require more than simply a careful reading of the lines for their most likely or intended meaning. (Jimmie Killingsworth's essay later in this volume takes up the poem in the context of ecocriticism.)

These few excerpts from Lucy's letters are sufficient, I think, to suggest the dedication she gave to the fulfilling of her self-assigned task — and clearly a poet's task — translating Whitman's *Leaves*. For those who never met Lucy, she comes alive in a story on the front page of the *New York Times* of February 6, 1988, with the headline: "Walt Whitman Sings Anew, but Now with a Chinese Lilt," carrying the byline of Edward A. Gargan.[3] There is an accompanying picture of Lucy, pen in hand, engaged in her translation at a desk in her home in Beijing. Gargan writes: "Her desk is small, a table really, its grainy rosewood polished by her palms, the frayed bindings of dictionaries, the tissue-thin paper she fills with tiny ideograms. For the last ten years, Zhao Luorui has sat here, at this desk carved four centuries ago during the Ming dynasty, putting Walt Whitman's boisterous, individualist, prodigious *Leaves of Grass* into Chinese. 'Whitman,' said this tiny woman, 'is the most American of the 19th-century poets.'"

For those fortunate enough to have visited Lucy in her courtyard house, Gargan's description of it is memorable: her rooms are "jammed with overflowing glass-fronted bookcases. . . . Volumes of Faulkner, Melville, Henry James, Emily Dickinson, all in . . . embossed cloth bindings . . . climb from floor to ceiling." What most impressed me when I first entered Lucy's home in 1994 was the picture of Whitman on the far wall, turning a "casual look" upon all who entered, "Leaving it to you to prove and define it, / Expecting the main things from you."

Lucy summarized her career to Gargan in this way: "'Thirty-five years of my life were lost,' she said, alluding to the political cataclysms that gripped China until 1978. 'I've poured everything into Whitman.'" This confession-like statement clearly reveals that her dedication to her translation was infinitely more than mere dedication to an assigned task. Her lost years were hanging in the balance. Only the successful completion of her translation could make up for those missing years. As for preparation, she had taken Napier Wilt's course on Whitman — but that had been in the 1940s — some thirty years in the past. To begin anew, she had to immerse herself in Whitmanian materials: "I began reading all the scholarly works on Whitman. . . . Then I read Whitman, both his prose and poetry. Then I began [the translation] right from the beginning."

On starting out on her translation, she made, she revealed to Gargan, an important discovery: "I began to feel that he was so different from T. S. Eliot. . . . I thought I didn't have to know much about Eliot to translate him. I had to know the writers Eliot read to know Eliot. But you have to know Whitman himself before you begin translating him." Her approach strikes a sympathetic reader as both complex and simple: "My theory is that translators should be faithful to the original form as well as to its spirit. The best translation will be faithful to the written form and spirit. But if you can't be faithful to both, you have to be faithful to the content. I'll sacrifice the form for the content." In conclusion, she summarized the challenge of translating *Leaves of Grass*: "Whitman . . . is American. He is not colloquial. Certainly he has the rhythm of the spoken language but it is not really colloquial. I try to follow that, the beauty of the spoken language. It's difficult to render idiomatic American style, but the thought is there."

Gargan completed his article by quoting the opening lines of "Song of Myself," the translation of which Lucy had just published in a small volume:

I celebrate myself, and sing myself,
And what I assume you shall assume,
For every atom belonging to me as good belongs to you.

I loafe and invite my soul,
I lean and loafe at my ease observing a spear of summer grass.
    (*LG* 28)

So that the reader could hear the sound of Lucy's translation, Gargan provided a rendering of the Chinese lines in pinyin. He then gave the last words of his story over to Lucy, who said: "The individual means everything to Whitman. . . . The individual should have a chance for self-development. Whitman talks a lot about sex, you know. I'm not afraid, being an old woman. I try to be faithful."

As I turn to a discussion of the relationship between T. S. Eliot and Whitman, the two poets Lucy faithfully translated, I find I must say some words about Ezra Pound as well. Both Pound and Eliot may be perceived as emphatically rejecting Whitman. In fact, I believe that each of these poets kept casting backward glances at the Good Gray Poet o'er their own traveled roads, and, after much resistance, came to terms with him as a primary predecessor poet. I should add, now that we have entered the twenty-first century, all the judgments critics have made about the poets of the twentieth century may well be called into question. If we glance back, for example, to the end of the nineteenth century, one of its major poets was barely known, and another was frequently dismissed as not only unpoetic but indeed chaotic. These two poets we now celebrate: Emily Dickinson and Walt Whitman.

Hugh Kenner entitled an enormous book he published in 1971 *The Pound Era*.[4] I have always believed that Kenner chose his title to preempt the publication of a volume entitled *The Eliot Era*. So far as I know, no literary historian has adopted Kenner's title for the modernist period. Both Pound and Eliot might be characterized by Lucy's phrase, "meticulous writers clotted with erudition." And there can be little doubt that they dominated the modernist movement, Pound with his critical acumen, Eliot with his flare for the poetic line. And I think now that there are many more people who have read Eliot's "Prufrock" and *The Waste Land* than have read Pound's "Hugh Selwyn Mauberly" and *The Cantos*. No other twentieth-century poets so dominated the literary scene as these two, and no others so emphatically distanced themselves from Whitman. Indeed, there were prominent poets who, one way or another, endorsed or celebrated Whitman as an important predecessor poet — for example, Hart Crane, William Carlos Williams, Allen Ginsberg, Charles Olson, D. H. Lawrence, and Dylan Thomas.

Moreover, the expatriates Pound and Eliot shared certain political views that set them radically apart. Pound became notorious for his celebration of Mussolini, both in his poetry and in his broadcasts from Italy to America condemning America's participation in World War II. In some ways and in retrospect, Pound seems to have been less alienated from America than Eliot, and his views of Whitman (despite his characterization of him as "an exceedingly nauseating pill") less severe. His 1909 two-page essay, "What I Feel about Walt Whitman," appears to be a strange and uneasy identification with a poet he considers to be a predecessor; one paragraph opens: "Mentally I am a Walt Whitman who has learned to wear a collar and a dress shirt."[5] His 1913 poem "A Pact" (beginning "I make a pact with you, Walt Whitman") is a kind of appeal to "make friends" and come together in a joint mission.[6]

But in one of his Pisan Cantos, written shortly before the end of the war when he was still in a prison cage in Pisa, Pound takes over the imagery of one of Whitman's most famous poems, "Out of the Cradle Endlessly Rocking," which in its conclusion portrays the sea as whispering over and over, "Death, death, death, death, death," repeated in a "low and delicious" whisper. Here are a few lines near the end of Pound's Canto 82:

> the loneliness of death came upon me
> . . . three solemn half notes
> their white downy chests black-rimmed
> on the middle wire.[7]

The lines clearly refer to the two birds whose drama of separation and loss forms the center of Whitman's poem. Kenner (in *The Pound Era*) writes: "This extraordinary homage, a structural X-ray of Whitman's poem, in articulating itself has stirred into life many voices [in Pound]. . . . The last page of Canto 82 is the voice, the spirit, of Whitman" (Kenner, 487–488).

Lucy Chen's translation of Eliot's *The Waste Land* appeared in 1937, at a time when Eliot's reputation was at its peak in England and America. Although no one, so far as I know, has written a book entitled *The Eliot Era*, many critics have written books about Eliot with that implicit assumption. I should admit at this point that I wrote a little-noticed article on Eliot back in 1958 entitled "Whitman and Eliot: The Poetry of Mysticism."[8] And I also wrote an infamous book on him entitled *T. S. Eliot's Personal Waste Land: Exorcism of the Demons*, published in 1977; although some reviewers attacked it at the time, more recent critics have found it persuasive.[9] I confess also that I have spent a good deal of time in the past few years writing a critical biography of Eliot. The biographers to date have been predominantly British, and they have tended to mischaracterize or overlook the American elements that shaped the first third of Eliot's life. Needless to say, however, I have approached my work on Eliot from a vastly different perspective from that I had when I first began my work on Whitman back in the 1950s.

I find myself pretty much in agreement with Harold Bloom, in his introduction to the volume he edited entitled *T. S. Eliot: Modern Critical Views* (1985). He wrote: "[Eliot's] disdain for Freud, his flair for demonstrating

James E. Miller Jr.

the authenticity of his Christianity by exhibiting a judicious anti-Semitism, his refined contempt for human sexuality — somehow these did not seem to be the inevitable foundations for contemporary culture."[10] The jacket for Bloom's book portrays a bewhiskered, easygoing Whitman in the dim background, his hand supporting his chin, gazing at the figure of the formally besuited Eliot in the foreground, his wrinkled forehead betraying a general if inexplicable uneasiness within.

There are innumerable dismissals of Whitman made by Eliot that could be quoted here, but one must suffice. It comes from Eliot's introduction to *Ezra Pound: Selected Poems*, published in 1928: "I did not read Whitman until much later in life, and had to conquer an aversion to his form, as well as to much of his matter, in order to do so. I am equally certain — it is indeed obvious — that Pound owes nothing to Whitman."[11] A reasonable reader might well find unpersuasive Eliot's sweeping dismissal of Whitman — including both his form and matter (one might ask, what else is there?) — and his insistence on the "obviousness" of the lack of any Whitman influence on Pound.

Eliot's gradual shift to some kind of appreciation of Whitman cannot be detailed here, but the climax came in 1952, in a lecture he delivered at Washington University in St. Louis, an institution founded by his grandfather. The lecture was entitled "American Literature and the American Language." In his discussion, Eliot selected three nineteenth-century American authors as what he called "landmarks": Poe, Whitman, and Twain. And he commented on Whitman:

> To Walt Whitman . . . a great influence on modern poetry has been attributed. I wonder if this has not been exaggerated. In this respect he reminds me of Gerard Manley Hopkins — a lesser poet than Whitman, but also a remarkable innovator in style. Whitman and Hopkins, I think, both found an idiom and a metric perfectly suited for what they had to say; and very doubtfully adaptable to what anyone else has to say.[12]

Eliot's comments begin with a complimentary tone but end in an ambiguous negativity. Indeed, Eliot here seems in his final sentence bent again on insisting, however obliquely, that Whitman could not have influenced him (or Pound).

By the time Eliot delivered his address, there were two nineteenth-century American writers whose reputations by the mid-twentieth century were at their peak: Emily Dickinson and Herman Melville. It is astonishing to me that Eliot, as widely read as he was in literature written in English and other languages, would not have at least noted their names in his Washington University address. I must conclude, however, that he had never read the poet who exclaimed in a tiny poem "I am nobody, who are you?" and the novelist who opened his enormous masterpiece with the brief command "Call me Ishmael." I have been unable to find any reference to these two great American writers in any of Eliot's innumerable critical writings.

I want to conclude by describing my encounter with someone my wife and I met when we visited Whitman's home in Camden, New Jersey. As we drove across the river from Philadelphia into Camden, we were shocked by the slums that seemed to appear at every turn in this famed city — indeed, a city scene that could have been comfortably included in an Eliot poem. Whitman's home stood in the middle of a block, many of the houses on either side having been demolished. There was a large penitentiary that could be viewed from Whitman's windows, but it was obviously a recent building. We found three or four people sitting on the front steps of the house. As we stood there wondering what to do, the curator came, having just arrived for her day's work in the house, and she said that they had a problem with prisoners' family members using the stoop to communicate with prisoners gathered at the prison windows. I could only wonder what poem Whitman might have written about his squatters.

After a tour of the house, including seeing the bed in which Whitman died, we decided to go see the massive mausoleum that Whitman had designed for himself and many members of his family. We drove through a decaying city to Harleigh Cemetery and made our way to the Whitman tomb. There was no one else about. As we lingered there, looking in silence at the somewhat shabby crypt overlooking a pond, we were suddenly joined by a young black man who came up to the monument and told us he was a poet and that he had just that day heard of Walt Whitman, a great American poet, who had lived in Camden in the latter part of his life. As a boy, this young man had often come here to fish in the pond, not knowing whose presence lurked behind him. We told him that the house Whitman lived in was still standing nearby and that we had an invitation to a birthday celebration that night, starting at the tomb, including poets reading their poems, and ending with a reception at the house. We gave him our invitation, which he accepted with delight and eager anticipation. We

James E. Miller Jr.

parted in friendship, but only after it was too late did we realize that we hadn't asked the poet his name.

As for Lucy, though we don't know her today as a poet, we do know her as a poet-translator, a tiny woman who entered Whitman's "whole personality" to translate him faithfully, "Leaving it to [the Chinese people] to prove and define it, / Expecting the main things from you."

NOTES

1. David Kuebrich, "Whitman in China," *Walt Whitman Quarterly Review* 1 (fall 1983), 33–35.

2. Kenneth M. Price, "An Interview with Zhao Luorui," *Walt Whitman Quarterly Review* 13 (summer/fall 1995), 59.

3. Edward A. Gargan, "Walt Whitman Sings Anew, but Now with a Chinese Lilt," *New York Times* (February 6, 1988).

4. Hugh Kenner, *The Pound Era* (Berkeley: University of California Press, 1971).

5. "What I Feel about Walt Whitman," in *Ezra Pound: Selected Prose, 1909–1965*, ed. William Cookson (New York: New Directions, 1973), 145.

6. "A Pact," in *Selected Poems of Ezra Pound* (New York: New Directions, 1962), 27.

7. "Canto LXXXII," in *The Cantos of Ezra Pound* (New York: New Directions, 1972), 523–527.

8. Reprinted in James E. Miller Jr., *Quests Surd and Absurd: Essays in American Literature* (Chicago: University of Chicago Press, 1967), 112–136.

9. James E. Miller Jr., *T. S. Eliot's Personal Waste Land: Exorcism of the Demons* (University Park: Pennsylvania State University Press, 1977).

10. "Introduction," in *Modern Critical Views: T. S. Eliot*, ed. Harold Bloom (New York: Chelsea House, 1985), 2.

11. T. S. Eliot, "Introduction," in *Ezra Pound: Selected Poems* (London: Faber & Gwyer, 1928), viii–ix.

12. T. S. Eliot, *American Literature and the American Language: An Address Delivered at Washington University on June 9, 1953; with an Appendix, The Eliot Family and St. Louis* (St. Louis: Department of English, Washington University, 1953), 16.

The Voluptuous Earth
and the Fall of the Redwood Tree
Whitman's Personifications of Nature

M. JIMMIE KILLINGSWORTH

The emergence of studies in "environmental rhetoric" and "ecocriticism" in the wake of environmentalist politics creates new possibilities for reading Whitman's poems. In the light of international ecopolitics, ecofeminism, the environmental justice movement, and the recent protests in the United States against "globalization," many nature poems seem to lose their innocence and acquire a cultural and political edginess.[1] Emerson, Thoreau, and the flock of nature writers who emerged from the tradition these two writers began have rightly received the greatest attention in ecocriticism focusing on nineteenth-century American literature, but a new project in ecopoetics — the aim of which is to understand the myths and metaphors by which human beings identify their own purposes with the creatures and processes of nature — might well turn to Whitman.[2]

No other writer before or after Whitman experimented so widely and warmly with the use of personification, a key trope of identity that since ancient times has taught people to think of the earth as a mother, a lover, and an analog of the human body. Whitman pushed the limits of this trope, as he did with so many others, especially in the energetic performances that filled the first three editions of *Leaves of Grass*. His infamous poetry of the body was not confined to contemplating physical beauty in human bodies alone but encompassed whole landscapes of life, as in these famous lines from "Song of Myself":

> Smile O voluptuous cool-breath'd earth!
> Earth of the slumbering and liquid trees!
> Earth of departed sunset — earth of the mountains misty-topt!

Earth of the vitreous pour of the full moon just tinged with blue!
Earth of shine and dark mottling the tide of the river!
Earth of the limpid gray of clouds brighter and clearer for my sake!
Far-swooping elbow'd earth — rich apple-blossom'd earth!
Smile, for your lover comes. (*LG* 49)

An ecocritical perspective asks us to question our own appreciation of such lines. The aesthetic value of the imagery is beyond question, in my view — the earth with cool breath and elbows, adorned in apple blossoms — as is the humor of the speaker's winkingly self-ironic hyperbole. But what about the political implications of personifying the earth as the voluptuous female lover of the male poet? After Annette Kolodny's ecofeminist critiques of the pioneering mentality that treats the land as a woman's body to be possessed and dominated, we may only dare to smile at Whitman's machismo.[3] As the linguistic philosophers George Lakoff and Mark Johnson have suggested, we not only love by our metaphors, we also live by them.[4] How does seeing nature as mother or mistress, or in any way seeing ourselves reflected in the environment, affect our conception of the human relation to nature? Such questions make even the innocent old clichés of personification seem suspicious, much less the wild troping of our pioneering poet.

And yet the science and nature writers who have been most influential in twentieth-century political ecology have employed a personifying rhetoric. Rachel Carson's 1962 book *Silent Spring*, the "mother text" of contemporary environmentalism, couches its most fervent appeals in personifications reminiscent of Whitman's best poems, conceptualizing the earth in terms of the human body. The "health of the landscape," in her words, sustains our own bodies in health; when the land grows sick, human health must decline as well. Surveying the damage from pesticides and industrial pollution, Carson laments the "scars of dead vegetation" and the "weeping appearance" of afflicted trees.[5] Each element of her trope, the earth's body and the human body, informs the other. Just as the earth experiences health and illness, she says, "[t]here is also an ecology of the world within our own bodies"— the cycles and chemical interrelations by which we live and die.[6] A precedent for Carson's wide-ranging personifications appears in Aldo Leopold's midcentury essay "Thinking Like a Mountain," which urges readers to abandon the short-term thinking of cattlemen who exterminate wolves to protect herds and thereby increase deer populations, only to ultimately unbalance the ecology of the land, leaving too many deer. The deer then destroy their own food supplies, stripping the mountain of its vegetation and driving themselves into starvation. From the vantage of its mighty stature and the wisdom of its many years, the mountain — quite clearly a personification of ecological consciousness — sees the big picture and understands the whole story that deer and humans cannot comprehend.[7] In another essay, "The Land Ethic," Leopold proposes that we extend ethical rights to the land, granting the earth the same ethical status that we grant other human beings.[8] Environmental rhetoric thus moves toward literalizing the personification of the earth. As René Dubos writes, "The phrase 'health of the environment' is not a literary convention. It has a real biological meaning, because the surface of the earth is truly a living organism."[9]

The personifying rhetoric of political ecologists like Carson and Leopold departs from the normal practices of two centuries in scientific discourse. As Lawrence Buell shows in *The Environmental Imagination*, both literature and science since the beginning of the nineteenth century, in theory if not in practice, have shied away from personification. While on the one hand Darwin's theories bring the human family closer to the animals, on the other hand the analytical imagination of modern science separates organisms from their world. Alienation and division, consonant with the prohibition of anthropomorphism, prevail over integration and holism. Division, implied in the very word "environment," signifying that which surrounds, finds its way into literary theory as early as Ruskin's concept of the pathetic fallacy. It informs literary naturalism's portrayal of nature as a force indifferent to human suffering. And it appears in the work of recent nature writers such as Edward Abbey, who reject personification as a sentimentalist relic that interferes with the zenlike contemplation of the earth as the wholly other.[10]

A particularly clear example of the assertion of difference in ecologically informed fiction appears in a fine descriptive passage in the recent novel *Soul Mountain* by the 2000 winner of the Nobel Prize in literature, the Chinese author Gao Xingjian. After observing that "the lush white flowers" on the ground beneath a wild azalea "have not begun to wither and are so charged with life that they exude a lust to exhibit themselves," the narrator backs away from the anthropomorphism that attributes lust to the wild thing. He remarks self-consciously, "This is pristine natural

M. Jimmie Killingsworth

beauty. It is irrepressible, seeks no reward, and is without a goal, a beauty derived neither from symbolism nor metaphor and needing neither analogies nor associations." At another point, fending off the pathetic fallacy, he says, "This unadorned splendour and beauty in nature fills me with another sort of indescribable sadness. It is a sadness which is purely mine and not something inherent in nature."[11]

In addition to the aesthetic and scientific objections we might raise against the drive of holistic ecology toward reintegration and identification with the earth, there is also a political concern. Division might actually be politically productive, as any attempt to figure the world in human terms invites the kind of human-centered understanding of existence that can lead to the unwise or immoral exploitation of the nonhuman. While anticipating the personifications of holistic ecologists, Whitman's poems embody some of the deepest conflicts of modern globalizing intelligence. We find in *Leaves of Grass* the contradictory impulses to stress on the one hand the unity of human and nonhuman nature, which may lead to exploitation through an uncritical assertion of identity, and on the other hand to preserve the integrity of the earth as an "environment," a natural system distinct from human interests and society.

A virtual laboratory for the study of personifying effects, Whitman's poetic practice varies so widely that it is hard to generalize from poem to poem, from period to period in his career, and even from section to section within long poems like "Song of Myself." But one identifiable trend follows a pattern familiar to Whitman scholars. The poems written before the Civil War, for the first three editions of *Leaves of Grass*, give us great clusters of vivid scenes and images that shock the conventional ear and suggest radically new, close-up perspectives on the world, while the later poems grow more distant, more politically conservative, and more traditionally "poetic" in diction and structure. The powerful sense of the particular yields to the kind of metaphysical abstraction that George Arms, among others, has associated with the genteel tradition and the "schoolroom poets"—Bryant, Longfellow, Whittier, Lowell, and Holmes.[12]

Signs of accommodating conventional public tastes are especially evident in poems published first in magazines rather than in *Leaves of Grass*. "A Noiseless Patient Spider," for example, which appeared first in an 1868 number of London's *Broadway Magazine*, echoes one of the most popular nature poems of the day, Oliver Wendell Holmes's "The Chambered

Nautilus," published a decade before Whitman's spider poem. Holmes's closing apostrophe "Build thee more stately mansions, O my soul" (Arms 118) — which turns on a metaphorical identification of the human spirit with the sea creature and its chambered shell, a partial personification, and a moral lesson taken from the observation of nature — resonates in Whitman's closing lines:

> And you O my soul where you stand,
> Surrounded, detached, in measureless oceans of space,
> Ceaselessly musing, venturing, throwing, seeking the spheres to
>   connect them,
> Till the bridge you will need be form'd, till the ductile anchor hold,
> Till the gossamer thread you fling catch somewhere, O my soul.
>   (*LG* 450)

Such moral-making poetry, though employing identity-forming tropes like metaphor and personification, requires a thoroughgoing and dualistic separation of nature and humankind, as well as of body and soul. As in another famous nineteenth-century poem, William Cullen Bryant's "To a Waterfowl" (Arms 30–31), the observation of nature leads the poet to reflect not on natural objects but on the supernatural. The mind drifts from its connection with the world and seeks some hold in "measureless oceans of space."

Abstraction and distance certainly predominate in a group of poems from the 1870s that I call the globalizing group. One of these is "Song of the Redwood-Tree," first published in *Harper's Magazine* in 1874. In linking manifest destiny to a view of nature as a boundless resource base for human expansion, the poem can only offend the sensibilities of modern environmentalists. As Gay Wilson Allen writes in an early ecocritical essay, "How Emerson, Thoreau, and Whitman Viewed the Frontier," "I know of no other literary work which so naively reveals the American national consciousness of the nineteenth century—though with most of the people it was probably an unconscious drive. But whether conscious or unconscious, it made the plunder of their natural resources inevitable—and tragic, courting hubris, as we can now see."[13] With its operatic structure and elegiac tone, the poem is similar to two earlier poems, "Out of the Cradle Endlessly Rocking" and "When Lilacs Last in the Dooryard Bloom'd." As in those poems, "Song of the Redwood-Tree" alternates between the poet's voice in roman type and the voice attributed to a nonhuman creature in italic type—not a mockingbird or a thrush this time, but the great sequoia tree itself, or rather the spirits that inhabit it— dryads and hamadryads, mythical figures, the kind that the poet studiously avoided in his earlier, less conventional elegies. Again, the poet takes comfort in the other's voice after experiencing an initial unquiet. But the unquiet is neither as profound nor as arresting as it is in "Out of the Cradle" and "Lilacs," and the resolution is far too rapidly enacted and disturbing in its implications. As Allen puts it, "A Conservationist or a Preservationist must find the logic of this poem maddening. The tree not only accepts annihilation, but glories in being 'absorb'd, assimilated' by these superior creatures who will 'really shape and mould the New World, adjusting it to Time and Space'" (Allen 126). The poet occupies a position of privilege, distant not only from the spirits of the trees, represented as an ancient race departing to leave the wood as dead material to be molded to new functions by the human race, but also from the nearly unconscious woodsmen who clear the trees:

> Riven deep by the sharp tongues of the axes, there in the redwood
> forest dense,
> I heard the mighty tree its death-chant chanting.
>
> The choppers heard not, the camp shanties echoed not,
> The quick-ear'd teamsters and chain and jack-screw men heard not,
> As the wood-spirits came from their haunts of a thousand years to join
> the refrain,
> But in my soul I plainly heard. (*LG* 206)

From an ecocritical perspective, one troubling quality of the poem is that it relies on old mythological conventions and traditional poetic language — such as "myriad leaves," "stalwart trunk and limbs," and "lofty top"— to portray the disappearance of one of the most distinctive natural features of North America (*LG* 206–207). Whitman's tree is an abstraction, a nonbeing, an idea that the poet inhabits in order to justify the ways of humans to nature. Admittedly, we hear of the forest "rising to two hundred feet," and we hear of the "foot-thick bark" (*LG* 207), but the poet's imagination seems far more attentive to the tools and operations of the logging camp. Whitman, who had never seen a redwood tree in the wild, retreats from his early commitment not to make poems distilled of other poems, as if lacking the experience or the energy to celebrate the redwoods with the evocative and suggestive images of his greatest poetry.[14]

Worse yet, the language of the poem—the mention of superior races and assimilation, for example—nods toward the darker side of manifest destiny, the racist logic that at the time Whitman wrote the poem was used to uproot indigenous peoples from their land so that white settlements could grow and dominate the western United States. The efforts to systematically exterminate tribal life during this era make Whitman's lines about "the new culminating man" coming in peace — *"Not wan from Asia's fetiches, / Nor red from Europe's old dynastic slaughter-house"* (*LG* 208) — seem naive at best. Even Whitman's treatment of the redwood's voice as emanating from a ghostly entity already departed from the scene of present-day life invokes a disturbing pattern, one that was conventionally applied to native peoples during the poet's day. As Renée L. Bergland points out in *The National Uncanny: Indian Ghosts and American Subjects*, "When European Americans speak of Native Americans"— from colonial days down to modern times — "they always use the language of ghostliness. They call Indians demons, apparitions, shades, specters, phantoms, or ghosts" and "insist that Indians . . . are ultimately doomed to vanish."[15] Bergland argues, "In American letters, and in the American imagination, Native American ghosts function both as representations of national guilt and as triumphant agents of Americanization"— representations conjured obsessively over the full span of American national history in a "dynamic of unsuccessful repression" (Bergland 4–5). In Whitman's poem, the all too easy substitution of red people for redwoods in the ghostly discourse suggests the nationalizing or globalizing impulse and the environmental racism against which contemporary protesters raise their voices.[16]

In "Passage to India," a poem written only a few years before "Song of the Redwood-Tree," the globalizing Whitman had celebrated the completion of Columbus's vision as a journey of the human spirit rather than a materialist fulfillment — and again, a fulfillment achieved at the expense of native peoples and through destructive uses of the land. Despite its celebration of peace and cross-cultural tolerance, "Passage to India" opens the door to the kind of abstraction and dualistic thinking all too easily enrolled in the service of exploitation. In a curious segment in the poem, Whitman actually questions the human connection with the earth, wondering whether "feverish children" with their "restless explorations" can count on the affections of the great mother:

M. Jimmie Killingsworth

Who speak the secret of impassive earth?
Who bind it to us? what is this separate Nature so unnatural?
What is this earth to our affections? (unloving earth, without a throb
   to answer ours,
Cold earth, the place of graves.) (*LG* 415)

By the end of the section, we find the questions answered. The "true son of God, the poet" will justify the earth to humankind: "Nature and Man shall be disjoin'd and diffused no more," we are told, "The true son of God shall absolutely fuse them" (*LG* 415–416). With its capitalized abstractions "Nature," "Man," and "God," these lines seem a far cry from the 1855 expressions of the poet's love for the earth in "Song of Myself," in which humility in the face of the earth's power often intervenes into the celebrations of selfhood. "The press of my foot to the earth springs a hundred affections," the poet had boasted, but he added a respectful qualification: "They scorn the best I can do to relate them" (*LG* 41). Although "Passage to India" lacks the subtlety and the imagistic energy of "Song of Myself," the idea of the earth fusing with human purposes, as well as the privileged position of the poet as the one who bridges the gap between nature and humanity, remains relatively intact from "Song of Myself" to the globalizing poems of the 1870s.

The structural movement in "Passage to India"— from the suspicion that the earth is indifferent to and forever separated from human purposes toward a sense of kinship and belonging — is also enacted in the 1856 poem "This Compost."[17] But the mood of this remarkable poem is far more welcoming to the modern ecological intelligence. It begins not with abstractions and distance, nor with affirmations of identity with the earth, but with a nearly physical repulsion. The poet walking in the woods to refresh himself in fine romantic form is confronted with something so offensive he leaves it unnamed, as if it is unspeakably hideous:

Something startles me where I thought I was safest,
I withdraw from the still woods I loved,
I will not go now on the pastures to walk,
I will not strip the clothes from my body to meet my lover the sea,
I will not touch my flesh to the earth as to other flesh to renew me.
   (*LG* 368)

His morbid fancy wonders that "the ground itself does not sicken" or that "the foul liquid and meat" of "distemper'd corpses" do not turn up when he plows or digs in the earth (*LG* 368). The arresting moment passes as the poet beholds the natural world as a great compost heap, its marvelous chemistry bringing forth the finest beauty and rebirth: "The resurrection of the wheat appears with pale visage out of its graves, . . . / The summer growth is innocent and disdainful above all those strata of sour dead" (*LG* 369). The personification finally survives, but the personifying imagination is chastened. While the poet again feels "That this is no cheat, this transparent green-wash of the sea which is so amorous after me, / That it is safe to allow it to lick my naked body all over with its tongues" (*LG* 369), something of the sense of awed distance will not go away. He remains "terrified at the Earth," he tells us in conclusion, "it is that calm and patient":

> It grows such sweet things out of such corruptions,
> It turns harmless and stainless on its axis, with such endless
> successions of diseas'd corpses,
> It distills such exquisite winds out of such infused fetor,
> It renews with such unwitting looks its prodigal, annual, sumptuous
> crops,
> It gives such divine materials to men, and accepts such leavings from
> them at last. (*LG* 369–370)

Faith in the earth's bounty — expressed in the last line with its questionable hint that, do what we will, the earth will reward us — is based in this poem not upon the pioneer's sense of the world as an inexhaustible storehouse for human exploitation but upon respect for the power of the earth's processes to restore health and complete its mighty cycles.

If, in view of ecocriticism, which "seeks to evaluate texts and ideas in terms of their coherence and usefulness as responses to environmental crisis," "Song of the Redwood-Tree" is the most reprehensible poem written in nineteenth-century America, "This Compost" may well be the most satisfactory.[18] As a celebration of the landscape in health, it stands as an able experiment in the special version of personification that reappears in Leopold's "Thinking Like a Mountain" and Carson's *Silent Spring*. It creates a kind of alternating consciousness that embraces the earth with signs of kinship and even identity but retains enough distance to keep the idea of environment alive as a realm of being distinct from human interests. The concept of protection would require as much in the second half of the twentieth century, when, for the first time in history, human beings gained

M. *Jimmie Killingsworth*

the power to destroy the world with a few concentrated acts of unbridled aggression. The discursive counterpart of using good judgment in protecting the environment may well be the act of keeping the personifying impulse in check, refusing to allow the demons of human imagination to fully possess the earth and reduce it to a mere reflection of self-serving desires.

NOTES

1. The most significant ecocritical studies of poetry have focused on British romantic literature. See, for example, Jonathan Bate, *Romantic Ecology: Wordsworth and the Environmental Tradition* (London: Routledge, 1991), and Karl Kroeber, *Ecological Literary Criticism: Romantic Imagining and the Biology of Mind* (New York: Columbia University Press, 1994).

2. Ecocriticism that canonizes prose nature writing as the central expression of the "environmental imagination" includes Scott Slovic, *Seeking Awareness in American Nature Writing: Henry Thoreau, Annie Dillard, Edward Abbey, Wendell Berry, Barry Lopez* (Salt Lake City: University of Utah Press, 1992); John P. O'Grady, *Pilgrims of the Wild: Everett Ruess, Henry David Thoreau, John Muir, Clarence King, Mary Austin* (Salt Lake City: University of Utah Press, 1993); Lawrence Buell, *The Environmental Imagination: Thoreau, Nature Writing, and the Formation of American Culture* (Cambridge: Harvard University Press, 1995); and Randall Roorda, *Dramas of Solitude: Narratives of Retreat in American Nature Writing* (Albany: SUNY Press, 1998). Of these, only Buell's magisterial work mentions Whitman. The trend in American studies to focus on prose works as the key texts for advancing thinking about environmental politics is reinforced in the field of environmental rhetoric, which emerged alongside ecocriticism in the 1990s. See, for example, M. Jimmie Killingsworth and Jacqueline S. Palmer, *Ecospeak: Rhetoric and Environmental Politics in America* (Carbondale: Southern Illinois University Press, 1992); James G. Cantrill and Christine Oravec, eds., *The Symbolic Earth: Discourse and Our Creation of the Environment* (Lexington: University Press of Kentucky, 1996); Carl Herndl and Stuart Brown, eds., *Green Culture: Environmental Rhetoric in Contemporary America* (Madison: University of Wisconsin Press, 1996); and Craig Waddell, ed., *"And No Birds Sing": The Rhetoric of Rachel Carson* (Carbondale: Southern Illinois University Press, 2000).

3. Annette Kolodny, *The Lay of the Land: Metaphor as Experience and History in American Life and Letters* (Chapel Hill: University of North Carolina Press, 1975). See also Gretchen Legler, "Body Politics in American Nature Writing: 'Who May Contest for What the Body of Nature Will Be?'" in *Writing the Environment: Ecocrit-*

icism and Literature, ed. Richard Kerridge and Neil Sammells (London: Zed, 1998), 71–87.

4. George Lakoff and Mark Johnson, *Metaphors We Live By* (Chicago: University of Chicago Press, 1980).

5. Rachel Carson, *Silent Spring* (New York: Fawcett Crest, 1962), 69, 70, 71.

6. Ibid., 170.

7. Aldo Leopold. "Thinking Like a Mountain," in *Sand County Almanac* (1949; rpt., New York: Oxford University Press, 1989), 129–133.

8. Aldo Leopold, "The Land Ethic," in *Sand County Almanac*, 201–226.

9. René Dubos, "The Limits of Adaptability," in *The Environmental Handbook*, ed. Garrett De Bell (New York: Ballantine, 1970), 27.

10. See Buell, 180–218.

11. Gao Xingjian, *Soul Mountain*, trans. Mabel Lee (New York: HarperCollins, 2000), 59, 61.

12. George Arms, *The Fields Were Green: A New View of Bryant, Whittier, Holmes, Lowell, and Longfellow, with a Selection of Their Poems* (Stanford, Calif.: Stanford University Press, 1953), 3–8.

13. Gay Wilson Allen, "How Emerson, Thoreau, and Whitman Viewed the Frontier," in *Toward a New American Literary History: Essays in Honor of Arlin Turner*, ed. Louis J. Budd, Edwin H. Cady, and Carl L. Anderson (Durham, N.C.: Duke University Press, 1980), 126. I am grateful to my colleague Jerome Loving for calling my attention to this essay by Allen, an early venture into ecocriticism and one of the few essays that consider Whitman's poems in light of environmental politics.

14. In a fascinating analysis of the cultural context of the poem, Diane Kirk observes that "Song of the Redwood-Tree" is "notably lacking in description of the visible features of the trees." The emphasis on the "foot-thick bark" and the height of 200 feet may well be traced, as Kirk argues, to an exhibit in New York in the early 1850s, called "Mother of the Forest." The bark of a giant sequoia was removed up to 116 feet and reassembled in the New York exhibit. Samuel Clemens saw a similar exhibit in Philadelphia in the early 1850s. Whitman makes no mention of the exhibit, but it is just the kind of event he relished, and the features of the bark and the impressive height could well have lodged in his memory and resurfaced in 1873 when the poem was written, a time when redwoods were the frequent subject of scientific writing, as Kirk shows. See Diane Kirk, "Landscapes of Old Age in Walt Whitman's Later Poetry" (Ph.D. diss., Texas A&M University, 1994), 8–12. I thank my friend and former colleague Kenneth Price, who directed this dissertation, for calling my attention to it.

M. Jimmie Killingsworth

15. Renée L. Bergland, *The National Uncanny: Indian Ghosts and American Subjects* (Hanover, N.H.: University Press of New England, 2001). I thank my colleague Siraj Ahmed for directing me to Bergland's fascinating book.

16. For a brief introduction to the notion of environmental justice and the protest against environmental racism in contemporary American literature, see M. Jimmie Killingsworth and Jacqueline S. Palmer, "Ecopolitics and the Literature of the Borderlands: The Frontiers of Environmental Justice in Latina and Native American Writing," in Kerridge and Sammells, *Writing the Environment*, 196–207.

17. I am grateful to Ed Folsom for pointing out the rhetorical similarity of the two poems.

18. Richard Kerridge, "Introduction," in Kerridge and Sammells, *Writing the Environment*, 5.

"O Divine Average!"

Whitman's Poetry and the Production of Normality in Nineteenth-Century American Culture

WALTER GRÜNZWEIG

Normality is a concept that evades analysis, reflection, and especially scientific inquiry. It is a self-justifying category. In popular usage, when something is referred to as "normal," there is no need to question what it means. The normal state is that to which we "naturally" aspire. "We just want a return to a normal life," said many inhabitants of Sarajevo, Bosnia, during and after the recent war, and what they meant was they wanted to walk around their city in peace, to have electricity and water and milk for their children. "I want to see a Serbia that is boring," the new Serbian leader Vojislav Kostunica said upon taking power. It sounds almost like a regret. What he meant, according to *Newsweek*, was that Serbia would become "'normal,' a country that would finally rejoin Europe — and put its pariah status behind it."[1] To reestablish diplomatic relations, cultural exchange, or trade between two countries is oftentimes referred to as a political process of "normalization."

Yet what may be normal for one person or culture may not be so for the next. When German citizens require their ethnic Turkish neighbors to behave in a "normal" way, they want them to accommodate to their German mode of living, which "normally" does not include shish kebabs grilled on condominium balconies. And when Westerners fill their cars with gasoline, they expect to be paying "normal" prices, which means *low* prices. In such cases, normality not only transports arrogance but implies force and violence against those who seemingly threaten that normality, although many oil-producing countries may depend on the natural resources for their economic development and survival.

Even these banal examples demonstrate that normality is not a given, never predefined, but rather something created, constructed. At Universität Dortmund, an interdisciplinary research group including specialists in American studies, German studies, history, statistics, sociology, business, media studies, and special education investigates normality as a constructed, culturally produced phenomenon. When we say "cultural" production, we refer to the term as used in cultural studies, meaning we include political, social, technological, and other conditions fashioning that culture. We are interested in studying the hegemonic processes that lead a culture or a society to define normality for itself and the tyrannical ways such notions of normality are used in order to censure others in that culture who are not part of that normality. We are also interested in the images, myths, and narratives that transport notions of normality textually.

Our project, then, is to investigate this category academically and systematically. It is an interdisciplinary project, but we in American studies and American literature believe that we have a special contribution to make. American culture, according to our point of view, is a "normalist" culture. In order to explain this, I must briefly address our theoretical framework.[2] We make a significant differentiation between "normal" and "normative." Norms and normative standards have little to do with what we consider normality. Most religions, such as Christianity, are ruled by norms, at least traditionally. That means that there are certain truths that are simply given and that nobody is allowed to question. They are true in an a priori sense, and discussions about them are pointless. Similarly, legal codes or authoritarian political orders are ruled by norms.

In 1776 the American colonies broke away from a normative European order. That order was variously characterized by such notions as the divine right of kings or legitimacy. The fact that the American colonies belonged to the home country did not need to be justified. It was a matter of course. As Americans left that normative order, it was they who needed to justify its rejection, the rejection of the norms that bound them to the New World. The problem was that once the normative principle was rejected, it could not be reestablished, even if there were attempts to do so. What evolved instead in the new republic was the notion of normality. Normality, unlike normativeness, would not be regulated by norms but by the will of the majority.

This, of course, does not mean that the term "norm" no longer appeared in American culture. But often, and in the course of its more than 200-year history increasingly so, it came to mean "normal." When Americans wanted to find out what was "normal," they would not look toward a king or a state church. They would look to themselves and ask what the majority view on a given question or topic was or was likely to be. That, then, would be defined as normal. Thus normality is closely tied to the democratic process and, interestingly enough, to statistics. Statistics, an essential element in all modern societies, are nowhere more integral to the culture than in the United States. When we look at present-day American media, we find them dominated by graphs and charts showing the views of Americans on every possible subject. Politicians are addicted to pollsters, and every day we see curious curves in the newspapers that supposedly present the public's opinions and feelings. The same is true of many other media cultures — for example, in Western Europe — that have followed this lead. We live in a landscape of curves.[3]

There are many who express strong and critical reservations regarding this development, asking, for instance, whether pictograms and polls of that sort do not shape peoples' opinion rather than reflect it. For the student of normality, this question is largely irrelevant. Normality's production is a complex and dialectical process that involves both the creation of patterns and their imitation. The many discourses of normality that rule people's lives in many Western societies we refer to as "normalism." Normalism has great significance for our lives, and our cultures can therefore be referred to also as "normalist."

One of the reasons why we discovered the significance of normalism for American culture is because of its prominence in the works of Walt Whitman. The chief American bard of democracy is indeed one of the earliest voices of normalism. "O such themes — equalities! O divine average!" Whitman sings right in the middle of his poem "Starting from Paumanok" (*LG* 21). It has often been observed that the poetry of the great equalizer Whitman lacks hierarchies, lacks the centuries-old criteria of what can be included in poetry and what cannot. In the center of his poetry, there is an "average," a statistical quantity in a culture which bypasses traditional orders of high and low and which defines as normal that which the average human being, the average American, holds to be true. It is noteworthy that in the line quoted from "Starting from Paumanok," this statistical metaphor is qualified by the adjective "divine." On the level of democratic

Walter Grünzweig

rhetoric, this means that the culture of averages — rather than, as previously, elite cultures — are divine, in other words, supreme. In our context, it means that the previously existing normative culture, which was guaranteed by religious dogma, is undercut. Ironically, statistics, rather than traditional religion, have become the basis of American society and culture.

This program of singing the "divine average" is realized in Whitman's poetry in famous ways. Average people, employed in average professions, are the subjects of his poetry. Their daily pursuits are the focus of hundreds of lines, as is their status as inhabitants of their various states and regions. In principle, such a statistical world view is liberatory, and not only because it emphasizes popular averages. Whereas normative culture was exclusive, a normalist culture is inclusive. The most popular graphic expression of statistics is the curve. Even though there clearly is a segment of the curve that best expresses the "average," there is no way of making a principled decision *where* on the curve an incision or a cut will separate the normal from the not-normal. In the history of normalism, both in the United States and elsewhere, there have, of course, always been attempts to define such borders between what is normal, acceptable, and what is not. But the decision of where exactly to draw that line has always been uncertain and fluid, and this fluidity has a revolutionary potential.

Jürgen Link, initiator and chair of the Dortmund research group, has called the attempt to narrow down the "normal" range "protonormalistic." This attitude can easily be understood psychologically. For centuries, indeed millennia, human beings were used to normative ways of life that did not require people to question their value systems and behavioral patterns. When normativeness gave way to the normalist world view and a statistical universe, human beings became fearful, worried that there was no longer a *guarantee* that their behavior would be normal.

Sexuality is a case in point. From a narrowly normalist point of view, it was important to distinguish between the normal range of sexual practices and the abnormal ones (those located outside of the normal range). However, the logic of the curve continuously threatens the borders between the normal and the abnormal. When the Kinseys conducted their investigations into the sexual behavior of Americans after World War II, they found significant percentages of men and women reporting sexual behaviors that previously had been defined as abnormal. Thus it was no longer possible to speak of a "weird" fringe of society, and the result was a new self-confidence on the part of the "marginal" as they demanded acceptance into the mainstream of society, into the spectrum of normality.

When we observe the development of American culture, we see that the boundaries of what is considered "normal" are, albeit slowly, expanding. For the most part, ethnic, sexual, and other minorities are not interested in establishing a separatist lifestyle within American society — traditionally, such separatism performs the function of helping disadvantaged groups gather strength and develop a political orientation. Eventually, minorities take up the fight for a place in the center of society, which requires the redefinition of normality and of that center. The spectrum of what is normal thereby becomes increasingly flexible; thus we refer to this type of normalism, which is characteristic of the twentieth century and especially of the second half of that century, as "flexible normalism."

What is fascinating about Whitman is that he adopts this strategy of flexible normalism already in the middle of the nineteenth century. His poetry processes American (and not only American) life and "normalizes" it. He is not content with the central segments of the curve but looks "To niches aside and junior bending, not a person or object missing, / Absorbing all to myself and for this song" (*LG* 40). There is nothing, then, that is not "normal": "What is commonest, cheapest, nearest, easiest, is Me" (*LG* 41).

Connected with this statistical approach toward the culture in which Whitman lives is a discourse of particles that make up the whole. The famous "atom belonging to me as good belongs to you" (*LG* 28) shows the essential randomness and exchangeability of individuals. Individuals are measured in minute units ("Not an inch nor a particle of an inch"), all of which are "familiar" and none of which are "vile" (*LG* 31). This not only suggests the fragility of the individual as a stable unit, it also shows these individuals existing in a normalized society where familiarity, a key attribute of normality, has replaced traditional moral standards ("vile"). It is not surprising, therefore, that the poet will not ask "the sky to come down to my good will," but that the "commonest, cheapest" will be "scattered . . . freely forever" (*LG* 41). The metaphorical form such a culture then takes is that of a huge field of grass, a "uniform hieroglyphic . . . Sprouting alike in broad zones and narrow zones" (*LG* 34).

Whitman's rhetoric of the masses is connected with this world of atoms and particles: "One's-Self I sing, a simple separate person, / Yet utter the word Democratic, the word En-Masse" (*LG* 1). Statistics is a discipline based

Walter Grünzweig

on phenomena occurring in masses and laws derived from their behavior. The individual, when part of a mass, becomes normalized.

It should come as no surprise that the rhetoric of normalization appears most prominently in the "Calamus" poems. There Whitman escapes most clearly from norms, the "standards hitherto publish'd," the "conformities" (*LG* 112). He escapes to the margin to search for standards not yet published, normalities that would include "the soul of the man . . . [who] rejoices in comrades" (*LG* 112). Standards, margin, conformities: this is the normalist vocabulary that we find right in the first poem of the "Calamus" series. These are paths untrodden, but they will merge into a new mass society. "I will plant companionship thick as trees all along the rivers of America . . . / I will make inseparable cities with their arms about each other's necks" (*LG* 117).

Whitman's poetry not only normalizes America but affects the whole world. As "latitude widens, longitude lengthens" (*LG* 137), these internal grids encompass the whole world as an extension of normalized American culture. Many might be inclined to interpret the "divine rapport" that has "equalized" (*LG* 148) him with people in other lands as a mystical force, but there are agencies that are less than mystical:

> I see the tracks of the railroads of the earth,
> I see them in Great Britain, I see them in Europe,
> I see them in Asia and in Africa. (*LG* 141)

These agencies bring the world together, all its parts, with none left out.

When Whitman's poetry was first translated into German, an early reviewer called it akin to the entries of an encyclopedia, only not alphabetized, a "dictionary-type poetry."[4] This was meant to be funny, yet it points to an essential quality in Whitman's works. Whitman is producing an inventory of American (and world) culture. I read Whitman's famous catalogs as a census of his world, as an inventory in his statistical poetry. In his catalogs, he collects data on America and the world, masses of data that are required for statistical purposes. The geographical regions of the United States and the world, the cities, the mountains, the rivers, the inhabitants — identified never by first or last name but always by ethnicity, race, profession, location, and so forth — standardize and thus normalize the diversity that makes up American culture. What the so-called pluralistic approach in statistics does is to try to find "a category of objects all satisfying a certain definition but varying in their individual characteristics."[5]

Whitman was trying to make a statement on masses of people, foremost Americans, and the definition he found for all the different Americans he described was the democratic man. Based on these masses of data, he was trying to establish a probability about what it meant to be an American: "Here is what moves in magnificent masses careless of particulars" (*LG* 343).

Whitman's samples of humans are always caught in the middle of their daily activities:

> The pure contralto sings in the organ loft,
> The carpenter dresses his plank, the tongue of his foreplane whistles
>   its wild ascending lisp,
> The married and unmarried children ride home to their
>   Thanksgiving dinner,
> The pilot seizes the king-pin, he heaves down with a strong arm.
>   (*LG* 41)

These are specific people, but they are important as a result of their everyday occurrence, which is the basis for the data pool Whitman establishes in *Leaves of Grass*. Note the insistence on statistics in a poem like "Our Old Feuillage":

> Always the vast slope drain'd by the Southern sea, inseparable with the
>   slopes drain'd by the Eastern and Western seas,
> The area the eighty-third year of these States, the three and a half
>   millions of square miles,
> The eighteen thousand miles of sea-coast and bay-coast on the main,
>   the thirty thousand miles of river navigation,
> The seven millions of distinct families and the same number of
>   dwellings — always these, and more, branching forth into
>   numberless branches,
> Always the free range and diversity — always the continent of
>   Democracy. (*LG* 171)

This statistical experiment thus is descriptive rather than prescriptive. Instead of censuring individuals' behaviors from a normative point of view, he takes account of differences in his "free range and diversity."

It is worth looking at the further development of the normalist discourse in order to appreciate Whitman's early flexibility. In 1920 American presidential candidate and later president Warren G. Harding stated in a famous election speech that America now needed "not heroics but healing, not rostrums but normalcy; not revolution but restoration." Thereby he not only provided a historiographical designation for a whole period — the period of normalcy — but he expressed, in a moment of crisis, the desire especially of the rural and small-town population for a restoration of earlier conditions. Just at the time when the urban element in the United States gained the upper hand numerically, traditionalist groups organized in order to restore the "normalcy" of the earlier period, which they considered threatened by the urban style of life — an attempt that gave the period of "normalcy" in the 1920s its ironic label.

One of the most important novels of the period, F. Scott Fitzgerald's *The Great Gatsby*, shows the centrality of the conception of normality for the 1920s but also its ambivalence. On the very first page of the novel, the first-person narrator, Nick Carraway, defines himself as a "normal person" to whom persons with "abnormal minds" are easily attracted.[6] Nick rejects the urban culture of the East Coast with a rhetoric strongly reminiscent of President Harding: "When I came back from the East last autumn I felt that I wanted the world to be in *uniform* and at a sort of *moral attention* forever" (Fitzgerald 2; my emphasis). Fitzgerald's novel presents the metropolis as a grandiose and extremely dynamic environment; at the same time, however, the logic of the protagonists' standards of what is normal rejects it. The literary and cultural texts of the 1920s abound with references expounding the cultural battle over normality.

One battleground is the literary canon itself. The so-called canon debate is no invention of the political correctness movement of the 1980s and 1990s. In 1925 Upton Sinclair states programmatically that his book *Mammonart* would "investigate the whole process of art creation, and place the art function in relation to the sanity, health and progress of mankind. It will attempt to set up new canons in the arts, overturning many of the standards now accepted."[7]

One area we have found to be particularly relevant with regard to our normality project is African American and ethnic studies and literatures. It is easy to imagine how marginalized groups would feel terrorized by a restrictive, limiting notion of what is "normal." In Toni Morrison's early novel *The Bluest Eye* (1970), Pecola, the African American girl yearning to have blue eyes, has internalized white racist standards of beauty. She and her mother, Pauline, experience a special and aggravated form of alienation because they accept these standards for themselves. Pecola's ability to identify with her own blackness, to view herself as desirable, acceptable, and "normal," is lost and replaced by self-hatred. The text from an old-fashioned reading primer frames the novel and contrasts the "normal world" of the white middle class with Pecola's experiences, which have little to do with these standards of beauty and family life.

This reference to post–World War II literature shows how much Whitman anticipated flexible versions of normality Americans (and Western Europeans) have come to appreciate since the countercultural revolution of the 1960s. However, this investigation of Whitman's exploration of normality is not merely of historical interest. In the past two decades, there have been many voices — and not only conservative ones — that have been lamenting the lack of defined standards and set norms. I believe that to do away with normality altogether is threatening to many and frequently leads to the ultraconservatism we encounter in so many of our Western societies. Whitman shows that normality may be defined flexibly, that indeed there might be several normalities in a pluralistic society. His insistence on *cohesiveness* in a non-normative society may beg the question of how to achieve it, but it outlines a problem we are all faced with. Maybe the ultimate normality of the twenty-first century, though we are far from it, will be that we can live without a narrow definition of the range of the normal. Whitman's poetry can definitely help us to understand that process.

NOTES

1. Rod Nordland and Zoran Cirjakovic, "Try a Little Boredom," *Newsweek*, October 16, 2000, 32.

2. The first systematic analysis of the development of "normalism" in Western cultures was undertaken by Dortmund scholar Jürgen Link in *Versuch über den Normalismus: Wie Normalität produziert wird* (Opladen: Westdeutscher Verlag, 1996; 2nd ed., 1998). This study also introduces and defines the terminology used in this essay. A comprehensive bibliography for various disciplines is offered by Jürgen Link, Rolf Parr, Matthias Thiele, eds., *Was ist normal? Eine Bibliographie der Dokumente und Forschungsliteratur seit 1945* (Oberhausen: Athena, 1999).

3. In fact, the Dortmund research project is entitled "Life in Landscapes of Curves: Flexible Normalism in Everyday Work and Life, Media, Literary and Non-Literary Texts."

4. J. V. Widmann, "Der amerikanische Lyriker Walt Whitman," *Das Magazin für die Litteratur des In- und Auslandes* 58 (1889), 585.

Walter Grünzweig

5. Jerzy Neymann, "The Emergence of Mathematical Statistics: A Historic Sketch with Particular Reference to the United States," in *On the History of Statistics and Probability: Proceedings of a Symposium on the American Mathematical Heritage to Celebrate the Bicentennial of the United States of America, Held at Southern Methodist University, May 27–29, 1974*, ed. D. B. Owen (New York and Basel: Dekker, 1976), 153.

6. F. Scott Fitzgerald, *The Great Gatsby* (New York: Scribner's, 1925), 1.

7. Upton Sinclair, *Mammonart* (Pasadena: The Author, 1925), 8.

Walt Whitman at the Movies
Cultural Memory and the Politics of Desire

KENNETH M. PRICE

In 1855 Walt Whitman claimed — bravely if not wisely — that "the proof of a poet is that his country absorbs him as affectionately as he has absorbed it" (*LG* 729). We've yet to experience what Whitman foresaw, a time when farmers, mechanics, and bus drivers routinely go to work with copies of *Leaves of Grass* in their back pockets. Yet the movie industry has in a sense justified his bold prediction, enabling versions of "Whitman" (ranging from the puerile to the subtle) to reach the vast audiences that eluded him in his lifetime. Whitman's relation to film is a complex, fascinating, and largely neglected topic.[1] This essay explores three interrelated matters. Initially, I note the affinities between Whitman's poetry and film and observe how his poetry developed concurrently with the earliest attempts at animated photography, coming to fruition in the Philadelphia area as artists and inventors, notably Eadweard Muybridge and Thomas Eakins, were advancing the field of motion studies. Next, I consider how in the silent era the groundbreaking American film theorist Vachel Lindsay, the leading director D. W. Griffith, and a pair of pioneering avant-garde filmmakers, Paul Strand and Charles Sheeler, all responded directly to Whitman. Finally, I analyze the appropriation of Whitman in films during the past sixty years, and especially the flurry of interest since 1980, for what it tells us about cultural memory and the politics of desire.[2]

Cinema, Leaves of Grass, *and Celebrity Culture*

Whitman's career coincided with the conceptual and technical breakthroughs that made possible the art of film. Animated photography was attempted as early as 1851, and in 1878 Muybridge published the first series of cinematographic pictures depicting a galloping horse taken on Leland Stanford's farm in Palo Alto, California (see fig. 1). The importance of Muybridge's pictures was immediately perceived by Whitman's friend Eakins. When Muybridge gained an appointment at the University of Pennsylvania in 1884 to continue his study of animal and human locomotion, Eakins served on the commission that supervised his work. In addition, Eakins engaged in his own motion studies and advanced beyond Muybridge in approaching the effect of a motion picture camera by using a single camera instead of a whole battery of cameras. In 1885 Eakins lectured on his photographic motion studies, and the following year he exhibited one of his works, *History of a Jump* (see fig. 2). In differing ways, Eakins, Muybridge, and Whitman each benefited from the Philadelphia-Camden locale, a center of interest in photography and in its new applications for art.[3]

Whitman did not live to experience the nickelodeon (the initial permanent exhibition outlets for films), but his contemporaries imagined cinema before it was realized. As André Bazin has argued, cinema, an "idealistic phenomenon," existed in a well-developed conceptual form long before the "obstinate resistance of matter" was overcome by a series of technical breakthroughs.[4] Whitman kept current about new applications in photography through his dealings with leading photographers and inventors, including Eakins and James Wallace Black, who was instrumental in the development of the magic lantern, a widely popular means of photographic display.[5] Early film visionaries yearned to advance beyond lantern slide lectures, to portray the world in a seamless fashion combining motion, sound, and color. Thomas Edison (who expressed a desire to "obtain a phonogram from the poet Whitman") sought to link sound and sight by attaching the phonograph to the kinetoscope (an apparatus for viewing recorded images that was widely available in Whitman's time). Like Edison and others, the poet welcomed new technological tools, as is suggested by the wax cylinder of what is apparently Whitman's own voice reciting lines from "America."[6] New inventions enhanced Whitman's tool kit, improving his ability to convey an illusion of presence. As Whitman remarked, "The human expression is so fleeting; so quick; coming and going; all aids are welcome" (*WWC* 5:479).

Leaves of Grass anticipated many techniques we now associate with filmmakers. When Whitman argued in 1872 that a "modern Image-Making

1. Eadweard Muybridge's serial photographs of Edgington trotting on Leland Stanford's farm in California. These photographs capturing high-speed motion inaugurated a new era in photography. Courtesy of Print & Picture Collection, Free Library of Philadelphia.

2. Thomas Eakins's History of a Jump, *with annotations by Eadweard Muybridge. Courtesy of Library Company of Philadelphia.*

creation is indispensable to fuse and express the modern Political and Scientific creations," he characterized poetry in ways that prefigured film.[7] He once remarked, "I approach nature not to explain nature but to picture. Who can explain?"[8] As early as the pre-*Leaves* poem "Pictures," Whitman began to develop his mature style that emphasized metonymy rather than metaphor, a style that gloried in the realistic details of life and moved freely across space and that linked images by a private logic. (As Ed Folsom has noted, early photographers were stunned by the clutter and debris in their pictures since the camera picked up details the eye had not noticed.)[9] "Pictures" stresses the democratic inclusiveness of photography, its capturing of all in its field in opposition to the selectivity of painting.

> For wherever I have been, has afforded me superb pictures,
> And whatever I have heard has given me perfect pictures,
> And every hour of the day and night has given me copious pictures,
> And every rod of land or sea affords me, as long as I live, inimitable
>   pictures. (*LG* 648–649)

The poet strove to give his work the dynamism that marked the best photography of his day, photography that seemed to him magically to catch life "in a flash, as it shifted, moved, evolved" (*WWC* 3:23).[10] Animated photography could, even more powerfully, convey both patterns and dynamics of information, the process of seeing, the unfolding of action. Whitman's own fidelity to process in a poem such as "Crossing Brooklyn Ferry" may have led Robert Richardson to the arresting claim that Whitman's example has had "at least as great an impact on film form as it has had on modern poetic practice."[11] I think Richardson overstates his case, but not badly so. Whitman's work was suggestive because of its compelling use of montage as a structural principle (what Sergei Eisenstein called "Walt Whitman's huge montage conception").[12] The poet's catalogs adumbrate the jump cutting, fluent mobility, and surprising juxtapositions frequently seen in films.

It is worth adding that Whitman's fashioning of himself as an artifact, a self-created star, prefigured developments in an industry that would thrive on public relations ingenuity. He set a new precedent for how a literary project could be advanced through photography, demonstrating photography's power to contribute to celebrity status. He included photographic portraits of himself in his books, portraits that contribute to and are inseparable from the meaning of some of his poems. He conceived of *Leaves* of *Grass* as his "definitive *carte visite* to the coming generations" (*LG* 562). In England, particularly among those interested in manly love, his photos took on special import, having a type of talismanic function. Recognizable yet elusive, Whitman endures in part because of this star quality. His blending of seeming opposites — intimacy and publicity — is analogous to one of the most powerful effects of film. Through a much commented upon metonymic trick, he collapsed the distinction between *Leaves of Grass* and himself, offering the illusion that he and his book were one. Alternately revealing and withholding information, he conveyed a curiously inscrutable familiarity.

"*I pass so poorly with paper and types*": Whitman and Silent Films

Whitman provided more than stylistic hints for early filmmakers. Beginning as early as 1913, filmmakers dramatized him in this new art form. The earliest cinematic treatment of Whitman is *The Carpenter* (see fig. 3), a silent film produced by the Vitagraph company.[13] This film, apparently no longer extant, was an adaptation of William Douglas O'Connor's short story of the same name. O'Connor's original story did not mention the poet by name, but the bearded visitor to hospitals, caregiver to the wounded of both North and South, unmistakably referred to Whitman. The emphases of the film are suggested by this review from *Motion Picture World*:

> Cast in war times and surroundings, the contentions which tore this nation cause severe division in this household; the son is opposed to the father, and espouses the opposite cause and is hated therefor[e] and as was not uncommon in those days, brothers fight against brothers. A second trouble arises in the coming financial ruin of the old home, while a third evil is seen in the advantage being taken of a young wife of one of the sons, by a visiting friend of alluring manners; hatred, ruin, and jealousy, are working their insidious way in dreaded canker-like manner, in this once happy and prosperous home.

The review notes that "there is an unknown Christ in the home moulding the control of events and bringing prosperity, peace, and happiness, if allowed to do by a willing yielding to his gracious influences."[14] Neither the

3. An illustration of The Carpenter *from* Motion Picture World.
Courtesy of the Library of Congress.

review nor an advertisement for the film mentions O'Connor as the author of the original story or Whitman as the prototype of the hero, suggesting that Marguerite Bertsch, the scriptwriter, may have pirated the story. In any event, the film treated one issue, the love triangle, that later would be pivotal in many Whitman films. O'Connor's original story explored the love of comrades, what he called the "love passing the love of women," though it is unclear how this issue figured in the film (an all-male triangle may be suggested by figure 4). The story associates the poet's hospital work with the healing powers of Christ and depicts him as uniting a family torn apart by sons fighting for opposing armies. The film also apparently emphasized the religious aspect of Whitman, an element that later would fade in importance as the dominant threads in Whitman's reception became not the political radical and the religious prophet but the secular poet and spokesman for mainstream liberal American democracy.

Writing two years after *The Carpenter*, Van Wyck Brooks, in *America's Coming-of-Age* (1915), reinforced the view that Whitman served as an in-

4. *A photo of the actor playing the Whitman figure in* The Carpenter.
Of interest here is the triangulated pattern of relationship and the carpenter's clothing:
the mixed coloring apparently attests to his lack of favoritism to either side.
Courtesy of the Library of Congress.

tegrating force in American culture. In this vital work in the development
of American modernism, Brooks declared Whitman to be part of the "us-
able past," a middle ground bridging highbrow and lowbrow. "The real
significance of Walt Whitman," Brooks asserted, "is that he, for the first
time, gave us the sense of something organic in American life. . . . In him
the hitherto incompatible extremes of the American temperament were
fused."[15] In the same year, Vachel Lindsay, champion of Whitman's legacy
in Hollywood, published *The Art of the Moving Picture* (1915), in which he
praised film as a new American hieroglyphics. Lindsay, seeking a solution
to the problem of Babel, hoped that the hieroglyph of film might be an in-
tegrating force on a large scale, that it might provide a universal language
because of the ability of narrative and image to cross cultural boundaries.

Kenneth M. Price

However, in an interesting turn, Lindsay argued that this universal language should have a national inflection: "We must have Whitmanesque scenarios, based on moods akin to that of the poem By Blue Ontario's Shore. The possibility of showing the entire American population its own face in the Mirror Screen has at last come. Whitman brought the idea of democracy to our sophisticated literati, but did not persuade the democracy itself to read his democratic poems. Sooner or later the kinetoscope will do what he could not, bring the nobler side of the equality idea to the people who are so crassly equal." Believing that those in "slums seem to be . . . most affected by this novelty," Lindsay underscored the social and political importance of film.[16] Lindsay does little, however, to mask his own feelings of superiority to those "so crassly equal," despite his advocacy of "Whitmanesque scenarios."

The idea that Whitman could underwrite an approach to filmmaking gained powerful support from D. W. Griffith. Griffith so admired Whitman that he said he "would rather have written one page of *Leaves of Grass* than to have made all the movies for which he received world acclaim."[17] Early in its history, film was associated with inexpensive popular entertainment, poorly educated city dwellers, and the immigrant working classes. As Lindsay's words and Griffith's practices showed, Whitman's ability to achieve high art standing while retaining populist credentials enabled him to be a resource for a new art form struggling to negotiate class boundaries and the sometimes conflicting claims of commerce and art. When classical film appropriated Whitman, the industry aligned itself with a poet who claimed (oxymoronically) special privilege as a spokesman for democracy.

With *The Birth of a Nation* (1915), Griffith achieved a stunning commercial and artistic success, even as controversy erupted over the film's racism and Griffith found himself confronting censorship battles. Whitman's own battles with censorship and his reputation as a poet of love increased his appeal for Griffith in the immediate aftermath of *The Birth of a Nation*, a time of both great achievement and great crisis. Griffith attempted mightily to secure middle-class respectability for the fledgling movie industry. Thus he strove to give *Intolerance* (1916), which explicitly invoked Whitman, the status of art, and he succeeded in that the film was greeted as an "epic poem" and "a film fugue."[18] Paradoxically, Griffith attempted to achieve a universal language of cinema *and* to ground cinema, as Lindsay had suggested, in a particular strain of U.S. culture directly related to Whitman, whom he "passionately admired" (Hansen 185). One of the central oddities of *Intolerance* is its use of intertitles, which often appear on tabletlike backgrounds displaying various scripts. Viewers encounter English intertitles superimposed upon nonphonetic and non-Western script. The effect is that of a palimpsest, with different systems of graphic notation visible in layered fashion within the same shot (Hansen 190). Even as *Intolerance* aspires to overcome textual limitations, the film multiplies textual forms, and if the film privileges any single text it is "Out of the Cradle Endlessly Rocking."

Griffith paralleled the approach of *Leaves of Grass* in his emphasis on the gritty materiality of life, his appreciation of detail, and his grandiose ambition to include seemingly everything. Epic in scope, *Intolerance* features four separate narratives set in radically different places and times. Interwoven by means of parallel montage, these narratives include a modern American story tracing a young couple's struggle with tenement violence and an unfair legal system; a French narrative treating the Saint Bartholemew's Day Massacre (A.D. 1572); episodes set in Judea focusing on the life of Christ; and a fourth narrative depicting the fall of Babylon to Cyrus (538 B.C.). Whereas the historical episodes all end in bloodshed, the modern story represents a variation in that catastrophe is averted when the young husband escapes execution at the last moment.

The four stories are linked only by a mysterious, mood-setting, shadowy shot of Lillian Gish rocking a cradle accompanied by intertitles that quote — sometimes inexactly — *Leaves of Grass* (see fig. 5). One intertitle reads: "A golden thread binds the four stories — a fairy girl with sunlit hair — her hand on the cradle of humanity — eternally rocking." The rocking cradle image is associated with no particular time (the woman's clothing could be from almost any period), as is true of the mysterious figures, the three Fates, visible in the background. The cradle image unifies *Intolerance*, marking transitions and introducing and concluding the film. The image conveys a common humanity linking all people and a view of history that is highly patterned and reiterative, as is suggested by the intertitle "endlessly rocks the cradle, Uniter of here and Hereafter."[19] Critical of this recurrent shot, Sergei Eisenstein noted that "the cradle could not possibly be *abstracted into an image of eternally reborn epochs* and remained inevitably simply a *life-like cradle*, calling forth derision, surprise or vexation in the spectator."[20] The cradle image is a jarring yet curiously powerful feature in this film: perhaps Eisenstein was bothered because the image remains outside the flow of all four narratives. Moreover, because the cra-

Kenneth M. Price

5. Lillian Gish rocking the cradle in Intolerance *with the Fates in the background.
Courtesy of the Museum of Modern Art/Film Stills Archive.*

dle image is often repeated, the viewer cannot help but notice the labori-
ousness of the attempt to convey an abstraction by means of a material object. The very oddity of mixing a prominent nonnarrative element in a
film notable for its four strong narratives produces a formal complexity
that is in keeping with, say, the experimentation of "Song of Myself," with
its mininarratives embedded within a nonnarrative structure.[21] To my way
of thinking, Griffith is reasonably successful in achieving a totality of effect
when he combines the visual image of the cradle and Whitman's words to
suggest "eternally reborn epochs." Through the invocation of "Out of the
Cradle Endlessly Rocking," Griffith taps into a poem that is profoundly
concerned with problems of "translation" across languages, species, and
time and that, like Griffith's film, reaches far back into Western tradition.

While Griffith developed cinema in the direction of narrative and kept
his camera focused on actors rather than on the space they inhabited,
Charles Sheeler and Paul Strand, more famous for their photography
and painting, adopted a starkly different approach. Sheeler and Strand's
seven-minute work, *Manhatta* (1921), has been called the first genuine

avant-garde film made in the United States.[22] Abandoning classical modes of address and the depiction of heroes and heroines, Sheeler and Strand present no story but instead depict a five-block area in lower Manhattan. Sheeler had proposed to Strand that they might make a kind of "experimental film about New York . . . — a silent film carried along by the titles . . . from Walt Whitman's poem." Shot mainly from the rooftops and streets, the film's disorienting vantage points remind viewers of their subjectivity and emphasize the geometric configurations of the cityscape. Humans, when seen at all, appear antlike, thus making the Whitman invocations strange given the poet's celebration of the larger-than-life "divine average" person.[23] *Manhatta* shifts curiously between a modernism that either shows humans as tiny or as part of well-functioning machines. The incongruity between words and images serves simultaneously as a commentary on the film's own modernist aesthetic and as a commentary on Manhattan itself, where, in panoramic shots opening the film, the picturesque waterways jut up against the stark angularity of skyscrapers.[24] The eleven intertitles drawn from various Whitman poems — "A Broadway Pageant," "Mannahatta," "Crossing Brooklyn Ferry" — give structure to the film and serve as a "lyric counter-point to the film's visual imagery."[25] *Manhatta* achieves a compelling and highly original visual style analogous to the pathbreaking nature of Whitman's "language experiment." Interestingly, Griffith, a narrative filmmaker, turns to "Cradle," one of the few narrative poems in Whitman's œuvre — while Sheeler and Strand turn to Whitman's various nonnarrative lyrics to enable their film to be "carried along," to explore methods of movement and organization in a film that lacks the forward drive of plot development.

Whitman Films in the Sound Era

FILMS AT MID-CENTURY

Two Warner Brothers films, *Now, Voyager* (1942) and *Goodbye, My Fancy* (1951), follow Strand and Sheeler in quoting Whitman in their very titles and follow Griffith's *Intolerance* in making explicit their invocations of the poet and their concern with textuality. *Now, Voyager*, directed by Irving Rapper and based on a novel by Olive Higgins Prouty, pivots on lines from Whitman's "The Untold Want."[26] This much-admired film treats problems of repression and a corresponding yearning for freedom as it traces the

6. An exchange between Dr. Jaquith and Charlotte in Now, Voyager.
Courtesy of the Museum of Modern Art/Film Stills Archive.

maturation of Charlotte Vale (Bette Davis). Charlotte achieves her sense of identity not through an orthodox heterosexual romance but through involvement with a married man, Jerry Durance (Paul Henreid). Moreover, the therapeutic approach of Dr. Jaquith (Claude Rains) hinges on his quoting of Whitman in a key scene with Charlotte in his sanitarium (see fig. 6). Dr. Jaquith turns to Whitman's poem "The Untold Want": "If old Walt didn't have you in mind when he wrote this, he had hundreds of others like you." He asks her to read for herself the lines: "Untold want, by life and land ne'er granted, / Now, Voyager, sail thou forth, to seek and find."[27] Whitman opens new possibilities for Charlotte by encouraging freedom from the sexual repression and rigidity of her former days. She finds her way to a new womanhood via a male doctor and a male poet by internalizing their messages and embarking on her own open-ended journey.

Charlotte's dilemma is scripted in terms of a rejection of Bostonian conventionalities, pretentiousness, and pieties.[28] The film opens with an image of the Vale name on a house stone and then shifts to a miniature statue of a black jockey, situating Charlotte's personal oppression and repression within a social context based on authority, division, and unequal access to power. The Bostonians depicted here — Charlotte's mother and Eliot Livingston, to whom Charlotte is briefly engaged — view the world very much in hierarchical terms. In opposition to the Boston elite, both Jerry Durance and Dr. Jaquith (and the outré Whitman) are figures foreign to the Boston world. Early in the film we see that Charlotte conceals her passionate inner life, hiding racy reading material behind stodgier tomes and hiding a notebook that records an earlier failed romance. Whitman is part of Charlotte's breaking away from the Puritan tradition to embrace a broader range of people and a less repressive outlook. Whitman helps Charlotte embrace her inner life and integrate it with her public personality.

Now, Voyager reconsiders and reconfigures family relations by depicting a woman who reaches full selfhood outside of the nuclear family and outside of marriage.[29] Charlotte cleverly responds to her mother's dim assessment of her marital future by remarking: "I'll get a cat and a parrot and enjoy single blessedness." The film not only explores Charlotte's affair with Jerry, a married man, but also subtly endorses the same-sex affectional bond she develops with Jerry's daughter, Tina, thus making the Whitman aura all the more apt. This film, described by one critic as "blatantly challenging monogamy," has a subtext of pedophilic lesbianism.[30] In a scene with Tina, Charlotte declares in a voice-over: "This is Jerry's child in my arms. This is Jerry's child clinging to me." Is she making a personal sacrifice to sanctify and sublimate her (heterosexual but illicit) love, or is her emphasis on an even more forbidden love, on the person in her arms? Is she emphasizing the man in her mind or the girl in her arms? Tina later kisses Charlotte's hand after causing a slight burn at a campfire. Even this level of tenderness prompts Tina to wonder over Charlotte's role: is she a friend, asks Tina? A mother figure? Or is she, as the film hints, moving into the role of intimate companion? Charlotte's caring, affectionate, and nurturing role with Tina exceeds typical categories and labels.[31] In this way, her affective life is like Whitman's own work in the Civil War hospitals, where he was simultaneously mother, father, lover, friend — a powerful and shifting emotional presence, giving and receiving a complicated set of signals in his work with young soldiers.

Like *Now, Voyager* in taking its title from Whitman's poetry, *Goodbye, My Fancy* addresses significant political issues in the immediate aftermath of World War II. The original play *Goodbye, My Fancy* (on which the film was based) was first copyrighted in 1947, one year after Malcolm Cowley's bold

Kenneth M. Price

treatment of the homosexual Whitman in the *New Republic* and in the same year that forty-three witnesses were subpoenaed in Washington, D.C., before the House Un-American Activities Committee investigating "Communist subversion" in Hollywood.[32] In 1950 discussions on the floor of the House of Representatives linked gays in government to Russians.[33] The film version of *Goodbye, My Fancy* (directed by Vincent Sherman) appeared in 1951, one year after National Security Council paper 68 inaugurated the Cold War as a problem not only of influence and ideology but of pressing military threat.[34]

The film adaptation of *Goodbye, My Fancy* also speaks to political issues, including academic freedom, women's rights, and unsanctioned sexuality. In *Goodbye, My Fancy*, when Congresswoman Agatha Reed (Joan Crawford) receives an invitation to return to Good Hope College for Women for homecoming, she eagerly accepts.[35] She is motivated by a desire to rekindle an old romance with James Merrill (Robert Young), whom she once knew as her Whitman-quoting history professor and who is now president of the college. Agatha's rise to public success, through an earlier career in journalism, occurred despite a scandal that kept her from graduating: she was dismissed from Good Hope for violating curfew (she was seeing James, then a young professor, whom she protected by disappearing). He tells her — as they reconsider the broken romance of the past — that he could never forgive himself for introducing her to the "beauties of Walt Whitman." He still has the departure note she had written him years earlier. They recite together "Good-bye My Fancy!" He offers the first two lines: "Good-bye my Fancy! / Farewell dear mate, dear love!" And she follows with the next three lines: "I'm going away, I know not where, / Or to what fortune, or whether I may ever see you again, / So Good-bye my Fancy" (*LG* 557). Agatha then rips up the old note and says "Hello my Fancy!" before they share a long kiss. This revived romance is doomed, however, because Matt Cole (Frank Lovejoy) arrives on campus intent on renewing his own lost love with Agatha and because she gradually perceives that James, as president, has become a tool of the trustees of Good Hope. The trustees fear the documentary Agatha has made about war-torn Europe. The specific cause of their fear remains unarticulated, but they clearly distrust open thought and debate.[36] Ultimately, Agatha is able to present her documentary, though we get no glimpse of it within the film. Perhaps to the male trustees the documentary's very title makes it something dangerous for women: "Command Your Future."

In Fay Kanin's original play, the documentary was an antiwar film, but the Hollywood scriptwriters switched matters to emphasize the (somewhat) less controversial issue of academic freedom. In the play, the admirers of Whitman are Agatha, Ginny (Merrill's daughter), and Dr. Pitt, a physics teacher who is concerned about the destructive capacity of atomic bombs and who encourages critical thinking and urges his students to read *Leaves of Grass*. Kanin's use of Whitman in the original play is more effective than Vincent Sherman's use of him on the screen. In the film, Merrill, stiff yet spineless, seems an unlikely admirer of the controversial, freethinking Whitman. In the original play, in contrast, Ginny and Agatha exchange the "Goodbye My Fancy" lines, not (as the film giddily has it) James and Agatha. In the early postwar period, Fay Kanin and, to a lesser extent, Vincent Sherman recognized Whitman's power as an icon of alternative thinking and anticipated the way the poet would be employed, more boldly and irreverently, by Jack Kerouac, Allen Ginsberg, and other beat writers.

REPRESENTING WHITMAN IN REAGAN'S AMERICA

A flurry of films appeared in the two decades between 1980 and 2000 that mention, depict, quote, picture, or in some other way make use of Whitman. The poet is invoked in the futuristic film *Until the End of the World* (1991).[37] He is quoted in the psychodrama *Dead Again* (1991). He is pictured as the image of devoted love of children in *The Blue Lagoon* (1980). He serves as a multicultural spokesman in *Fame* (1980), *With Honors* (1994), and *Quiz Show* (1994). He represents the quintessential American poet to various Europeans in *Down by Law* (1987), *Little Women* (1994), and *Love and Death on Long Island* (1997). He highlights the contrast between the U.S. dream of freedom and the U.S. nightmare of wide-scale imprisonment in, again, *Down by Law* and *Road Scholar* (1993).[38] He has most cultural resonance, however, as a poet of love. Alicia Ostriker once remarked that Whitman "permitted love": the "degree and quantity and variety of love in Whitman are simply astonishing."[39] Often he serves as a type of love currency in heterosexual settings. In *Postcards from the Edge* (1990), a speech about Whitman works as the standard pickup ploy for Jack Faulkner (Dennis Quaid). In *Patch Adams* (1998), a medical student (Robin Williams) takes up reading Whitman instead of his medical books to reorient his education and to woo a female medical student. In *Doc Hollywood* (1991), a character recites "Out of the Cradle Endlessly Rocking" in a scene that first signals ultimate romantic pairings. In *Reds* (1981), just before marrying Jack Reed (Warren Beatty), Louise Bryant (Diane Keaton) hides a love poem written by Eugene O'Neill (Jack Nicholson) in *Leaves of Grass*, a book serving simultaneously as a love intensifer and as an affirmation of their leftist principles.[40]

Somewhat more bold and thus more interesting are filmic treatments of Whitman in connection with same-sex love. James Baldwin once remarked that "men do not kiss each other in American films."[41] This cinematic prohibition on male intimacy held until only recently. In "Gay Love and the Movies" (1969), Ralph Pomeroy discussed the love that had a social life but no screen life:

> Watching love stories on the TV,
> watching a movie,
> I wonder where we are.
> I've wondered for a long time.
> I've never seen any of us there,
> straight on, like nouvelle vague lovers,
> like psychedelic dancers.
> I've never seen us, arms akimbo, standing in the morning, waiting,
> lying around in grassy meadows[42]

Here, yearning for a love made visible, Pomeroy exploits the potential of Whitman, whose force as an icon is all the more persuasive in that he need not be named. Instead, Pomeroy calls to mind the poet of *Leaves of Grass*, his famous daguerreotype with arm akimbo, and his key symbol of manly love, the phallic calamus reed found in marshes and grassy meadows. Pomeroy's poem was prescient given the role Whitman has since played in films that have broken through old codes of silence and invisibility about gay life.

Filmmakers have appropriated Whitman as a relatively unthreatening entryway into consideration of same-sex love.[43] Whitman's sexual ambiguity, sanctified status (especially because of his hospital work in the Civil War), and stature as a revered poet have made him a figure granted latitude. But why did this intensified consideration of same-sex love, mediated by Whitman, occur in the 1980s? The timing involves the confluence of the history of Hollywood, the history of sexuality, and the history of Whitman criticism. Between 1930 and 1968 Hollywood production codes precluded overt treatment of homosexuality. The new readiness to invoke

Whitman occurred after the lifting of these codes, after the Kinsey report, after Stonewall and the first gay pride marches, and concurrently with post-1980 conservative efforts to curtail modest advances gays were making within society. In the last two decades of the twentieth century, Whitman's cultural stock was on the rise, while scholars, many of them gay, began to be much more assertive in countering the rather tepid accounts of Whitman's sexuality that had dominated American critical discourse.[44] The early 1980s, the beginning of an intensified interest in Whitman in films, was also a time of anxiety about gay life because of the AIDS crisis. Whitman's treatment of male-male love and his remoteness from the era of AIDS rendered him a safe object of contemplation.

The films discussed below from the 1980s and 1990s make Whitman "gay" for a popular audience, gay in a way he could only be in a post-Stonewall world when new terminology contributed to new shapes of psychic lives. Most of these films are market-driven Hollywood productions. Not surprisingly, then, daring is more superficial than real, and while these filmmakers have broken through to new topics, they haven't shattered old patterns and conceptions. Homosocial films, ranging widely in quality, do not all attempt to construct Whitman as gay.[45] In discussing how these films treat Whitman and gay issues, I move from least direct to most direct, from the homosocial to the homosexual, though not necessarily from the least to the most artful or honest.

One especially effective film, a non-Hollywood production, is Jim Jarmusch's black-and-white *Down by Law*, which turns to Whitman at a pivotal moment in its study of the world of three men in prison and their escape. A concern with comradeship rather than carnal attachment is at the center of this clever, poignant, and thoughtful film. The film contrasts the grand aspirations of poetry with the depressing realities of the down-and-out. It opens by tracing the declining lives of Zack (Tom Waits), a New Orleans disc jockey who has been set up to take a murder rap, and Jack (John Lurie), a pimp who, though certainly corrupt, is innocent of the crime he is charged with, soliciting a minor. Jack and Zack mirror one another, as their names imply, though they are unable to work together or sacrifice for one another. The opening scenes depict Zack and Jack in emotionally empty relationships with women, and their inability to interact with others does not improve when they enter the all-male world of the jail. Zack and Jack dislike each other and barely speak. But with the en-

Kenneth M. Price

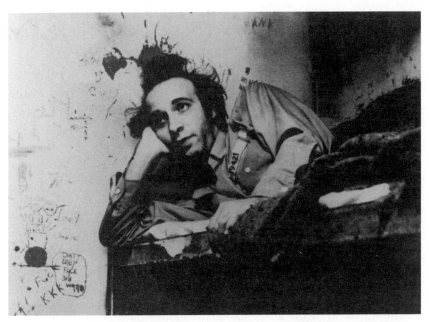

7. *Roberto Benigni on the cot from which he will recite* Leaves of Grass *in Italian translation. Courtesy of the Museum of Modern Art/Film Stills Archive.*

trance of Roberto (Roberto Benigni), the dynamic gradually begins to change (see fig. 7). Ostracized by Zack and Jack, Roberto breaks through isolation by conversing with himself. He asserts "I love Walt Whitman: *Leaves of Glass*! [*sic*]" Then, in stirring Italian, he recites lines from "The Singer in Prison":[46] "Vision di pietà, di onta e afflizione, / Orribil pensiero, un'alma in prigione"[47] [*O sight of pity, shame and dole! / O fearful thought — a convict soul (LG 376)*]. The incongruous humor of the scene underscores a serious matter: Zack and Jack are imprisoned souls not merely in their physical incarceration. We never learn why Zack and Jack were set up, but the Whitman lines suggest that the cause is irrelevant, that the real issue is the imprisoned soul: that is, Zack and Jack, especially, were more imprisoned *before* their incarceration than they were during and after it. Jack and Zack have little patience with Roberto and only gradually and grudgingly come to accept him. Yet he is the prisoner who draws a window on the prison wall, who can see, as it were, through the walls toward escape and toward another life. Roberto, against all odds, stumbles upon a café in the Louisiana bayou during their escape and falls in love with the Italian woman who owns it. His example of love and generosity eventually has an effect on Jack and Zack in the final scene when they swap coats as they part ways, their first cooperative action.

Two years later, another homosocial film, *Dead Poets Society*, repressed homosexual content with as much thoroughness as in the days of the Hollywood production codes. Although in this film homosexuality is never discussed as such, it is the submerged topic of concern: the drama of the story hinges on the main student character, Neil Perry (Robert Sean Leonard), who is allied with his teacher John Keating (Robin Williams) against Neil's authoritarian father. Neil's father prohibits him from taking part in a theatrical production (a stereotypical site of homosexual activity), forbidding him to play Puck, a fairy, in *A Midsummer Night's Dream*. Also gratuitously added is a picture of the teacher's girlfriend who is supposedly away in England while he is teaching at a boarding school, a touch apparently meant to reassure the audience that this Whitman-identified teacher in an all-male environment is safely heterosexual.

The film is strangely divided about key issues. *Dead Poets* stresses male bonding and invokes a recognizable gay icon. The teacher, Keating, blurs his own identity with that of Whitman: he urges his students to call him "Captain" (as in Whitman's "O Captain! My Captain!"). Whitman is the patron saint of Keating's classroom: a Whitman photograph from the 1860s hangs directly behind him in numerous shots. Furthermore, "Song of Myself," and specifically Whitman's primal yawp, becomes a resource to help a shy and repressed student to find his creativity. Yet the film blinks at a homosexual interpretation of Whitman, emphasizing instead the patriotic poet. Just as curiously, the film calls for independent thought while celebrating a reverential attitude toward a particular teacher and his pseudo-philosophy. As Tania Modleski remarks, because the sexual content of the film has been repressed and excluded from the narrative, it returns to haunt the film through textual inconsistencies and absurdities.[48]

The opportunities and pitfalls of working with Whitman as a film icon are manifest in *Beautiful Dreamers* (1990), a treatment of a romantic triangle that opens up intriguing issues. The combined fascination with and fear of homosexuality that befuddles *Dead Poets Society* also undermines *Beautiful Dreamers*. The film stars Rip Torn, who had broken new ground with his bold treatment of Whitman's love of men in "Song of Myself" (1976), a made-for-television movie produced by CBS in the *American Parade* series. In *Beautiful Dreamers*, Torn struggles with a script that is deeply flawed. Set in the late 1870s and early 1880s, the film, directly depicting Whitman, focuses on his friendship with his admirer Richard Maurice Bucke ("Maurice") (Colm Feore), director of the Asylum for the Insane in Ontario, Canada. The film presents Bucke, who ran the largest asylum in North America at the time, as a gentle, enlightened, forward-thinking man who opposes benighted beliefs about male masturbation and indignantly rejects the practice of removing women's ovaries in order to combat "moral insanity."[49] The film's portrayal of Bucke as unambiguously enlightened distorts his actual role. The historical Bucke was an aggressive intervener, using gynecological surgery to treat mental disorders (at least 200 women had their sexual organs removed while he served as superintendent), and he "approached the insane [male] masturbator with a sense of cleansing vengeance." A common treatment involved electric shocks applied to the penis.[50] If anything, then, Bucke was a steadfast enforcer of sexual norms.

Beautiful Dreamers is both inaccurate as history and weak as a story. It fails as a fictional account because it does not pursue the questions it raises. To its credit, the film addresses the erotics of discipleship. The conflict is not between Richard Maurice Bucke and Whitman over Maurice's wife, Jessie Gurd Bucke (Wendel Meldrum), but between Walt and Jessie over Maurice. Letters between the Buckes indicate that Maurice fell for Whitman so hard that he almost lost his wife. But the film, in treating this triangulated relationship, does not capture the urgency this situation had in life. After raising the idea of Jessie's jealousy of Walt, the film seems to imply — in a scene in which Jessie apparently masturbates while reading *Leaves of Grass*— that her romantic rival is also her savior whose words help her achieve a newly passionate relationship with her husband. By too easily emptying the triangulated conflict of all tension, the film deprives viewers of a satisfactory resolution of an issue raised by the film. The key scene, as often in Whitman-related works, involves bathing. At the edge of a pond, Walt and Maurice sing Italian opera in the nude, dangle their legs in the water, and sling mud on one another. When Jessie arrives to witness this scene, she joins the group instead of fleeing. In fact, she strips off her clothes, providing the only full frontal nudity in the film (Walt and Maurice have by this time modestly plunged into the water). She challenges Walt to explain why he never married, asserts that nature intended for men and women to be together, and shifts the dynamic to male-female, restoring a dyadic bond with Maurice. The scene affirms heterosexual bonds and, in the perspective it assumes and the gaze it invites, imagines a heterosexual male audience. Although Walt is not victorious in the romantic competition, his general doctrine of love prevails, or so the film's ending would have it. *Beautiful Dreamers* closes with a celebratory cricket match in which the hospital inmates play against a local club. We are led to believe through a flashing of dates and historical time cards in the final shots that Whitman was the source of the newly loving and gentle treatment of patients at Bucke's asylum. The film highlights a suggestive proximity of dates and events: the visit of the poet to Canada (1880), the lifting by Bucke of restraints on inmates (1882), and the publication of Bucke's biography of Whitman (1883).

The handling of nudity offers a key to the film's shortcomings. Despite his location outside of Hollywood, John Kent Harrison, a Canadian filmmaker, nonetheless adheres to the strict Hollywood prohibition against male frontal nudity. A more daring film would not have repressed the possibility of female fetishization of the male body or of male fetishization of the male body. (The breaking of this taboo would be, arguably, the filmic equivalent of Whitman's own experimental techniques and bold treatment of the body.) As a trope of unregulated desire, the nude male body, open for the scopophilic gaze of the female or the homosexual male, would be a defeat of regulation.[51] Instead, like Bucke himself, *Beautiful Dreamers* only appears to be unconventional but finally reinforces a compulsory heterosexuality.[52]

Much more honest and emotionally convincing are two other films treating Whitman and same-sex attachments by means of triangulated relationships, *Sophie's Choice* (1982) and *Bull Durham* (1988). The striking difference in subject matter between the two films, one treating the Holocaust and the other baseball, should not blind us to a fundamental similarity they share. These two films use Whitman and love triangles — involving two men and a woman — to explore the complexity of erotic desire. Filmmakers temper courage with caution, managing to treat homosexuality while offering a popular audience multiple possible identifications in considering these relationships. *Sophie's Choice*, set in 1947, involves a love triangle between Sophie (Meryl Streep); her schizophrenic husband, Nathan (Kevin Kline); and a writer they befriend, Stingo (Peter McNichol) (see fig. 8). Alan J. Pakula's script tells the story from Stingo's perspective and adheres fairly closely to the original novel by William

8. Nathan, Sophie, and Stingo on the magic-carpet ride at Coney Island.
Courtesy of the Museum of Modern Art/Film Stills Archive.

Styron. Intriguingly, however, the crucial Whitman material in the film is added by Pakula. The film, unlike the novel, opens with a gift of *Leaves of Grass* to the new writer on his arrival in Brooklyn. Later, in another scene interpolated into the film, the three friends drink champagne on the Brooklyn Bridge, toast one another, and pay homage to "the land that gave us Whitman, gave us words." Whitman's prestige as a writer, his Brooklyn roots, and his homoeroticism make him a fitting addition to the story line. Conveniently, he also reinforces a key aspect of the triadic relationship explored by Styron. However much Stingo lusts for women, he also longs for Nathan. As both film and novel make clear, Stingo finds Nathan to be "utterly, fatally, glamorous."[53] He is smitten with Nathan, loving him with an intensity rivaling his devotion to Sophie. Sophie, a Holocaust survivor from Poland, has faced an unthinkable life choice: to select one of her children for death so that the other might survive. She is a broken woman who can neither forget the past nor forgive herself. Her alliance with the troubled Nathan seems to result from a belief that through him may come punishment and, perhaps, salvation. Stingo's tangled love of Sophie is partly a desire to ease her pain and to rescue her from further tragedy. In Styron's novel, Whitman receives only the most brief, passing mention: *Leaves of Grass*, after all, explores a world in which hopefulness and human kindness are dominant forces, in which the central force in the universe, a "kelson of the creation" (*LG* 33), is love. What can such hopes mean in a world haunted by the grim historical events that frame Styron's almost unbearably painful narrative, a world scarred by the *shoah*? Pakula's judicious decision to include references to Whitman suits the film, which, though dark, is considerably less bleak than the novel.

The three-sided romance of *Bull Durham* is set in happier circumstances. Early in the film Annie Savoy (Susan Sarandon) reports in a voice-over: "Walt Whitman once said: 'I see great things in baseball. It's our game, the American game. It will repair our losses and be a blessing to us.'" *Bull Durham*, written and directed by Ron Shelton, a former minor league baseball player, explores everything from Whitman to New Age metaphysics while analyzing the homoerotic underpinnings of the national pastime. The film explores a three-sided romance involving Ebby Calvin "Nuke" LaLoosh (Tim Robbins) and Crash Davis (Kevin Costner) and Annie. In *Bull Durham*, traffic in men serves to cement the bond between Annie and Crash. That is, we have a shifting triangle with Crash and Nuke sometimes competing for Annie, and Annie and Crash sometimes competing for Nuke. The script, with neatly echoing lines, emphasizes the nearly identical roles of Annie and Crash: both are to give Nuke life experience and guide him to the majors. In one scene, Annie ties Nuke, stripped to his underwear, to her bedposts, but instead of engaging in some strange sexual act, or perhaps *as* some strange sexual act, she reads to him assorted lines from Whitman's "I Sing the Body Electric" (see fig. 9):

> I sing the body electric,
> The armies of those I love engirth me and I engirth them,
> They will not let me off until I go with them, respond to them,
> And discorrupt them, and charge them full with the charge of the
>   soul.
> . . . .
> But the expression of a well-made man appears not only in his face,
> It is in his limbs and joints also, it is curiously in the joints of his hips
>   and wrists,

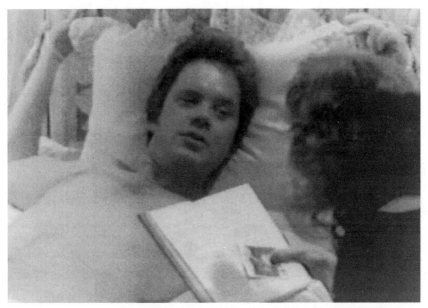

9. *Annie reading to "Nuke" from* Leaves of Grass *in the movie* Bull Durham.

. . . .
. . . love-flesh swelling and deliciously aching,
Limitless limpid jets of love hot and enormous . . . (*LG* 93–94, 96)

In a more subtle use of the poet, Crash announces his credo in strikingly Whitmanian fashion, through a catalog of parallel items.[54] The film explores what many fans refuse to acknowledge: the homosocial and homoerotic aspects of baseball, a game that depends on the effective wielding of bats. Fittingly, Annie remarks early in the film that the rivalry between Nuke and Crash is "really just some redirected homoeroticism." At its best, *Bull Durham* probes the complexity of erotic desire and explores the unstable boundary between homosocial and homoerotic relations.

Other films unmistakably invoke Whitman as a homosexual icon, as, for example, in the low-budget film *The Incredibly True Adventure of Two Girls in Love* (1995). Writer-director Maria Maggenti's film features one high school girl, Evie (Nicole Parker), who signals her affection for another, Randy (Laurel Holloman), with a gift of *Leaves of Grass*, an illustrated edition once owned by Evie's grandmother. This particular volume is granted a quasi-spiritual force. They swear eternal love — in a besieged hotel room — over *Leaves of Grass*, as if laying hands on a Bible.[55] A volume of Whitman is used rather than other possibilities — Sappho, Emily Dickinson, Adrienne Rich — presumably because he is the most prominent gay icon in the United States and because Maggenti concluded that it was more important to affirm same-sex love in general than to particularize that love as lesbian. In the concluding sequence, the two lovers embrace one another (with ears covered) as the zaniness of society rages on behind them. The film's concluding voice-over quotes "Song of Myself" about "a word unsaid": "It is not in any dictionary, utterance, symbol. / Something it swings on more than the earth I swing on, / To it the creation is the friend whose embracing awakes me" (*LG* 88). Evie and Randi then agree to change "friend" to "girlfriend."

Love and Death on Long Island (1997), another independent film, also provides an unusually insightful treatment of a love triangle and stands as perhaps the best example of effective treatment of Whitman and gay issues in a widely distributed release. The film explores the life of a reclusive widower, the British writer Giles De'Ath (John Hurt), who has lived shielded from modernity in his study and who accidentally locks himself out of the house during a rainstorm. He finds shelter at a nearby movie theater, selecting a film based on E. M. Forster's *The Eternal Moment*. After taking a wrong turn, Giles find himself viewing not Forster but *Hot Pants College II*, featuring randy undergraduates bent on voyeurism. These male gazers are contrasted with Giles, who, dismayed, begins to leave until he is mesmerized by a face, that of a young actor named Ronnie Bostock (Jason Priestley) (see fig. 10).

Whereas Gilbert Adair's novel *Love and Death on Long Island* negotiates its relation to fiction and the homosexual past by invoking E. M. Forster, the film negotiates its relation to cinema and previous depictions of homosexuality by invoking a distinguished predecessor, Irving Rapper's *Now, Voyager*. In both of the films, textuality is presented via a slip of paper containing Whitman's poetic lines, and precisely the same lines from "Untold Want" are quoted (see fig. 11). The differences between the films are also instructive. Charlotte in *Now, Voyager* is the object of the audience's gaze, whereas Giles in *Love and Death* is the gazer through whom we see. Charlotte "learns to be herself under the scrutiny of others' gaze, while Giles learns to accept and understand his own gaze."[56] The film version of *Love and Death on Long Island* makes extensive use of Whitman: Giles quotes *Leaves of Grass* when he arrives on Long Island, and Ronnie quotes *Leaves*

Kenneth M. Price

10. Ronnie preparing to quote Whitman at his mother's gravesite.
Courtesy of the Museum of Modern Art/Film Stills Archive.

11. Giles De'Ath scripting Ronnie's speech at his mother's gravesite.

of Grass again at the end, suggesting that he has benefited from his encounter with De'Ath, though their relationship never reaches a fully realized romance. The references to Whitman, though they are nowhere to be found in the original novel, are apt. Director Richard Kwietniowski, in creating a fresh work of art guided by but not limited by the original source, responds sensitively both to his source text and to the history of the genre in which he works. One can see why Kwietniowski concluded that interjecting Whitman would highlight themes already present in Adair's novel. Whitman's erotic attachments were with significantly younger men, and Kwietniowski explores precisely this type of bond. This film also considers the question of cultural crossing: Whitman's importance in the development of gay consciousness is directly related to an Atlantic crossing, whereby his ideas were put to use by a group of writers and sex radicals led by John Addington Symonds and Edward Carpenter who were striving to establish a positive homosexual identity within a hostile British cultural context. The class politics of Whitman's sexuality were key to his reception in Britain, and this film fittingly highlights the class contrast between a stuffy, elegant, and refined upper-class Englishman who reverses the directional flow across the Atlantic in his pursuit of an American B-movie star who, though he is rich, lacks taste and other markers of class. The handling of homoeroticism here avoids the clichés of many films in which older men fall for younger ones, and it also refuses to accept the deathly ending of many of those novels and films such as *Death in Venice.* In this case, the yearning of an older man for a younger doesn't lead to desperation and destruction; on the contrary, Giles, though unsuccessful in his quest, is filled with joy. He has opened himself up to a new life and presumably to a new ability to write novels.[57]

Interestingly, scriptwriters frequently turn to Whitman when he is not in their original source. In the novels *Little Women, Love and Death on Long Island, A Midnight Clear, Postcards from the Edge,* and *The Object of My Affection,* no mention is made of Whitman, and in *Sophie's Choice,* Whitman is mentioned only in passing. In each of the film adaptations, however, he plays a significant role.[58] Whitman has now become a convenient shorthand in American film culture, in a way analogous to his functioning for British readers at the end of the nineteenth century, when, as Eve Kosofsky Sedgwick has noted, a picture of Whitman or a letter from him served as a homosexual badge of recognition. Despite his crucial role in the construction of Anglo-American gay identities, Whitman's meanings are not

Kenneth M. Price

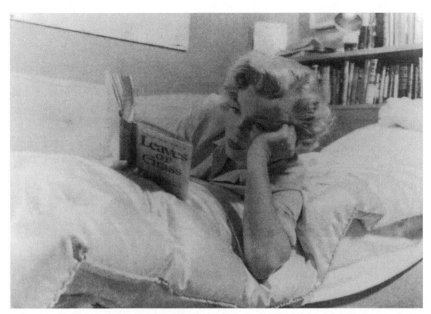

12. Marilyn Monroe photographed in her apartment. Reproduced with permission from James Haspiel, Young Marilyn: Becoming the Legend *(New York: Hyperion, 1994).*

limited to a particular type of sexuality. Indeed, he is attractive to many filmmakers for his more general aura of being the "tenderest lover." In 1951 in a "candid" shot reproduced in the volume *Young Marilyn*, Marilyn Monroe is seen reading *Leaves of Grass* as she reclines on a bed in her apartment (see fig. 12). What poem was she reading? Perhaps "So Long!" —

> Camerado, this is no book,
> Who touches this touches a man,
> (Is it night? are we here together alone?)
> It is I you hold and who holds you,
> I spring from the pages into your arms . . . (*LG* 505)

Walt and Marilyn — two American icons — exude irresistible sexuality. No wonder films found them and they found each other.

NOTES

1. Whitman's relationship to film has received little sustained treatment. Particular questions and topics have been pursued effectively in Alice Ahlers, "Cinematographic Technique in *Leaves of Grass*," *Walt Whitman Review* 12 (Decem-

ber 1966), 93–97; Robert Richardson, *Literature and Film* (Bloomington: Indiana University Press, 1969); Ben Singer, "Connoisseurs of Chaos: Whitman, Vertov, and the 'Poetic Survey,'" *Literature/Film Quarterly* 15 (1987), 247–258; Barry K. Grant, "Whitman and Eisenstein," *Literature/Film Quarterly* 4 (1976), 264–270; Michael Lynch, "Putting Whitman Back in the Closet," (Toronto) *Globe and Mail* April 17, 1990, A7; and in other commentary noted below. Special thanks to Brett Barney for help in locating illustrations for this essay.

2. This study makes no attempt to examine the many documentaries treating Whitman.

3. Philadelphia was home to the country's oldest photographic society and to the journal *Philadelphia Photographer* (see Kathleen A. Foster, *Thomas Eakins Rediscovered* [Philadelphia: Pennsylvania Academy of the Fine Arts, and New Haven, Conn.: Yale University Press, 1997], 108). Susan Danly notes that "in Philadelphia there was an active group of photographers and publishers who ardently believed that photography also had an aesthetic component" ("Thomas Eakins and the Art of Photography," in *Thomas Eakins* [Washington, D.C.: Smithsonian Institution Press, 1993], 180). Eakins even offered suggestions to Muybridge, which were ignored (Foster, 112). Meanwhile, during their collaboration, Eakins and Muybridge both experimented with the Marey wheel technique, a means of recording a sequence of images on a single plate, requiring the use of a perforated disk that rotated at a constant speed behind the camera lens (see Danly, 191 n.6).

4. André Bazin, *What Is Cinema?* as reproduced in part in *Film Theory and Criticism*, ed. Gerald Mast and Marshall Cohen (New York: Oxford University Press, 1979), 23.

5. It is commonly thought that Whitman and Eakins met in 1887, though they may have met earlier, perhaps in 1883. See Ed Folsom, "Whitman's Calamus Photographs," in *Breaking Bounds*, ed. Betsy Erkkila and Jay Grossman (New York: Oxford University Press, 1996), 215. Lantern slide lectures were available to Whitman. In the early 1880s the Pennsylvania Academy of the Fine Arts hosted a series of such lectures and photographic exhibitions (Danly, 180).

6. For a discussion of this wax cylinder recording and the reasons for concluding that it is probably authentic, see Ed Folsom, "The Whitman Recording," *Walt Whitman Quarterly Review* 9 (spring 1992), 214–216. Folsom quotes Edison's letter about wanting to "obtain a phonogram" from Whitman.

7. Ben Singer makes this point in "Connoisseurs of Chaos," 247. Singer goes on to note remarkable parallels in the works and rhetoric of Whitman and Dziga Vertov and suggests "a direct influence on Vertov by Whitman." Whitman had a pow-

Kenneth M. Price

erful impact on Russian letters, especially during the 1910s and 1920s. Kornei Chukovsky's translation of *Leaves of Grass* went through multiple printings, including one edition of 50,000 copies issued shortly after the revolution by the Petrograd Soviet of Workers and Red Army Deputies. Vertov's brother, Mikhail Kaufman, confirmed in a 1976 interview that Vertov's intertitles were directly indebted to Whitman's poems. Singer argues that the clearest example is *One Sixth of the World* (1926) with its repetition of "I see" (248).

8. Whitman made this remark to Horace Traubel (quoted in Milton Hindus, ed., *Leaves of Grass: One Hundred Years After* [Stanford, Calif.: Stanford University Press, 1955], 7).

9. See Ed Folsom, *Walt Whitman's Native Representations* (Cambridge: Cambridge University Press, 1994), chapter 4.

10. That Whitman was successful is suggested by a remark of a student: "Whitman's poetry is like a film on fast forward" (mentioned at a Whitman session at the British Association of American Studies, Swansea, Wales, April 2000).

11. Richardson, 24.

12. Quoted (from Eisenstein's *Film Form*) in Harry K. Grant, "Whitman and Eisenstein," *Literature/Film Quarterly* 4 (1976), 264.

13. For discussion of the film (based on advertising copy and letters), see Florence B. Freedman, "A Motion Picture 'First' for Whitman: O'Connor's 'The Carpenter,'" *Walt Whitman Review* 9 (June 1963), 31–33. *The Carpenter* was commissioned by J. H. Johnston, a friend of Whitman, who some decades earlier arranged for a series of photos that depicted him as a paternal or grandfatherly figure.

14. Rev. W. H. Jackson review of *The Carpenter*, *Motion Picture World* (August 9, 1913), 616–617.

15. Van Wyck Brooks, *America's Coming-of-Age* (1915; rpt., New York: Octagon Books, 1975), 112.

16. Vachel Lindsay, *The Art of the Moving Picture* (New York: Macmillan, 1916), 65–66. Interest in hieroglyphics had been intense in nineteenth-century America, and Whitman in particular was fascinated by the new discoveries of Egyptology, including the discovery of the Rosetta stone and the decipherment of Egyptian hieroglyphics. In the early 1850s Whitman was a frequent visitor to Dr. Henry Abbott's Egyptian museum in New York. For Whitman, hieroglyphics held appeal as a communication system escaping the customary limits of language.

17. Quoted in Kenneth Joseph Pierson, "Dramatizing Whitman: A Doctoral Dissertation with a Creative Component," (Ph.D. diss., University of Minnesota, 1994), 176. Further evidence of Griffith's admiration for Whitman is provided by

the recollections of cameraman Karl Brown: "When we ran out of things to do with the Assyrian army, we went back to the studio and did some shots of Lillian Gish rocking a cradle, all to the tune of Walt Whitman's poetry, which Griffith recited with great feeling and surprisingly good delivery, considering how outstandingly lousy he was as an actor." See Brown, *Adventures with D. W. Griffith* (New York: Farrar, Straus, Giroux, 1973), 166.

18. Miriam Hansen, *Babel and Babylon: Spectatorship in American Silent Film* (Cambridge: Harvard University Press, 1991), 165. Despite the film's initial reception — first warm, then chilly — it is now regarded as an extraordinary achievement.

19. Richard J. Meyer, "The Films of David Wark Griffith: The Development of Themes and Techniques in Forty-two of His Films," in *Focus on D. W. Griffith*, ed. Harry M. Geduld (Englewood Cliffs, N.J.: Prentice-Hall, 1971), 118.

20. Sergei Eisenstein, *Film Form*, ed. and trans. Jay Leyda (New York: Harcourt, Brace, 1949), 241.

21. Similar formal complexity is found, of course, in *Moby-Dick*, a novel that constantly tests and disrupts typical definitions of genre.

22. The original title of the film is a matter of some debate. When reminiscing about the film, Strand alternately called it *Manhatta* and *Mannahatta*. The Rialto Theatre probably chose the title used when the film was first released commercially: *New York the Magnificent*. See Jan-Christopher Horak, "Paul Strand and Charles Sheeler's *Manhatta*," in *Lovers of Cinema: The First American Film Avant-Garde 1919–1945*, ed. Jan-Christopher Horak (Madison: University of Wisconsin Press, 1995), 269. With regard to the title, I would add that the very use of the word "Manhatta" or "Mannahatta" is a poeticizing of the more literal choices also available: Manhattan or, perhaps, even less poetically, New York. Sheeler and Strand follow Whitman's preference for the original Algonquin term for the "place encircled by many swift tides and sparkling waters" (*PW* 2:683).

23. Jan-Christopher Horak writes: "Another difference separating *Manhatta* from films like *Berlin, Symphony of a City*, and *Man with a Movie Camera* is its lack of interest in human subjects. Considering the humanist impulse inherent in Strand's 'Photography and the New God,' it seems ironic than *Manhatta* would almost totally exclude images of city dwellers in its portrait of the urban environment. . . . *Manhatta's* view remains distanced, perching the spectator on skyscrapers, away from any day-to-day activity." See Horak, "Modernist Perspectives and *Manhatta*," *Afterimage* 15 (November 1987), 14.

24. The same experimentation, a comparable emphasis on the city, and a similar interest in Whitman underlie Vertov's *Man with a Movie Camera* and *One Sixth of the World*. The latter film uses catalogs in the intertitles and a type of parallel struc-

ture that is quite similar to Whitman. For more on the Vertov-Whitman connection, see Singer, 247–258.

25. Horak, 277–278.

26. Olive Higgins Prouty, *Now, Voyager* (Boston: Houghton Mifflin, 1941). Prouty's title page includes the following epigraph: "Untold want, by life and land ne'er granted, / Now, Voyager, sail thou forth, to seek and find." These lines are quoted again within the body of the text. The expression "Now, Voyager" also appears in Whitman's poem "Now Finalè to the Shore." See M. Lynda Ely, "The Untold Want: Representation and Transformation: Echoes of Walt Whitman's *Passage to India* in *Now, Voyager*," *Literature Film Quarterly* 29 (2001), 43–52, for another view of how Whitman's poetry, Prouty's novel, and Rapper's film interrelate; Ely's article appeared after my essay was completed.

27. *Now, Voyager*, ed. Jeanne Thomas Allen (Madison: University of Wisconsin Press, 1984), 84–85.

28. The film makes this point when Jerry is reintroduced to Charlotte and is described as a "nice chap . . . not Boston, you know." In Prouty's novel, however, Jerry has a stronger association with Boston and New England (he was a student at MIT and lives in New Hampshire). The film, vaguer about Jerry's background, makes him seem non-Bostonian and even a bit exotic because of Henreid's accent.

29. Allen, 17, argues that "Charlotte turns her new-found energies to parenting Jerry's child, applying the knowledge Jaquith offered her to become the mother she needed as a child. And since it is one of Jaquith's patients she is caring for, she implicitly becomes a partner to Jaquith. Although the novel ends with Charlotte's insistence that caring for Tina unites her with Jerry through a sublimation of their love affair, character development suggests that Charlotte has outgrown the father-lover she met on the boat and become the peer of the father-doctor, joining in his work and supporting it."

30. Allen, 24.

31. Lea Jacobs notes: "The question of how, and through whom, Charlotte Vale's desire will express itself engenders a dizzying chain of displacement and counter-displacement which never comes to rest. . . . Tina, the stars, they all serve as replacements for the man, yet the fact remains that Charlotte refuses the man. In a gloriously perverse gesture the narrative does not bring Charlotte's desire to fruition and an even more perverse sub-text would lead one to suspect that she likes it that way." See Jacobs, "*Now, Voyager*: Some Problems of Enunciation and Sexual Difference," *Camera Obscura* 7 (spring 1981), 103.

32. Malcolm Cowley, "Walt Whitman: The Secret," *New Republic*, April 8, 1946, 481–484.

33. See <http://www.english.upenn.edu/~afilreis/50s/gays-in-govt.html> and *Congressional Record* 96, part 4, 81st Congress 2nd Session, March 29–April 24, 1950, 4527–4528.

34. Mark Goble, "'Our Country's Black and White Past': Film and the Figures of History in Frank O'Hara," *American Literature* 71 (March 1999), 76. At this time, Warner Brothers was speaking in contradictory fashion politically. In the same year that the company brought forth the liberalism of *Goodbye, My Fancy*, it also produced *I Was a Communist for the FBI*, a film suggesting that any labor meeting or race riot stemmed from Communists.

35. Fay Kanin's original play makes clear that the college is set in Massachusetts. Thus, like Prouty, Kanin turns to Whitman to reconstruct the United States on more egalitarian lines and away from what each author sees as a more narrow and patriarchal mode associated with New England.

36. Anticommunist fervor led to distrust of open, lively discussion in the academy. For an interesting discussion of this point shedding indirect light on *Goodbye, My Fancy*, see Alan Filreis, "'Conflict Seems Vaguely Un-American': Teaching the Conflicts and the Legacy of the Cold War," *Review* 17 (1995), 155–69.

37. A paperback copy of *Leaves of Grass* is present on a table at the key moment of the film, the attempt to restore vision to a woman who has been blind for years.

38. Two other uses of Whitman in film can be noted here. In *Sub Down* (1997), a character quotes *Leaves of Grass* at a moment of great crisis, perhaps because the filmmaker wanted to add a touch of culture to a film of little value. Much more interesting and challenging is D. W. Harper's award-winning alternative film *Delicate Art of the Rifle* (1996), based on a story by Stephen Grant, which makes haunting use of Whitman. This student-made film is loosely based on the 1966 University of Texas sniper shootings by Charles Whitman. The filmmakers have rechristened Charles Whitman "Walt Whitman," a move that has both resonance and disorienting effects.

39. Alicia Ostriker, "Loving Walt Whitman and the Problem of America," in *Walt Whitman: The Measure of His Song*, ed. Jim Perlman, Ed Folsom, and Dan Campion, rev. ed. (Duluth, Minn.: Holy Cow! Press, 1998), 458.

40. *Reds* is a rare U.S. film treating Whitman's appeal for leftist groups.

41. James Baldwin, *The Devil Finds Work* (1976; rpt., New York: Dell, 1990), 67.

42. Byrne S. Fone, ed., *The Columbia Anthology of Gay Literature* (New York: Columbia University Press, 1998), 732–733.

43. Threatening and scandalous in his own time, Whitman's relatively tame current status is seen in the frequent use of him in television programs, including the April 5, 1997, episode of the CBS-TV series *Dr. Quinn, Medicine Woman*. The epi-

sode treats the Peter Doyle–Whitman relationship. For discussion of this program, see Joann Krieg, "Walt and Pete in the Family Hour," *Walt Whitman Quarterly Review* 14 (spring 1997), 201–202, and Desirée Henderson, *"Dr. Quinn, Medicine Woman* and the Prime-Time 'Outing' of Walt Whitman," *Walt Whitman Quarterly Review* 17 (summer/fall 1999), 69–76. The entire matter of the representation of Whitman in television shows deserves thoughtful treatment. Some of the key shows for study include a *Twilight Zone* (old series) adaptation of Ray Bradbury's "I Sing the Body Electric" and a *Northern Exposure* episode in which the disc jockey, Chris, is fired by his boss (the superpatriotic ex-astronaut) for mentioning on the air that Whitman was gay.

44. Robert K. Martin's *The Homosexual Tradition in American Poetry* (Austin: University of Texas Press, 1979), was an especially important critical and cultural intervention.

45. Of this group, one of the more interesting films is the non-Hollywood production *Urinal*. Though it makes only passing reference to Whitman, the film is more daring aesthetically and politically than most of the films discussed here, popular films that reached a broad audience but challenged that audience only minimally.

46. "The Road Not Taken" is also quoted in Italian translation.

47. Benigni seems to quote from the standard Italian translation of *Leaves of Grass*. See *Foglie d'erba e Prose di Walt Whitman*, ed. Giulio Einaudi (Turin: Francesco Toso, 1950), 459.

48. Tania Modleski, *Feminism without Women: Culture and Criticism in a "Post-feminist" Age* (New York: Routledge, 1991), 137.

49. One irony is that Bucke's asylum held that the "solitary vice" (masturbation) caused insanity, but the film provides a glimpse of his wife apparently masturbating while reading *Leaves of Grass*.

50. Lynch, A7; S. E. D. Shortt, *Victorian Lunacy: Richard M. Bucke and the Practice of Late Nineteenth-Century Psychiatry* (Cambridge: Cambridge University Press, 1986), 125.

51. Gwendolyn Audrey Foster, "No Male Frontal Nudity: The Denial of Female Fetishism in Hollywood Cinema," *Mid-Atlantic Almanack* 4 (1995), 37.

52. I am indebted to Ed Folsom for this idea.

53. This remark is made in the film *Sophie's Choice*, but comparable sentiments can be found in the novel.

54. Crash's speech, if lineated in the style of *Leaves of Grass*, would break into parallel units reminiscent of Whitman's own work. When Annie asks, "What do you believe in then?" he responds: "Well, I believe in the soul, the cock, the pussy, the

small of a woman's back, the hanging curve ball, high fibre, good scotch, that the novels of Susan Sontag are self-indulgent, overrated crap, I believe Lee Harvey Oswald acted alone, I believe there ought to be a constitutional amendment outlawing Astroturf and the designated hitter, I believe in the sweet spot, softcore pornography, opening your presents Christmas morning rather than Christmas eve, and I believe in long slow deep soft wet kisses that last three days." Few would mistake Crash for Whitman, of course, yet his fondness for lists and rough parallelism shows a rhetorical affinity with the poet who was also willing to announce a credo:

I believe a leaf of grass is no less than the journey-work of the stars,
And the pismire is equally perfect, and a grain of sand, and the egg of the wren,
And the tree-toad is a chef-d'œuvre for the highest,
And the running blackberry would adorn the parlors of heaven,
And the narrowest hinge in my hand puts to scorn all machinery,
And the cow crunching with depress'd head surpasses any statue,
And a mouse is miracle enough to stagger sextillions of infidels. (*LG* 59)

55. The film is both a celebration of lesbianism and an acknowledgment that lesbianism is under siege. Randy's lesbian family gives thanks at night routinely for getting through another day.

56. Nicole Cloeren, "Whitman as Signpost to Self-Discovery in *Now, Voyager* and *Love and Death on Long Island*," unpublished paper, quoted with permission.

57. With regard to Ronnie, the novel is much bleaker in its ending than is the film.

58. I refer to the most recent film adaptation of *Little Women* (1994).

Kenneth M. Price

"Where's Walt?"

Illustrated Editions of Whitman for Younger Readers

JOEL MYERSON

Anyone writing on representations of Whitman seems to be going over old ground, in terms of both the poet himself and the scholarship on him. After all, the special double issue of the *Walt Whitman Quarterly Review* edited by Ed Folsom (fall/winter 1986–1987) devoted to Whitman photographs is striking not just because of the total number of pictures there of Whitman (130) but also because of the way these photos present a series of "representative" Whitmans: "one of the roughs" in the frontispiece of the 1855 *Leaves of Grass* eventually metamorphosing into the Good Gray Poet of the last decades of his life.[1] Should anyone doubt Whitman's shrewdness in controlling his image or his posturing when doing so, they need only to consult the famous picture of him with a butterfly used in the 1889 "Birthday Edition" of *Leaves*, in reality a cardboard model employed to "enhance" the scene. He was equally careful in controlling the prose depictions of his life: anonymous "interviews" with himself published in friendly newspapers helped to counteract otherwise unfriendly comments; *Leaves of Grass Imprints* (1860), which he edited and to which he contributed reviews of his own work, certainly placed *Leaves* and its author exactly where Whitman wanted them to be in the literary world; his uncredited work on John Burroughs's *Notes on Walt Whitman as Poet and Person* (1867) and Richard Maurice Bucke's *Walt Whitman* (1883) allowed others to create the biographical portrait he himself desired; and his almost daily conversations with Horace Traubel, eventually published in nine volumes (1906–1996), enabled Whitman to refine his image as much as he wanted.

Still, what I propose to do in this essay — to study representations of

Whitman in relation to books for young readers—may seem a strange undertaking. He is, after all, the poet who describes himself in *Leaves of Grass* as "Walt Whitman, a kosmos, of Manhattan the son, / Turbulent, fleshy, sensual, eating, drinking and breeding" (*LG* 52), not exactly the sort of chap from whom you tell your children it's safe to take candy. But my topic is not as far-fetched as it may seem: back on March 12, 1891, Whitman's poem "Ship Ahoy!" was published in the *Youth's Companion,* one of the major nineteenth-century American children's periodicals. What I'd like to do here is to make some general observations about these illustrated editions and then examine how some specific poems have been treated.

Not surprisingly, most early illustrated anthologies of poetry aimed at young readers had generic illustrations. That is, an artist drew a sunrise, and that picture was placed near a poem about a sunrise. This generic approach carries over to modern editions, where volumes organized by theme or topic predominate over more general collections. There are many more volumes of favorite cat or dog or teddy bear or whatever poems than there are of general anthologies for young readers. These thematic or topical collections take a generic approach to their illustrations by having the requisite number of cats or dogs or teddy bears posing in the appropriate emotional states appearing next to the corresponding poems. For these reasons, looking for visual significance in the ways Whitman poems have appeared in illustrated anthologies in the last fifty years has proven a fruitless exercise: the pictures generally seem drawn for the book rather than to illustrate a particular poem.

Even within the books devoted entirely to Whitman, a great degree of selectivity takes place. Illustrators, like all anthologists, choose from what is available to suit their own purposes. Whitman was a prolific author, with the standard scholarly edition of his poems consisting of three volumes totaling 779 pages. When editors make their selections for young readers, for whom a book of poetry by one author is rather short and usually contains no more than one poem per page, they obviously sacrifice a great deal of what the author has written. As a rule of thumb, the poems that get included are those dealing with concrete, rather than abstract, subjects. In the Whitman books, for example, his Civil War poems and his poems on Abraham Lincoln are the most popular ones for inclusion.

Two other factors seem to influence illustrators of Whitman's poetry. First, Whitman generally wrote long poems. As a practical matter, this means that fewer Whitman poems are included in their totality, unlike, say, the poems of Emily Dickinson, which (since they are typically between four and twenty lines long) require little or no paring down. Whitman was expansive, and a poem like "Song of Myself" runs to eighty-three pages in the New York University Press edition. While Whitman's anthologists and illustrators show a preference for the shorter verses, they also freely choose which sections to extract from the longer writings, an ability that becomes much appreciated when we discuss the third factor.

That third factor is the subject matter of the poems. The Fireside poets (such as Henry Wadsworth Longfellow and James Russell Lowell) produced verses that not only rhyme and are understandable but also ones that generally do not deal with controversial subjects. To use my Dickinson parallel again, the idea that her poems might contain erotic or homoerotic overtones actually went unnoted until a 1951 biography made the case for such a reading, some sixty years after her first book had been published. There's no question of the potential eroticism contained within her verse, but it is masked by the traditional language of nineteenth-century poetry, a poetic tradition of which younger readers are unaware, and therefore they can believe, along with Sigmund Freud, that "sometimes a cigar is just a cigar."

Whitman, on the other hand, had to fend off queries during his own lifetime about the homosexual aspects of his verses, and this line of inquiry has been a strong one in Whitman studies ever since. Indeed, Whitman's latest biographer, Jerome Loving, states that because of "the ongoing debate over the place of homosexuality in America today, the discussion of Whitman's sexual orientation will probably continue in spite of whatever evidence emerges."[2] This aspect of Whitman's personality is not a problem for adult-oriented illustrated editions of his poetry, such as the recent *Whitman's Men: Walt Whitman's Calamus Poems Celebrated by Contemporary Photographers* (1996). But imagine a child reading these lines about a woman watching a group of men bathing outdoors:

The beards of the young men glisten'd with wet, it ran from their
    long hair,
Little streams pass'd all over their bodies.

An unseen hand also pass'd over their bodies,
It descended tremblingly from their temples and ribs.

The young men float on their backs, their white bellies bulge to the
    sun, they do not ask who seizes fast to them,

They do not know who puffs and declines with pendant and
   bending arch,
They do not think whom they souse with spray. (*LG* 38–39)

And then imagine that child asking his or her parents to explain what this poem means. Not surprisingly, then, the omissions from Whitman's longer poems are almost as telling as what parts are included.

The illustrators and their books that I'll be discussing are Zhenya Gay's *There Was a Child Went Forth* (1943), Alexander Dobkin's *I Hear the People Singing* (1946), James Daugherty's *Walt Whitman's America* (1964), Charles Mikolaycak's *Voyages* (1988), Robert Sabuda's *I Hear America Singing* (1991), and Jim Burke's *Poetry for Young People: Walt Whitman* (1997).[3] There is a long tradition of illustrated editions of Whitman — he has always been a favorite of fine presses, and his works have been published by the likes of the Gehenna Press, Lime Kiln Press, Spiral Press, and the Limited Editions Club, which has done three titles by him — and they have been illustrated by such distinguished artists as Valenti Angelo, Rockwell Kent, and Boardman Robinson. In addition, there have been numerous editions illustrated with photographs (Hallmark contributing two of these); nearly all these latter works invoke a Whitman who represents American optimism, as can be seen by titles such as *America the Beautiful in the Words of Walt Whitman*, *Miracles: Walt Whitman's Beautiful Celebration of Life*, *Miracles: The Wonder of Life*, and *A Most Jubilant Song*.[4]

Many of Whitman's works have been illustrated for younger readers in a straightforward fashion, either one that serves to provide a visual narrative to accompany a text, or a series of pictures to make a visual point to accompany the meaning that the artist has imposed on the entire work. Gay's drawing (fig. 13) shows how her pictures form a parallel narrative to the text of "There Was a Child Went Forth." The dust jacket flap for Sabuda's *I Hear America Singing* calls the poem "a lyrical celebration of the American spirit as it gives voice to the many faces of this land." The illustrations begin with a picture on the dust jacket (fig. 14) of a man playing a fiddle with two children, invoking a type of storyteller figure for the poem that follows. This is one of Whitman's catalog poems, and the pictures do little more than flesh out the occupations described by Whitman (figs. 15 and 16). Mikolaycak invokes the Civil War in such pictures as one in which the image of Lincoln overlooks a battle scene, where the dead sleep both peacefully and in unbloodied fields (fig. 17).

13. Zhenya Gay, There Was a Child Went Forth *(Harper and Brothers, 1943).*

There are some books where the form of the pictures is influenced by political forces. *I Hear the People Singing* begins with an introduction by Langston Hughes about how "the vast sweep of democracy is still incomplete even in America" in 1946, when the book was published, and many of the pictures reinforce this theme of the masses still being oppressed.

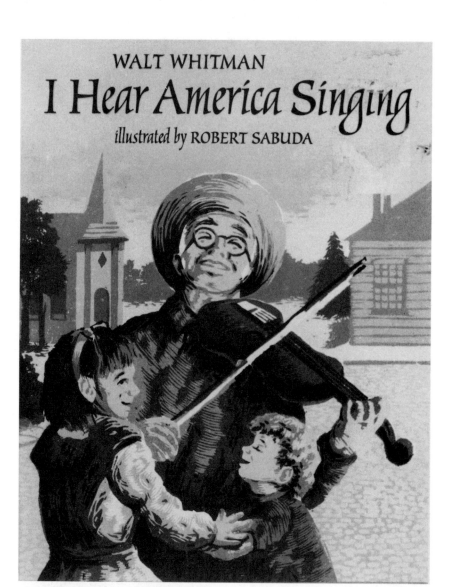

14. Front dust jacket illustration, copyright © 1991 by Robert Sabuda, from I Hear
America Singing *by Walt Whitman, illustrated by Robert Sabuda. This figure and figures
15 and 16 are used by permission of Philomel Books, an imprint of Penguin Putnam
Books for Young Readers, a division of Penguin Putnam Inc.*

The carpenter singing his as he measures his plank or beam.

15. Illustration of the carpenter, copyright © 1991 by Robert Sabuda, from I Hear America Singing, *17.*

The book's title page shows a picture of working people (fig. 18), a visual reminder of the sources and possibilities of democracy. In the text, there are warnings about the chains of the past, as in Dobkin's picture of "Starting from Paumanok" (fig. 19). This drawing seems to have little to do with any specific line from the poem, but, in showing a miner trapped

the deckhand singing on the steamboat deck,

16. *Illustration of the deckhand, copyright © 1991 by Robert Sabuda,
from* I Hear America Singing, *9.*

17. Illustration from Voyages: Poems by Walt Whitman, *illustration copyright © 1998 by Charles Mikolaycak, reprinted by permission of Harcourt, Inc.*

claustrophobically in his shaft underneath the urban and industrialized countryside, Dobkin suggests how the labor of the common person underlies all visible progress; in having the miner reach upward with his tool, he suggests that the masses want to break out and share in the riches as well.

Daugherty wishes to stress Whitman's Americanness, which is how the book affected him when he first read it while in London. *Leaves of Grass* "got under my skin and into my bones," he writes in the introduction to his selection. "For the first time I felt the meaning and power of that majestic word 'America,' and through Whitman's eyes I dimly glimpsed the grandeur of its possibilities." And to continue the thread of his remarks about Whitman's relevance to his audience of 1964, he says, "We too have felt the terrible shock of a beloved President assassinated. It is as if Whitman had written for us today his great funeral dirge 'When Lilacs Last in the Door-yard Bloom'd'" (13). Daugherty's pictures bear out the force of his identification of Whitman with America by presenting a series of studies that look almost like figures from William Blake on steroids (figs. 20– 22). At one point he suggests the iconographic status he wishes to bestow upon the poem "I Hear America Singing" by identifying it with that supreme American symbol, the Statue of Liberty (fig. 23). And he also picks up on Whitman's descriptions of the many types of people that go toward making up America, showing, as few of the illustrators do, adult women (as opposed to female children) representing the gamut from a narcissistic society woman, to a mother and child, to a factory worker (fig. 24).

The book illustrated by Burke is a more sophisticated rendering of Whitman because the editor, Jonathan Levin (an English professor at Columbia University), tries to present a broader range of poems, and he glosses the hard words for his readers. Indeed, the jacket flap states that the book wishes to "inspire young people both to appreciate the poetry and to understand what is being said between the lines." Burke often lets a single symbol stand for a complete poem, as when he prints a poem titled "I Tramp a Perpetual Journey" (fig. 25), identified as lines from "Song of Myself," and allows a pair of unlaced shoes to speak for the poem. Ironically, Burke's illustration for a verse entitled "The Spotted Hawk Swoops By" (really section 52 of "Song of Myself") shows the male figure as fully clothed (fig. 26), whereas Daugherty (fig. 27) has more accurately caught the sense of the narrator exposing himself, both figuratively and literally.

"I Sing the Body Electric" is not a poem we would expect to find in a book for young readers, and only Dobkin and Burke deal with it; both

I Hear the People Singing

SELECTED POEMS OF WALT WHITMAN

INTRODUCTION BY LANGSTON HUGHES

ILLUSTRATED BY ALEXANDER DOBKIN

YOUNG WORLD BOOKS

PUBLISHED BY INTERNATIONAL PUBLISHERS, NEW YORK

18. Title page of I Hear the People Singing *(New York: Young World Books, International Publishers, 1946), illustrated by Alexander Dobkin.*

Land of the eastern Chesapeake! land of the Delaware!
Land of Ontario, Erie, Huron, Michigan!
Land of the Old Thirteen! Massachusetts land! land of Vermont and
Connecticut!
Land of the ocean shores! land of sierras and peaks!
Land of boatmen and sailors! fishermen's land!
Inextricable lands! the clutch'd together! the passionate ones!
The side by side! the elder and younger brothers! the bony-limb'd!
The great women's land! the feminine! the experienced sisters and the
inexperienced sisters!
Far breath'd land! Arctic braced! Mexican breez'd! the diverse! the
compact!
The Pennsylvanian! the Virginian! the double Carolinian!
O all and each well-loved by me! my intrepid nations! O I at any rate
include you all with perfect love!
I cannot be discharged from you! not from one any sooner than another!

40

19. Illustration by Alexander Dobkin from I Hear the People Singing.

20. Dust jacket of Walt Whitman's America *(Cleveland: World, 1964),*
illustrated by James Daugherty.

21. *Frontispiece and title page of* Walt Whitman's America,
illustrated by James Daugherty.

concentrate on the section about the slave at auction (fig. 28). The poem appeared in the "Children of Adam" section in the 1860 edition of *Leaves of Grass,* and its polymorphous sexuality has been commented upon by many critics. M. Wynn Thomas reads this poem as an economic statement, saying "the auction of a slave meant something much more general to Whitman than the insufferable plight of Southern blacks. It meant a system that threatened to degrade the beauty of the human body, and with it the dignity of human labor, to the status of an economic commodity." M. Jimmie Killingsworth sees the auction as a disjuncture between physicality and democracy, as the pairing of the slave and, in the next section, the woman (a slave or a prostitute) shows how the "antidemocratic institutions of society" are "those most clearly out of register with the morality of the body." And Betsy Erkkila sees politics at work here, arguing that "Whitman continues to interrogate his readers directly, insisting that they probe and resolve the contradictions in their own racial attitudes. To the economics of slavery and Negrophobia of his age, he counters with a vision of blacks as coequal citizens in the process of personal and national creation."[5]

The pictures by Dobkin and Burke are very different. Dobkin (fig. 29)

Joel Myerson

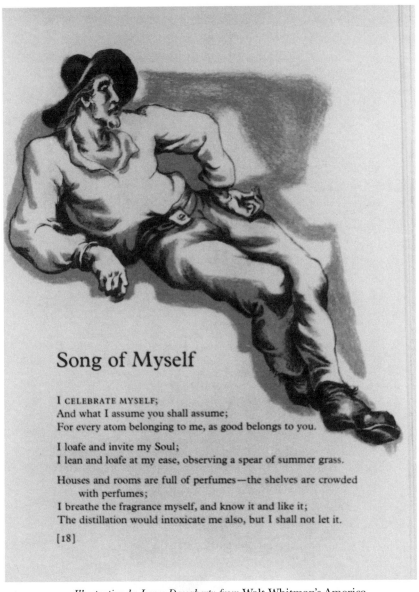

Song of Myself

I CELEBRATE MYSELF;
And what I assume you shall assume;
For every atom belonging to me, as good belongs to you.

I loafe and invite my Soul;
I lean and loafe at my ease, observing a spear of summer grass.

Houses and rooms are full of perfumes—the shelves are crowded
   with perfumes;
I breathe the fragrance myself, and know it and like it;
The distillation would intoxicate me also, but I shall not let it.

[18]

22. *Illustration by James Daugherty from* Walt Whitman's America.

presents (in his usual artistic style) figures in outline, with the auctioneer
a caricature of a mean-visaged Southern planter, complete with a floppy
planter's hat. Beside the podium (which is labeled "Sale") and viewed
from the side stands a figure holding one hand against his other wrist; the
sense of enslavement is obvious, but so, too, is the sense of resignation

23. *Illustration by James Daugherty from* Walt Whitman's America.

24. *Illustration by James Daugherty from* Walt Whitman's America.

(and, visually speaking, self-enslavement). Burke (fig. 30), on the other hand, works in color and with a full-figure frontal portrayal to convey his sense of the poem. The white planter or auctioneer is gone, allowing the reader to focus entirely on the African American slave, who is now chained by his owner (rather than being self-restrained) and whose open hands and

I Tramp a Perpetual Journey

This poem, taken from "Song of Myself," explores one of Whitman's favorite themes, the romance of travelling the open road. One of Whitman's key ideas here is that you must travel the road "for yourself."

I tramp a perpetual journey, (come listen all!)
My signs are a rain-proof coat, good shoes, and a staff cut from the woods,
No friend of mine takes his ease in my chair,
I have no chair, no church, no philosophy,
I lead no man to a dinner-table, library, exchange,
But each man and each woman of you I lead upon a knoll,
My left hand hooking you round the waist,
My right hand pointing to landscapes of continents and the public road.

Not I, not any one else can travel that road for you,
You must travel it for yourself.

It is not far, it is within reach,
Perhaps you have been on it since you were born and did not know,
Perhaps it is everywhere on water and on land.

Shoulder your duds dear son, and I will mine, and let us hasten forth,
Wonderful cities and free nations we shall fetch as we go.

If you tire, give me both burdens, and rest the chuff of your hand on my hip,
And in due time you shall repay the same service to me,
For after we start we never lie by again.

This day before dawn I ascended a hill and look'd at the crowded heaven,
And I said to my spirit *When we become the enfolders of those orbs, and the pleasure and knowledge of every thing in them, shall we be fill'd and satisfied then?*
And my spirit said, *No, we but level that lift to pass and continue beyond.*

duds—*clothes*   level that lift—*reach that height*
chuff—*probably the palm*

45

---

25. *Illustration by Jim Burke. This figure and figures 26, 28, 30, and 31 are used with permission of Sterling Publishing Co., Inc., from* Poetry for Young People: Walt Whitman, *edited by Jonathan Levin, illustration copyright © 1997 by Jim Burke.*

26. Illustration by Jim Burke from Poetry for Young People: Walt Whitman; *illustration copyright © 1997 by Jim Burke.*

wearied look contrast with his muscled figure. This is much more like the "wonder" to which Whitman refers than is suggested by Dobkin's figure.

But, to me, Burke does not do as well with the final poem I'll discuss, "The Dalliance of the Eagles" (fig. 31). This is another poem one would not expect to find in a book for children, with lines like

The atmosphere is not a perfume—it has no taste of the distilla-
tion—it is odorless;
It is for my mouth forever—I am in love with it;
I will go to the bank by the wood, and become undisguised and
naked;
I am mad for it to be in contact with me.

*　　*　　*

The spotted hawk swoops by and accuses me—he complains of
my gab and my loitering.

27. *Illustration by James Daugherty from* Walt Whitman's America.

28. Page from Jonathan Levin, ed., Poetry for Young People: Walt Whitman.

The rushing amorous contact high in space together,
The clinching interlocking claws, a living, fierce, gyrating wheel,
Four beating wings, two beaks, a swirling mass tight grappling,
In tumbling turning clustering loops, straight downward falling,
Till o'er the river pois'd, the twain yet one, a moment's lull,
A motionless still balance in the air, then parting, talons loosing,

Bodies at Auction

(FROM "I SING THE BODY ELECTRIC")

The man's body is sacred and the woman's body is sacred,
No matter who it is, it is sacred—is it the meanest one in the laborers'
  gang?
Is it one of the dull-faced immigrants just landed on the wharf?
Each belongs here or anywhere just as much as the well-off, just as much
  as you,
Each has his or her place in the procession.

(All is a procession,
The universe is a procession with measured and perfect motion.)

Do you know so much yourself that you call the meanest ignorant?

57

29. *Illustration by Alexander Dobkin from* I Hear the People Singing.

30. Illustration by Jim Burke from Poetry for Young People: Walt Whitman*;
illustration copyright © 1997 by Jim Burke.*

Upward again on slow-firm pinions slanting, their separate
    diverse flight,
She hers, he his, pursuing. (*LG* 274)

Robert K. Martin calls this poem "as erotically powerful as anything Whitman ever wrote," saying that in it "Whitman has freed the depiction of sex-

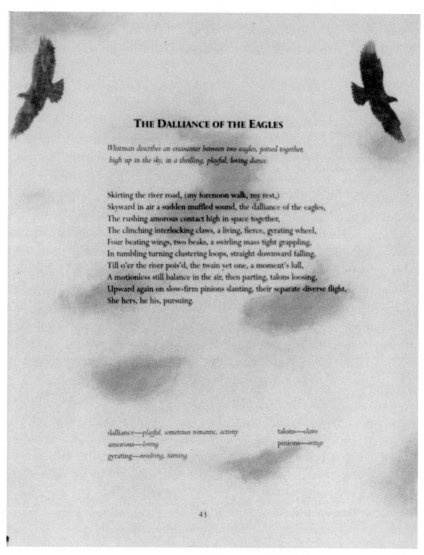

THE DALLIANCE OF THE EAGLES

Whitman describes an encounter between two eagles, joined together, high up in the sky, in a thrilling, playful, loving dance.

Skirting the river road, (my forenoon walk, my rest,)
Skyward in air a sudden muffled sound, the dalliance of the eagles,
The rushing amorous contact high in space together,
The clinching interlocking claws, a living, fierce, gyrating wheel,
Four beating wings, two beaks, a swirling mass tight grappling,
In tumbling turning clustering loops, straight downward falling,
Till o'er the river pois'd, the twain yet one, a moment's lull,
A motionless still balance in the air, then parting, talons loosing,
Upward again on slow-firm pinions slanting, their separate diverse flight,
She hers, he his, pursuing.

dalliance—*playful, sometimes romantic, activity*   talons—*claws*
amorous—*loving*   pinions—*wings*
gyrating—*revolving, turning*

43

31. *Illustration by Jim Burke from* Poetry for Young People: Walt Whitman; *illustration copyright © 1997 by Jim Burke.*

uality from the confines of romantic evasion, allowing for a sexual desire to be seen in violently physical terms."[6] Nor is Martin alone in holding such an opinion: "The Dalliance of the Eagles" was cited by the district attorney of Massachusetts as one of the poems that had to be deleted entirely from the 1881–1882 *Leaves of Grass* when he banned the volume for sale as being "obscene literature." More recently, James E. Miller Jr. believes that it "contains in its symbolic drama . . . the delirious abandon to the sexual merge, but with the persistence of personal identity and individuality," and Betsy Erkkila sees "in the figure of two eagles copulating in midair, a fierce and erotically compelling female desire that was unrelated to any maternal or reproductive drive."[7] Not surprisingly, Levin and Burke play down this aspect of the poem, as Levin's headnote calls this an encounter between two eagles "in a thrillful, playful, loving dance," thus translating the sexuality of the poem into a type of friendship or romantic love (depending, of course, on the age of the reader) suitable for children. Burke's illustration runs even farther away from the energy of the poem: two eagles appear against a blue and white clouded sky, one at the top left and the other at the top right of the page. As Whitman says, the eagles are pursuing "their separate diverse flight," but the choice of a clearly postcoital moment (and the need not to deal with what went before) reinforces to the child reader that these birds are merely going away to find other eagles with whom to play. A poem comprised of complex linguistic and symbolic acts has been turned into a charming and innocent rhyme.

I hope this brief examination of the illustrated editions of Whitman that were produced for young readers suggests the planning that went into preparing the illustrations for these works, as well as the ways in which these illustrations affect our interpretation of the poems. Sometimes literary critics forget the interpretive role that may be assumed by people besides themselves and the author. That is, anthologists or editors who select which poems to use in a book help to define the poet's concerns (or even sexuality) by deciding which works to include and which to omit. In a similar fashion, illustrators affect how we see poems by presenting their vision of the poem's meaning, not in words like literary critics do, but in pictures. And in our very visual age, these pictures sometimes speak (if I may mix metaphors) for the poem on a subliminal level; much as the special occasion on which we hear a song will forever define how we react to it when we hear that song in the future, these pictures will come to represent the poem as children grow up and reflect back on the visual rendering of a poem that they read or had read to them when they were young. For all these reasons, it is important to remember the power that visual images have as symbolic markers that often replace the very works upon which they are supposed to comment.

NOTES

1. Ed Folsom, "'This Heart's Geography's Map': The Photographs of Walt Whitman," *Walt Whitman Quarterly Review* 4 (fall/winter 1986–1987), 1–72.

2. Jerome Loving, *Walt Whitman: The Song of Himself* (Berkeley: University of California Press, 1999), 19.

3. Zhenya Gay, illus., *There Was a Child Went Forth* (New York: Harper and Brothers, 1943); Alexander Dobkin, illus., *I Hear the People Singing* (New York: International Publishers, 1946); James Daugherty, ed. and illus., *Walt Whitman's America* (Cleveland: World, 1964); Lee Bennet Hopkins, ed., and Charles Mikolaycak, illus., *Voyages: Poems by Walt Whitman* (San Diego: Harcourt Brace Jovanovich, 1988); Robert Sabuda, illus., *I Hear America Singing* (New York: Philomel, 1991); and Jonathan Levin, ed., and Jim Burke, illus., *Poetry for Young People: Walt Whitman* (New York: Sterling, 1997).

4. See, for example, *America the Beautiful in the Words of Walt Whitman* (Waukesha, Wis.: Country Beautiful, 1970); *American Bard* (Santa Cruz, Calif.: Lime Kiln Press, 1981, rpt., New York: Viking Press, 1982); *Call of the Open Road* (New York: Limited Editions Club, 1989); *The Half-Breed and Other Stories* (New York: Columbia University Press, 1927); *Miracles: Walt Whitman's Beautiful Celebration of Life* (Kansas City, Kans.: Hallmark Editions, 1973); *Miracles: The Wonder of Life* (Chicago: Rand McNally, 1969); *A Most Jubilant Song* (Kansas City, Kans.: Hallmark Editions, 1973); *The Open Road* (Mesa, Ariz.: Four Corners Edition, 1996); *Overhead the Sun: Lines from Walt Whitman* (New York: Farrar, Straus and Giroux, 1969); *Salut au Monde!* (New York: Random House, 1930); *The Sleepers* (Paris: F. Bernouard, 1919); *Song of the Broad-Axe* (Philadelphia: Centaur Press, 1924); *The Tenderest Lover: The Erotic Poetry of Walt Whitman* (New York: Delacorte/Seymour Lawrence, 1970); *To Love Free: The Great Romantic Poems of Walt Whitman* (N.p.: April Editions, 1972); *Whitman's Men: Walt Whitman's Calamus Poems Celebrated by Contemporary Photographers* (New York: Universe, 1996); and *Wrenching Times* (Newtown, Wales: Gwasg Gregynog, 1991).

5. M. Wynn Thomas, *The Lunar Light of Whitman's Poetry* (Cambridge: Harvard University Press, 1987), 32; M. Jimmie Killingsworth, *Whitman's Poetry of the Body: Sexuality, Politics, and the Text* (Chapel Hill: University of North Carolina Press, 1989), 9; Betsy Erkkila, *Whitman the Political Poet* (New York: Oxford University Press, 1989), 127.

6. Robert K. Martin, "The Dalliance of the Eagles," in *Walt Whitman: An Encyclopedia*, ed. J. R. LeMaster and Donald D. Kummings (New York: Garland, 1998), 161.

7. James E. Miller Jr., *Walt Whitman* (New York: Twayne, 1990), 93; Erkkila, 310.

A Dream Still Invincible?

The Matthiessen Tradition

ROBERT K. MARTIN

An aging gay man, Reeve, lies in a hospital bed, the victim of gay-bashing by a young hustler he had picked up in a bar. In the adjoining bed, a working-class boy spends his time watching television waiting for his thumb to heal. Reeve's friend, Howard, openly gay and effeminate, brings some reading matter, copies of George Eliot's *Daniel Deronda* and T. F. Slater's *The Invincible City*, the latter a barely concealed echo of F. O. Matthiessen's *American Renaissance*.[1] This is the opening of Mark Merlis's 1994 novel, *American Studies*, concerning the narrator and protagonist who passes much of his time recalling the life and work of Slater/Matthiessen.[2] The phrase "the invincible city" is taken from one of Whitman's "Calamus" poems, the first line of which is "I dream'd in a dream, I saw a city invincible to the attacks of the whole of the rest of the earth" (*LG* 133). Merlis's use of this line makes it clear that, for him, Matthiessen's citation of Whitman is a central part of a revaluation of Matthiessen's (and Whitman's) politics. Merlis alludes to this relatively little known Whitman poem at several places in the novel. Merlis sees Matthiessen (as I shall call him when thinking of the critical voice) as caught in an impossible contradiction of idealism — wanting a perfect world and knowing it is impossible to find — just as literature of the American Renaissance period was torn between a necessary idealism and a tragic knowledge that such perfection could only exist in a dream. Merlis's comment about Slater speaks perfectly of Matthiessen: "He was looking for a ticket to the impossible city that lived only in his book" (64).

This comment can also apply to Whitman and particularly to the "Calamus" poems, product as they are of unfulfilled desire and longing. Of course, one must feel that deep need in order to write, one must dream even if one knows that most dreams are not realized. The "impossible" dream is also the "fabulous city," a term taken in both its colloquial and formal meanings. Slater's death is a product of the homophobic hysteria of the 1950s, of his internalization of guilt. (Merlis has advanced the action of the Slater section by two years, to 1952, to make clear the connections between the persecution of homosexuals and that of Communists, although the public denunciations of homosexual "security risks" had already begun in early 1950.) Slater kills himself because he cannot, like Matthiessen, reconcile the ideal love presented positively in Whitman and ironically in Fuzzy Walgreen's Pindar with the reality of the gay bar of the violent hustler. That Fuzzy should specialize in the author of the Olympian odes adds an extra note of irony. Fuzzy teaches Greek but cannot bear to think of the sexuality of Greece. This does not, however, mean rejection of all hope, of all ability to (in Forster's term) "connect"; it means recognizing the moments of joy when they present themselves. It means, as Merlis puts it, thinking of Whitman's democratic vision and Matthiessen's socialism, "the revolution isn't ever coming, the city of friends is beyond the margins of the map. All you can do is wait for the intervals when the guns are silent and grab whatever you can" (235). It is a diminished form, a somewhat chastened realistic idealism and an echo of Foucault's micropolitics.

Admirers of Matthiessen (and they are still many) have tried to claim that *American Studies* does not give an accurate portrait of Matthiessen. Merlis makes a number of conscious changes, focusing, for instance, on Slater's romantic obsessions with his male students, and he leaves out entirely Matthiessen's lover, painter Russell Cheney. But he very accurately captures the witch-hunts of the postwar period and offers what is probably the best reading of *American Renaissance* anywhere. Craig Seligman, reviewing *American Studies* in the *New Yorker*, sees the novel as "abject in its resignation," but it would be more accurate to speak of accepting, of the loss of a dream. Seligman claims that "Matthiessen was anything but tragic," but in fact Matthiessen saw a tragic spirit in America and viewed his own life as tragic.[3] To have endured the interrogation of his loyalty, he who founded that project of studying and celebrating American culture, is the supreme and awful irony. Although often praised for his politics and his refusal to cooperate in the witch-hunt, Matthiessen turns out to be far less revolutionary than he perhaps imagined. As David Bergman puts it, "he had a little of the patrician concern for the social form as well as social obligation."[4] Eric Cheyfitz has shown in a brilliant and moving essay on

Robert K. Martin

Matthiessen that *American Renaissance* is a fundamentally liberal text that seeks to "repress crucial conflicts" (most notably in Matthiessen's outrageous omission of both African American and women writers).[5] The price of that vision of a homogeneous progressive society must exclude any sense of the real, lived marginality and oppression. And Cheyfitz goes on to point out that the political blindness of Matthiessen is repeated in his repression of sexuality, both in his own life and in the works he is studying. Obviously, there was no model for discussing homosexuality in 1941, and indeed the accusation of deviant sexuality was used by the Left to attack an alleged collaboration between fascism and homosexuality. Thus Matthiessen's strange and troubling passing comment on Whitman's "pathological" sexuality (his *only* comment on the subject) has its origins partly in a popular American Freudianism and partly in a Stalinist view of homosexuality as a bourgeois disorder. Only by locating Whitman in terms of medical control could Matthiessen ever raise the subject of sexuality. Still, it is not accurate to say, as Kermit Vanderbilt has, that "as teacher and critic [Matthiessen] apparently never broached homosexuality in Whitman or James."[6]

The problem, as Cheyfitz puts it, is the need to "translate . . . social vision into social action."[7] The metaphor for this translation in *American Studies* lies in the space between the two hospital beds, and the two men of different age and class: "How to cross the abyss between the two beds" (41) is a feat that is indeed accomplished in a wonderfully comic triumph of eros (pace Seligman) and a phrase that probably owes something to the space between in Melville's *Billy Budd*.

Matthiessen famously entitled his Whitman chapter "Only a Language Experiment," thereby joining in Whitman's own effort to sublimate or simply conceal his own sexuality. As a major project of denial, it bears comparison with T. S. Eliot's denial of any sexual meaning in *The Waste Land*. Matthiessen claims to believe in honesty; it is not clear how much about himself he acknowledged. In an earlier novel about Matthiessen, May Sarton's *Faithful Are the Wounds*, there is no hint of the Matthiessen character's sexuality.[8] This silence always seemed odd to me, and when the occasion arose once, in 1977, I took advantage of the opportunity to question her, why had she, herself a lesbian, chosen to omit such a large part of her friend Matthiessen's sexuality and his long relationship with Cheney, the two men even living near Sarton in southern Maine. Sarton's amazing response to me was that she had no idea about Matthiessen. Either she was lying or Matthiessen lived a very closeted life. Matthiessen was indeed very closeted, even by the standards of the time. When Newton Arvin brought along his lover, Truman Capote, to dinner at Harry Levin's, Matthiessen fled from Arvin's campy manner. Matthiessen's virtual excision of Whitman's sexuality in *American Renaissance* is strangely at odds with Whitman's more personal meanings. Whitman was in fact crucial as the guiding star of the Matthiessen-Cheney relationship, although you would never guess it from *American Renaissance* or, for that matter, even from Matthiessen's published correspondence with Cheney. In 1977 Louis Hyde, a friend of Matthiessen, published a selection of the enormous (1.6 million words) correspondence.[9] The index has no entry for Whitman, so that many readers looking for information on Matthiessen and Whitman may not have gone any further. However, even in this collection, despite the index, there are important Whitman references (and it may be that the editing process eliminated many more).

Writing at the very beginning of the relationship, in 1924, Matthiessen tells Cheney, "I carried Walt Whitman in my pocket. That's another thing you've started me doing, reading Whitman. Not solely because it gives me an intellectual kick the way it did last year [that is, before meeting Cheney], but because I'm living it" (*Rat* 26). This is precisely the split that Matthiessen has been charged with failure to heal, the connection he is accused of not making. But in fact, from the earliest days, Matthiessen saw that the personal and the intellectual must be joined and that it is precisely under the sun of Whitman that this can be accomplished. To this comment, Matthiessen appends three lines from "So Long!" It is hard to imagine a more appropriate passage to preside over the beginning of the relationship. Just as Matthiessen had carried the physical Whitman in his pocket, so it is here that Whitman announces, "Camerado, this is no book, / Who touches this touches a man" (*LG* 505). "So Long!" insists on the corporeal Whitman, but it also locates that erotic Whitman in a national context. First published in 1860, on the eve of the Civil War, Whitman's poem speaks for the Union, calling for one "more and more compact, indissoluble" (*LG* 504), only to shift to the incarnation of this union in adhesiveness. The theoretical self leads to the personal. The following year Matthiessen returned to this subject, telling Cheney of his desire to be a Whitmanian hero, to bring together body and soul in "a mighty symphony." "In our union . . . I feel that I have followed the deepest voice of my nature" (*Rat* 88). Whitman's presence, indeed concluding proof, in *American Renaissance* is no accident. As the poetic force that led to the

Robert K. Martin

establishment of a lifelong union with Cheney, Whitman also became the spirit that presides over Matthiessen's work. In ways that he did not feel able to express, Whitman was what enabled Matthiessen to unite the national and the personal. So, too, in Merlis's account, Slater's book offers Reeve a way to cross the "abyss" between the beds and embrace the working-class boy.

In an autobiographical sketch, "The Education of a Socialist," Matthiessen remarks on the "almost complete isolation of Harvard Yard from Central Square [which] generally prevents the inhabitants of Widener Library from even glimpsing [the city]."[10] The problem can be put another way: how has Whitman's democratic project succeeded in overcoming difference or, even better, in recognizing difference? It is obvious that Matthiessen produces not a democratic canon but a white male New England canon. Whitman is the only exception — as a working-class man from Brooklyn. But Whitman was canonized by being washed clean, his rough edges filed down. Whitman could not be eliminated, but he could be straightened up. Harvard Yard could efface Central Square.

Of course, it has often been mentioned that Whitman was a participant in his own sexual cleansing. The "invincible city" poem offers a good example. In the manuscript, the threat to the city is not mentioned, but rather "all the men were like brothers." As in a number of the "Calamus" poems, the emphasis is on public physical affection between men. They are "walking hand in hand," they "tenderly love each other." At the core of this utopia is what he originally calls "manly love" and then euphemistically "robust love." Robust or manly, the love between men must be masculine, as Whitman insists, and can be seen in the "looks and words" of the men in the city of friends.[11] Desire is visible and audible, there is already a code that permits one gay to recognize another. Whitman begins the project of making the private public, of erasing the boundaries of pleasures and politics, by reclaiming public space for "private" desires.

But what of those who are not, in our modern vocabulary, gay? Did all of those men whose names and descriptions Whitman jotted down think of themselves as gay? The letters from the soldiers to Whitman after the war would indicate no, at least to me. But this need to binarize sexuality seems as strange in Whitman's day as in our twenty-first century, even as Whitman repeatedly relies on his model of the gay man as other. Oddly enough, our famous "100 years of homosexuality" seems in the age of queer to have returned to another model, one that is universalizing rather than minoritizing. Let us go back to those two men sharing a hospital room in *American Studies*. The gay man has clearly not become a democratic hero, while his democratic roommate devotes himself to cartoons and sports on television. Can these two come together? Merlis's Slater can fall in love with boys who represent upper-middle-class white privilege, but can he manage to learn the semiotics of the gay bar? Does the gay bar indeed mark the accomplishment of a socialist dream? Slater's preference for platonic romance makes him unable to function in Central Square and even less in a Boston gay bar. Like his model, Matthiessen, Slater has supported the Spanish Republic, headed the faculty union at Harvard, and in many ways deserved a place on a list of fellow travelers. But his love life has remained safely at Harvard. The narrator accomplishes the feat that his mentor could not, of crossing the abyss and returning to paradise: "I am in Eden; his cock salutes me guilelessly as he mutes the television. Like a flag, sweetflag, a shoot of Calamus" (Merlis 241). Whatever personal affection may be possible, the dream city is not achieved, nor, according to Merlis, can it ever be. Slater's book is "a travel guide to a fanciful place the world never did find its way to" (274). It is as likely to be achieved as Howard's videos of acrobatic youth. Still, this time there is no bashing but a silent conspiracy, signaled by a wink.

What happened to gay male academics in the 1950s? One possible fate is suggested by Merlis, who says after Slater's exposure, "You could go to Smith, there [is] an opening" (117). The allusion, of course, is to Newton Arvin, whose career both intellectually and personally was so often parallel to Matthiessen's. Author of books on Melville and Whitman, essays on Emerson, a National Book winner, professor at Smith, Arvin saw his career ruined in 1960 when he was arrested for the distribution of gay male pornography and was forced to retire. His fate was also tied to Cold War politics, as he was compelled to appear before a Massachusetts legislative inquiry in a time when it seemed, according to the press, that all gay men were security risks. There is always a Captain Vere, a stern father. What Slater claims he wanted, and what Matthiessen wanted, was a "revolution built on love and not on bloodletting" (Merlis 67). In many ways, that is what many American Renaissance heroes wanted. In the footsteps of Fourier, they sought a "commune built on love" to which the narrator can only reply, comically, "I need to go to the men's room" (68).

For those of us who began writing about Whitman in the 1960s and

1970s, his sexual paradises, like Melville's, although less corrupted, seemed real and attainable. As I put it, thinking of Whitman in the 1970s, "homosexuality meant a heightened political awareness, a sensitivity to the situation of women in a patriarchal society, and a belief that a homosexual society, freed from the impulse to power, might devote itself to pleasure."[12] I had been reading, you will realize, Herbert Marcuse and Norman O. Brown, and although I do not want to retract what I said then, I do want to acknowledge a certain naïveté. I was severely taken to task for suggesting that the steam bath might provide a model of such a commune.[13] While I certainly no longer would want to see the steam bath as *inherently* homosexual, I would still argue for such a site of pleasure as potentially transformative. The extravagance of disdain with which my remark was met and its recourse to a discourse of the family remind us, as Michael Warner has, of the ways in which moralism produces and employs sexual shame. Why not consider, instead, enforced monogamy as a form of property law, as Melville suggests in "Fast Fish and Loose Fish"? Matthiessen has been praised for his "marriage" to Cheney, which may have been modeled on the tradition of the "Boston Marriage," but marriage is a means of assimilating homosexuals, once again through a form of liberal consensus.

Is there a danger in taking Whitman's idealism too seriously? Surely less danger than in having no dream at all. Whitman, as "I Dream'd in a Dream" shows, always seeks the embodied word, the dream of reality — the actions, "walking hand in hand" as the manuscript has it. One of Matthiessen's first letters to Cheney quotes Whitman precisely on the union body and soul: "And if the body does not do fully as much as the soul? / And if the body were not the soul, what is the soul?" (*LG* 94).

Merlis's book does capture brilliantly the fears and very real dangers of gay life in the 1950s. He also places a certain blame on Matthiessen, who swerved away from the very texts he was studying in private. There was in the end a failure of nerve. But we must, I think, remember that, as Reeve puts it, "Tom died because he was queer" (Merlis 111). So, I think, did Matthiessen. Whitman, of course, survived. As to the dream, it recorded a goal that often seems farther and farther away, much as the bourgeois privileges of gays seem to increase daily. Love, in the end, is perhaps not enough. We can dance all night, but to what end? The dream remains elusive partly because we do not know quite what we want. Reeve's crossing of the abyss, his redefining of space from private to public, his politics of the body, like Whitman's claim to public space, indicate what that dream might be. Merlis's account suggests that such deconstructions of identity still coexist fragilely with the near-fatal beating of the gay man. It is necessary to remember that the price of living that ideal can still be death.

NOTES

1. F. O. Matthiessen, *American Renaissance: Art and Experience in the Age of Emerson and Whitman* (New York: Oxford University Press, 1941).

2. Mark Merlis, *American Studies* (Boston: Houghton Mifflin, 1994).

3. Craig Seligman, *New Yorker* (October 24, 1994), 25.

4. David Bergman, *Gaiety Transfigured* (Madison: University of Wisconsin Press, 1991), 37.

5. Eric Cheyfitz, "Matthiessen's American Renaissance: Circumscribing Revolution," *American Quarterly* (1989), 349.

6. Kermit Vanderbilt, *American Literature and the Academy* (Philadelphia: University of Pennsylvania Press, 1986), 470.

7. Cheyfitz, 358.

8. May Sarton, *Faithful Are the Wounds* (New York: Norton), 1955.

9. Louis Hyde, ed., *Rat and the Devil: Journal Letters of F. O. Matthiessen and Russell Cheney* (Hamden, Conn.: Archon, 1978); hereafter cited as *Rat*.

10. F. O. Matthiessen, "The Education of a Socialist," in *F. O. Matthiessen: A Collective Portrait*, ed. Paul M. Sweezy and Leo Huberman (New York: Schuman, 1950), 8.

11. *Whitman's Manuscripts: Leaves of Grass (1860)*, ed. Fredson Bowers (Chicago: University of Chicago Press, 1955), 114–115.

12. Robert K. Martin, *The Homosexual Tradition in American Poetry* (Austin: University of Texas Press, 1979), xviii.

13. Robert Boyers, "The Ideology of the Steam-bath," *TLS* (May 30, 1980), 603.

Whitman's En Masse Aesthetics

SHERRY CENIZA

It all started this past summer when I read, once again, *Leaves of Grass*. Shortly afterward, I read Jay Grossman's essay "Epilogue" in *Breaking Bounds: Whitman and American Cultural Studies*. Grossman's angry tone is understandable, when toward the end of his essay he recounts gays' "being asked to submit to the fundamentally anti-intellectual regime of 'Don't ask, don't tell'" and notes the fact that "almost two-thirds of the U.S. Senate voted to deny funds to school districts that attempt to acknowledge the presence of their young gay and lesbian students through curricular or extracurricular activities."[1] He mentions gay teenage suicide and deaths from AIDS. But, finally, Grossman's overall tone in the essay works against him, at least it did for me. Toward the end of "Epilogue," Grossman comments on the "current visibility of homosexuality in the public sphere," saying that it is "everywhere appearing since the 1980s as the very public, sometimes shouting, and increasingly angry proclamations of a queer love that had previously, even recently, dared not speak" (258). As Whitman scholars, we cannot ignore the fact of homophobia, but we can choose how to address it. Grossman's own tone in "Epilogue" "sometimes [shouts]" and contains "angry proclamations." Well and good, his choice of tone is his call.

I went to Grossman's essay for ideas of ways to respond to the question students frequently ask where I teach: "Was Whitman gay?" This question comes with assumptions on the asker's part. Certainly in the United States, the question is not innocent, for gays and lesbians can be, have been, and are killed for their sexual orientation. I did not, however, come away from reading Grossman's "Epilogue" with ideas I could use. But I have come up with my own approach, which is to respond to my students' question with the question, "What does being gay mean?" I pose my question because the assumption behind the question "Was Whitman gay?" all too often assumes gays as a homogenous group based on the group's homogenous differing from the so-called homogenous norm. In the book *Gays/Justice: A Study of Ethics, Society, and Law,* Richard D. Mohr writes: "The most effective way of changing nongays' views about gays is for nongays to interact personally with some openly gay people."[2] Whitman said that democracy and his poetry were inextricable. In our present climate, the discussion of democracy might get short shrift, but not the question of sexual orientation. And that's the problem: a discussion of sexual orientation and of the concept of democracy do not belong in two different categories. Surely, living under a democracy and a person's living openly, without threat, his or her own sexual orientation are not oxymoronic.

Mohr speaks of the trap of reductiveness when he argues that the collective noun "gay" does not voice a monolithic view. An individual's stance cannot unproblematically be lumped into a group stance; to do so, Mohr says, "naively assumes that gays uniformly have the same interests and espouse the same views on any given gay issue, so that one simply needs to know one sociological fact — the percent of gays in the general population — to know the extent to which some publicly espoused gay interest is held" (171). Whether a person is straight or gay or bisexual or asexual does not in itself tell us about that person's stance toward any issue, not just those dealing with sexual orientation. Sexual orientation does not denote a person's essence. Creating camps labeled "straights" and "gays" does not break down boundaries; it creates them.

> I cannot tell how my ankles bend, nor whence the cause of my
>   faintest wish,
> Nor the cause of the friendship I emit, nor the cause of the friendship
>   I take again.
>
> That I walk up my stoop, I pause to consider if it really be,
> A morning-glory at my window satisfies me more than the metaphysics
>   of books. (*LGV* 1:34)

As to metaphysics: talking with Whitman on a Sunday in April 1889, Horace Traubel told him about his walk the night before when he joined the Saturday crowds busying themselves shopping. Whitman asked Traubel to tell him all about the people, the crowds, saying, "I am an outdoors man serving an indoor sentence." Then, in a clipped, three-sentence addendum, Whitman says, "Tell me about things — don't tell me theories. I have theories of my own" (*WWC* 4:510). And, talking with Whitman about Richard Maurice Bucke's belief that drinking alcohol was unhealthy, Traubel asks Whitman if he had read "Bucke's pamphlet on the subject." Whitman responds, "Probably, but I don't remember: I guess I was not convinced: I go on as I have gone on. You can't make rules of diet or rules of anything else to suit everybody. I am more likely to have feelings than theories about things" (*WWC* 2:465).

Reading Whitman's poetry, a reader can hardly avoid having feelings. Though there is no way to predict the outcome of those feelings, at the very least, reading *Leaves of Grass* opens up for discussion the issue of knee-jerk reactions based on perceived difference. The persona Whitman will, more likely than not, become the person Whitman, and, through extension, readers will — assuming that they *like* this person Whitman — question their own reactions concerning sexual orientation. I make a connection between Mohr's comments on gay group-speak and a closed reading of Whitman's poetry.

When Whitman uses words such as "yearning," "comrade," "love," "lover," "unrequited love," "linked," "fusing," "friend," and "friendship," the words signify according to their context and to their reader. Whitman sets us up for open readings in section 6 of "Song of Myself," the passage that starts, "A child said *What is the grass?* fetching it to me with full hands." The persona—"Walt Whitman, a kosmos, of Manhattan the son"—answers, "I guess it must be the flag of my disposition . . . Or I guess it is the handkerchief of the Lord . . . Or I guess the grass is itself a child . . . Or I guess it is a uniform hieroglyphic . . . And now it seems to me the beautiful uncut hair of graves" (*LGV* 1:31, 6–7). The "I guess . . . or" structure denies a definitive response to the question, "What is the grass?" This denial of a one-voiced reading allows a wide range of readers, distinct one from the other, to feel comfortable with their own readings of passages, of words, in *Leaves*, thus allowing readers to feel included in Whitman's world rather than shut out because of differences. Take, for instance, the term "comrade":

Ashes of soldiers South or North,
As I muse retrospective murmuring a chant in thought,
The war resumes, again to my sense your shapes,
. . . .

Phantoms of countless lost,
Invisible to the rest henceforth become my companions,
Follow me ever — desert me not while I live.

Sweet are the blooming cheeks of the living — sweet are the musical
  voices sounding,
But sweet, ah sweet, are the dead with their silent eyes.

Dearest comrades, all is over and long gone,
But love is not over — and what love, O comrades!
Perfume from battle-fields rising, up from the fœtor arising.

Perfume therefore my chant, O love, immortal love,
Give me to bathe the memories of all dead soldiers,
. . . .
Make these ashes to nourish and blossom,
O love, solve all, fructify all with the last chemistry. (*LGV* 2 : 510–512)

"Companions" and "comrades" and "lovers"— the desire here is for immortal love, possible for Whitman through his poems. In the last edition of
Leaves, Whitman moved "Ashes of Soldiers" to the cluster "Songs of Parting." By the time the reader has read *Leaves* in its entirety up to this point
and reads "Ashes," the tone sounds somber and reverent and, yes, dignified — dignified in a positive sense. His desire that the dead soldiers shroud
the poems, that the dead cover the poems "all over with tender pride" (*LG*
492), speaks of the disinterested but intense love Whitman felt for those
killed in battle, fighting for, he believed, the concept of American democracy, or the "IDEA," as he expressed it in *Democratic Vistas* (*PW* 2 : 368). The
tone of the poem brings to mind Bach, an elegiac tone.

The word "comrades" calls up a different relationship in the poem "In
Paths Untrodden," the opening poem of the "Calamus" cluster, in which
the word "comrades" holds the privilege of place, ending the poem:

I proceed for all who are or have been young men,
To tell the secret of my nights and days,
To celebrate the need of comrades. (*LGV* 2 : 365)

Just as the "Songs of Parting" cluster works on a reader's emotions, so,
too, does the "Calamus" cluster, but in a different way. Here, if tone comes
to mind, perhaps it's "Lush Life" I hear, a song by jazz composer Billy

Strayhorn, who, for some, ranks right up there with Bach, but the harmonies and melodies in "Lush Life" speak of longing, of regret, of deep feeling on a personal, sexual level, just as speak many of the "Calamus" poems. In the "Calamus" poems, "comrade" can be read as a coded term for lover, male lover. That reading does not mean, however, that "comrade" cannot also signify nonsexual bonding. As in the "What is the grass?" passage in "Song of Myself," the sense of the word "comrade" admits multiple readings. Whitman himself uses the word "comrade" in an all-inclusive sense when he says to Traubel: "I think there is nothing beyond the comrade — the man, the woman: nothing beyond: even our lovers must be comrades: even our wives, husbands: even our fathers, mothers: we can't stay together, feel satisfied, grow bigger, on any other basis" (*WWC* 3:581). And, at another time: "Comradeship — yes, that's the thing: getting one and one together to make two — getting the twos together everywhere to make all: that's the only bond we should accept and that's the only freedom we should desire: comradeship, comradeship" (*WWC* 2:371).

As to the "Calamus" poems, in an 1888 conversation with Traubel, speaking about a letter he, Whitman, had written to a friend named Hugo, Whitman says to Traubel: "I want you some day to write, to talk, about me: to tell what I mean by Calamus" (*WWC* 3:385). I do not know what Whitman was alluding to; no one does. It's anyone's guess. I don't believe that there's any one reading of "Calamus." Traubel notes the date of this conversation as December 25, 1888, twenty-eight years after the publication of the third edition of *Leaves*, the first edition to create the "Calamus" cluster. In his 1871 *Democratic Vistas*, Whitman meditates on comradeship: "Intense and loving comradeship, the personal and passionate attachment of man to man — which, hard to define, underlies the lessons and ideals of the profound saviours of every land and age, and which seems to promise, when thoroughly develop'd, cultivated and recognized in manners and literature, the most substantial hope and safety of the future of these States, will then be fully express'd" (*PW* 2:414).

I find it hard to believe that Whitman meant here simply genital contact. Certainly on one level, the "Calamus" poems speak through the persona of the personal love of a male for a male lover, and some suggest sexual contact. What does this signify? The fact that a male and female sleep together, a male with a male, or a female with a female — who cares, I say. I say this because I don't consider it any of my business who sleeps with whom, and also I see no prize belonging to heterosexuals because of their being heterosexual; perhaps my being heterosexual leads me to this conclusion. But the reaction "who cares?" is one I can make in the relative safety of my own life. In the United States, anyway, it's not smart to react with "who cares?" In the United States, we have only to look at the issue of abortion to see the conflation of private/public or personal/political. I see the consequences of a laissez-faire attitude. And so, what is at issue when reading Whitman's poems and questioning his sexual orientation? What happens when the personal becomes public?

In the 1876 preface, Whitman speaks about what seems to be personal affection, but in the context of his readers, present and future, he makes the personal public since he would not literally know his many readers personally: "I say, the subtlest, sweetest, surest tie between me and Him or Her, who, in the pages of 'Calamus' and other pieces realizes me — though we never see each other, or though ages and ages hence — must, in this way, be personal affection. And those . . . are at any rate *my readers*."[3] Whitman uses the phrase "political significance" in this same passage:

> Besides, important as they are in my purpose as emotional expressions for humanity, the special meaning of the "Calamus" cluster of "Leaves of Grass," (and more or less running through that book, and cropping out in "Drum-Taps,") mainly resides in its political significance. In my opinion, it is by a fervent, accepted development of comradeship, the beautiful and sane affection of man for man, latent in all the young fellows, north and south, east and west — it is by this, I say, and by what goes directly and indirectly along with it, that the United States of the future . . . are to be most effectually welded together, intercalated, anneal'd into a living union. (*PW* 2:471)

Here, "comradeship" is defined as "the beautiful and sane affection of man for man," but just what acts make up "beautiful and sane affection" are not spelled out. Whitman's indirectness leaves it open for readers to supply the terms.

When Whitman says that the "special meaning of the 'Calamus' cluster of 'Leaves of Grass,' (and more or less running through that book, and cropping out in 'Drum-Taps,') mainly resides in its political significance," part of what he means by "political significance" lies in his sense of democracy, which extends to democracy of the body. Robert H. Wiebe, in *Self-Rule: A Cultural History of American Democracy*, writes that "one of the crucial concomitants to democratic individualism early in the 19th century

Sherry Ceniza

was a new sense of owning one's body. Its origins lay in various Enlighten-ment propositions." Wiebe goes on to say: "Starting in the 1820s, the right of control over one's body was democratized. . . . The abolition of flogging in the navy capped this movement at midcentury, by which time the right of each white man to dispose of his own body was a well-established dem-ocratic principle. . . . Within the leeway that life allowed, democracy de-creed that each white man would make his own decisions about the dis-posal of his own body."[4] By extension, the phrase Whitman uses in the 1876 preface, "political significance," could have implied for Whitman the right for all to live their sexual orientation openly, without censure.

Whitman's 1876 preface and his 1871 *Democratic Vistas* strain to balance the scale Whitman recognizes early in his writing, the tension between what he called in the 1855 preface "sympathy" and "pride" (*PW* 2:443). In the aftermath of the war, when Whitman published *Democratic Vistas*, he clarifies what he sees as this tension:

> And, topping democracy, this most alluring record, that it alone can bind, and ever seeks to bind, all nations, all men, of however various and distant lands, into a brotherhood, a family. . . . Not that half only, individualism, which isolates. There is another half, which is adhesive-ness or love, that fuses, ties and aggregates, making the races comrades, and fraternizing all. Both are to be vitalized by religion. . . . For I say at the core of democracy, finally, is the religious element. All the religions, old and new, are there. (*PW* 2:381)

"Calamus" and "Drum-Taps" speak on multilevels — just as they read into our consciousness the physical love of man for man, so also do they read of the need for the phrenological sense of adhesiveness, a nonsexual bonding between human beings, regardless of sexual orientation. Sympa-thy and pride. Just as Whitman does not separate the body and the soul, so also does he not separate love into categories of carnal love only, same-sex love only, man-woman love only, or noncarnal caring love only. By and large, our society does make those separations. And, regrettably from my point of view, so do many of us scholars.

In Whitman's 1871 *Democratic Vistas* and his 1876 preface, the language weighs heavily on communal bonding, but the language likewise speaks of physical sexual desire and also of the plain old desire for sharing, sharing one's joy as well as one's fears, one's tenderness as well as one's frustration — male and female. Yearning. Whitman's words can hardly miss "itch[ing] at [our] ears" (*LGV* 1:77).

Why is this point about open readings important to me? I am pushing my own Walt Whitman, one whose poetry succeeds because it *does* address multiple readers. To tie the poetry down robs it of its richness.

"When I Heard at the Close of the Day," from "Calamus," speaks of a man's tender, passionate, yearning love for his lover:

> When I heard at the close of the day how my name had been receiv'd
>   with plaudits in the capitol, still it was not a happy night for me
>   that follow'd,
> And else when I carous'd, or when my plans were accomplish'd, still
>   I was not happy,
> But the day when I rose at dawn from the bed of perfect health,
>   refresh'd, singing, inhaling the ripe breath of autumn,
> When I saw the full moon in the west grow pale and disappear in the
>   morning light,
> When I wander'd alone over the beach, and undressing bathed,
>   laughing with the cool waters, and saw the sun rise,
> And when I thought how my dear friend my lover was on his way
>   coming, O then I was happy,
> O then each breath tasted sweeter, and all that day my food nourish'd
>   me more, and the beautiful day pass'd well,
> And the next came with equal joy, and with the next at evening came
>   my friend,
> And that night while all was still I heard the waters roll slowly
>   continually up the shores,
> I heard the hissing rustle of the liquid and sands as directed to me
>   whispering to congratulate me,
> For the one I love most lay sleeping by me under the same cover in
>   the cool night,
> In the stillness in the autumn moonbeams his face was inclined
>   toward me,
> And his arm lay lightly around my breast — and that night I was
>   happy. (*LGV* 2:381–382)

I search for words to articulate the beauty in this poem, the poignant beauty. This poem speaks to all. Depending on how the reader imagines the speaker of the poem, the poem speaks of a gay union or a heterosexual union. Until I started teaching this poem, I was oblivious to this since I read the speaker as male and the poem as a poem about the male speaker's love for his male lover. However, many of my students — probably because of compulsory heterosexuality, to use Adrienne Rich's term — do not imagine the sexual orientation to be male-male.[5] In our discussion as we come to the ending of the poem, some one or two of my students will use the pronouns "him" and "her," "he" and "she." I then propose my reading. My hope is that my students will see that, just as they can empathize with the speaker of the poem if they read the poem as male-female, so can they also empathize once they think of the relationship as being same-sexed. And gay or lesbian students will have the pleasure of reading a love poem addressed outside the heterosexual context. Is that too much to ask?

Consider the "Calamus" poem "To a Stranger":

Passing stranger! you do not know how longingly I look upon you,
You must be he I was seeking, or she I was seeking, (it comes to me
    as of a dream,)
I have somewhere surely lived a life of joy with you,
All is recall'd as we flit by each other, fluid, affectionate, chaste,
    matured,
You grew up with me, were a boy with me or a girl with me,
I ate with you and slept with you, your body has become not yours
    only nor left my body mine only,
You give me the pleasure of your eyes, face, flesh, as we pass, you take
    of my beard, breast, hands, in return,
I am not to speak to you, I am to think of you when I sit alone or
    wake at night alone,
I am to wait, I do not doubt I am to meet you again,
I am to see to it that I do not lose you. (*LGV* 2:392)

Depending on a reader's sexual orientation, the "you" can be determined male or female, or for those not looking for self-validation, the "you" remains fluid, as it is in the poem. A poignancy exists when the poem says, "I am not to speak to you, I am to think of you when I sit alone or wake at night alone." A reader of Whitman will recall other points when Whitman speaks of not voicing or wanting to have voiced personal feelings, personal attractions. Is it society's lack of valorization for same-sex unions that causes this desire for silence? Or is it something else? It's as if yearning meant more to the Whitman persona than actualization.

Finally, it's the ties between people, not the differences, that Whitman's poetry enacts.

"It is interesting — even odd — how many things come into, stay in, a man's mind which he cannot account for," Whitman said to Traubel (*WWC* 3:119).

> When I read the book, the biography famous,
> And is this then (said I) what the author calls a man's life?
> And so will some one when I am dead and gone write my life?
> (As if any man really knew aught of my life,
> Why even I myself I often think know little or nothing of my real life,
> Only a few hints, a few diffused faint clews and indirections
> I seek for my own use to trace out here.) (*LGV* 2:561)

NOTES

1. Jay Grossman, "Epilogue: Whitman's Centennial and the State of Whitman Studies," in *Breaking Bounds: Whitman and American Cultural Studies*, ed. Betsy Erkkila and Jay Grossman (New York: Oxford University Press, 1996), 261.

2. Richard D. Mohr, *Gays/Justice: A Study of Ethics, Society, and Law* (New York: Columbia University Press, 1988), 177.

3. Walt Whitman, *Two Rivulets* (Camden: Author's Edition, 1876), 11.

4. Robert H. Wiebe, *Self-Rule: A Cultural History of American Democracy* (Chicago: University of Chicago Press, 1995), 91, 92.

5. Adrienne Rich, "Compulsory Heterosexuality and Lesbian Existence," in *Blood, Bread, and Poetry: Selected Prose 1979–1985* (New York: W. W. Norton, 1986).

Public Love

Whitman and Political Theory

BETSY ERKKILA

Gaze, loving and thirsting eyes, in the house or street or public assembly!
Sound out, voices of young men! loudly and musically call me by my nighest name!
    — *Whitman*, Leaves of Grass, 1856

One's-Self I sing, a simple separate person,
Yet utter the word Democratic, the word En-Masse.
    — *Whitman*, Leaves of Grass, 1871

In 1783, at the close of the American Revolutionary War, George Washington broke into tears as he silently embraced, kissed, and said good-bye to each of his officers at the Fraunces Tavern in New York. As it was remembered and circulated in the American cultural imaginary, this revolutionary scene of public emotion and tears, which Whitman later recast as part of the simultaneously homoerotic and democratic dream fantasy of "The Sleepers" in 1855, came to signify the new forms of antipatriarchal authority imagined by the American republic: the commander in chief and later president of the United States as sentimental friend. Publicly divesting himself of authority as commander in chief through speechless acts of physical affection, mutuality, and exchange, Washington symbolically embodied the republican ideal of military authority returning to the self-sovereign citizen soldiers of the American republic and the Continental army dissolving into an affectionate union among friends.

This ideal of republican union is, of course, very far from the reality of violence and blood that have marked and continue to mark American and democratic history. Although the preamble to the Constitution of the United States makes its appeal to "justice," "domestic tranquillity," "the blessings of liberty," and the creation of "a more perfect union" in the name of "We, the people," the Constitution was in fact an illegal document put together in secret by an elite group of property-holding white men who literally feared for their lives in the wake of the rebellion of debtors led by Daniel Shays in Massachusetts in 1786–1787 and other turbulent signs — inside, outside, and on the borders of the American republic — that the "Union" was on the verge of collapse into anarchy and blood.

At the center of the struggle over the Constitution as it was defended by Alexander Hamilton, James Madison, and John Jay in *The Federalist Papers* (1787–1788) was the problem and paradox of liberty and union: how to reconcile the ideal of an American republic grounded in liberty and the self-sovereign rights of the individual with the need for order, law, and government. "Among the difficulties encountered by the convention," wrote Madison in *Federalist* No. 37, "a very important one must have lain in combining the requisite *stability and energy in government* with the inviolable attention due to *liberty and the republican form*."[1] The founders sought to resolve the problem of the passions and self-interests of human nature, states, and nations legally through a written constitution, representative government, the separation and balance of powers, and "the *federal principle*" of power divided between state and nation (No. 51, 293). This liberal model of government was grounded in conflict, in what Madison called "contending interests" (No. 37, 198); it left unresolved when it did not overtly repress or privatize the role that passion, eroticism, sympathy, and love might play in bringing about what Whitman would later call democracy as "a living union" among people (*PW* 2:471). It is the relations among public emotion, homoeroticism, political union, and democratic theory that I want to explore in this essay.

In recent years, Whitman's work has received increasing attention from political theorists and philosophers of democracy. Taking Whitman "seriously as a social scientist," the former Harvard professor of the science of government Samuel H. Beer compares Whitman's model of the state as an organic union held together by a diversity of interests to Émile Durkheim's argument in *The Division of Labor in Society* (1893) that in modern industrial society, the diversities of the division of labor are "the principal source of cohesion" (Durkheim, cited in Beer 365).[2] Poems such as "Song of Myself" and "Crossing Brooklyn Ferry," Beer argues, "confirm Whitman as a master of the sociological imagination" (377). Whereas Beer emphasizes Whitman's "nation-centered purpose," the political theorist George Kateb contends that Whitman "is perhaps the greatest philosopher of democratic culture" as the setting for the development of "democratic individuality."[3] Reading "Song of Myself" as a "work in political theory," Kateb (548) argues that Whitman's notion of the individual as composite, multiple, and "strange" becomes the means through which individuals are connected to each other in a democratic, rights-based polity. "To admit one's compositeness and ultimate unknowability," Kateb writes, "is to open oneself to a kinship to others that is defined by receptivity or responsiveness to them. It intensifies the mutuality between strangers that is intrinsic to the idea of rights based–individualism in a democracy" (556).

While Beer and Kateb have pioneered in opening a space for public discussion of Whitman as a serious philosopher and theorist of democracy, their work is also characteristic of a long tradition of liberal literary and political criticism that has bracketed or erased the collective, adhesive, and homoerotic dimensions of Whitman's theory of democracy.[4] Like social philosophers from Plato to Edmund Burke to Durkheim to Herbert Marcuse, Beer recognizes the erotic nature of the bonds that attach individuals to each other and to the state, but he does not elaborate on this insight; nor does he make any allusion to the specifically homoerotic sources of Whitman's notions of adhesiveness, comradeship, and love. Like Hannah Arendt, Kateb in his turn sees democratic individualism as a form of resistance to various forms of statism, from nationalism to totalitarianism to communitarianism. He explicitly rejects the importance of American nationality, "group identity," and adhesiveness to Whitman's theory of democracy (547). "Connectedness," as Kateb understands it, is an ideal of "receptivity and responsiveness" *within* the individual that "is not well illustrated by Whitman's notion of adhesive love, or love of comrades." He writes: "Adhesiveness threatens to suffocate the very individual of personality that Whitman is trying to promote, while it despiritualizes and falsifies the superior idea of oneself as composite, and hence as indefinite, and hence not properly amenable to an all-enfolding merger. It does not go with the spirit of rights-based individualism. It also serves the sinister project of nationalism. The comradely side of Whitman is not his most attractive because it is not the genuinely democratic one" (564).

As I have argued elsewhere, it is simply not possible to take Whitman seriously as a philosopher of democracy without taking seriously the importance of the collectivity and the en masse to his theory of democracy; the centrality of Whitman's concept of adhesiveness — or affectionate and usually same-sex love — to his political thinking; and the inseparability of his erotic and sexual experience as a man who loved other men (sometimes strangers) to his poetic, visionary, and theoretical writings about the future of democracy in America and worldwide.[5]

I want to use the work of one of the major democratic theorists of our time, Jürgen Habermas, as a means of reflecting on the relations among sex, tears, politics, poetry, and public love that undergird Whitman's theory of democracy. In *The Structural Transformation of the Public Sphere: An Inquiry into a Category of Bourgeois Society* (1962), Habermas describes the public sphere as a space between civil society (the family and the market) and the state (government) in which private persons engage in public talk about issues of common interest to all. As it emerged out of the privacy of the family and the intimacy of letters as the "containers for the 'outpourings of the heart'" in the eighteenth century, the public sphere of letters became the base for political criticism and resistance to public and state authority.[6] Habermas's concept of a public sphere of political dialogue separate from the state provides a useful model for understanding Whitman's theory of democracy and its inseparability from his effort to resist liberal privatization — the increasing distinction between a private sphere of intimacy, sex, women, and the family and a public sphere of politics, reason, manhood, and the state under liberal capitalism.

As it developed in the United States in the nineteenth century, the public sphere of speech, print, and popular assembly — protected by the constitutional guarantees of freedom of speech, press, and assembly — became the space where those social and sexual outsiders excluded by the Constitution or marginalized by society might find public voice through nonstate forms of participation, citizenship, and resistance.[7] As a popular writer, journalist, and poet, Whitman participated in this movement toward giving public and written voice to the masses of common men and women who made up the American people. He was also at the origins of a movement to resist sexual oppression and liberal privatization by publicly naming the taboo subjects of sex and the body and by giving public and print expression to the multiple — and sometimes secret and forbidden — forms of erotic attraction, pleasure, desire, and love that bring and hold people together not only in forms of social and political union but in all forms of daily life.

Whitman came of age at a time when the racial, sexual, economic, and class contradictions that were left unresolved at the time of the nation's

Betsy Erkkila

founding were beginning to tear the American union apart at the seams. At the center of Whitman's effort to address the problem of political union and, in effect, to make public love was the role of print, publication, and literature. Like "The Child's Champion" (1841), Whitman's popular temperance novel, *Franklin Evans; or the Inebriate, A Tale of the Times* (1842), was published by the *New World*, a mass-circulation newspaper, which, as Whitman wrote, gave him the power of reaching and shaping "mighty and deep public opinion" by "diffusing" his story "by every mail to all parts of this vast republic."[8] Written "*for the mass*" — not "for the critics but for THE PEOPLE" — and framed by the language of sentimental and "Temperance Reform," *Franklin Evans* seeks to teach the value of a "prudent, sober, and temperate course of life" as part of a broader movement of national republican regeneration (36, 37). "Victory! Victory! The Last Slave of Appetite is free, and the people are regenerated!" (170), the multitude proclaim in a Washingtonian dream sequence that is one part temperance meeting and one part national revival. But as Michael Moon and Michael Warner have argued, in Whitman's early temperance tales, the rhetoric of temperance reform functions as a fluid medium for voicing, at the same time that it condemns, a seductive urban underworld of male desire, pleasure, cruising, dissipation, same-sex eroticism, fluid identities, and border crossings that erode the illusory boundaries of class and identity, sex and blood.[9]

Whereas in *Franklin Evans* the desire to name and tell the "seductive enchantments" and erotic pleasures available to young men in the new urban space of the city exists in uneasy dialectical tension with the republican ideal of personal and national regeneration, by the time Whitman gets to the 1855 edition of *Leaves of Grass*, he is determined to give public voice to hitherto unnamed sexual, erotic, and homoerotic urges that in effect tie individuals, the body politic, and the entire universe together. "And . . . a kelson of the creation is love," the poet declares, in a mystical vision that literally comes out of the erotic and homoerotic union at the outset of the long opening poem (later entitled "Song of Myself"):

I mind how we lay in June, such a transparent summer morning;
You settled your head athwart my hips and gently turned over
    upon me,
And parted the shirt from my bosom-bone, and plunged your tongue
    to my barestript heart,
And reached till you felt my beard, and reached till you held my feet.

Swiftly arose and spread around me the peace and joy and knowledge
    that pass all the art and argument of the earth;
And I know that the hand of God is the elderhand of my own,
And I know that the spirit of God is the eldest brother of my own,
And that all the men ever born are also my brothers . . . . and the
    women my sisters and lovers,
And that a kelson of the creation is love;
And limitless are leaves stiff or drooping in the fields,
And brown ants in the little wells beneath them,
And mossy scabs of the wormfence, and heaped stones, and elder
    and mullen and pokeweed.[10]

Here as in the "Twenty-eight young men," "Thruster holding me tight,"
and "Is this then a touch?" sequences, scenes of sexual and orgasmic pleasure with another man, with twenty-eight young men, with the "voluptuous coolbreathed earth," or with oneself become the source of political
and spiritual vision — the ideal of "form and union and plan" toward
which the poem moves (*LG* 1855, 34, 45, 53, 85).

The democratic knowledge that the poet receives and gives of a universe
bathed in an erotic force that joins God, men, women, and the natural
world is not only linked with the ecstasy of same-sex union among and between men. The democratic "sign" that the poet gives is also linked with giving public voice to the socially marginalized and sexually repressed. "I speak
the password primeval. . . . I give the sign of democracy," Whitman writes:

Through me many long dumb voices,
Voices of the interminable generations of slaves,
Voices of prostitutes and of deformed persons,
Voices of the diseased and despairing, and of thieves and dwarfs,
. . . .
Through me forbidden voices,
Voices of sexes and lusts . . . . voices veiled, and I remove the veil,
Voices indecent by me clarified and transfigured. (*LG* 1855, 48)

Although Whitman's reference to clarifying and transfiguring "indecent"
voices has been read as a capitulation to bourgeois propriety, the lines suggest just the opposite. "Sexes and lusts" are not "indecent" because they
are bad but because they are socially "forbidden." In accord with the
Habermassian principle of publicity, the poet clarifies and transfigures

"sexes and lusts" by removing the veils of bourgeois decorum and liberal privacy, by making them public and common.

As Robert K. Martin, Gary Schmidgall, and other gay critics have shown, Whitman's poems might be read as a virtual handbook of the multiplicity of sexual and erotic pleasures men find with each other.[11] In fact, as I want to elaborate in this essay, it is in daring to structure his poetry and his political vision around a sexual and specifically "homosexual" symbolics that Whitman is at his most radical as a democratic theorist.[12] Having said this, however, it is also important to recognize that the social and political force of erotic attraction in Whitman's work is not always sexual — or genital; and it is not always — though it is mostly — between men. In the 1855 poem later entitled "The Sleepers," for example, Whitman presents two historical scenes of Washington weeping in a public display of affection for his troops. The first is at "the defeat of Brooklyn." Standing "amid a crowd of officers," Washington "cannot repress the weeping drops" as he "sees the slaughter of the southern braves confided to him by their parents" (*LG* 1855, 110). In the second, Washington stands in "the old tavern" at the close of the war as "the well-beloved soldiers all pass through":

> The officers speechless and slow draw near in their turns,
> The chief encircles their necks with his arm and kisses them on
>   the cheek,
> He kisses lightly the wet cheeks one after another . . . . he shakes
>   hands and bids goodbye to the army. (*LG* 1855, 110)

By incorporating these scenes from the beginning and end of the American Revolution into the seemingly private homoerotic dream fantasy of "The Sleepers," Whitman gives to the private, the sexual, and the imaginary a public, democratic, and national inflection. He embodies in the figure of Washington himself the public and political role that emotion, tears, and bodily affection between men will play in creating new and more democratic forms of leadership, citizenship, and friendship as the foundation of the new American nation.

This founding scene of public affection and love is immediately paired in "The Sleepers" with Whitman's account of his mother's "remembrance" of the bodily attraction and love that she felt for an American Indian woman — a "stranger"— "when she was a nearly grown girl living home with her parents on the old homestead":

My mother looked in delight and amazement at the stranger,
She looked at the beauty of her tallborne face and full and pliant
 limbs,
The more she looked upon her she loved her,
Never before had she seen such wonderful beauty and purity.
 (*LG* 1855, 110–111)

Here, as in the "Twenty-eight young men" sequence in "Song of Myself," in which a socially repressed woman (and ultimately Whitman himself) fantasizes a scene of group sex with twenty-eight male bathers, Whitman imagines democratic culture as the broadest possible opening up of society to the energies of erotic and homoerotic attraction and love in all their various social and sexual forms.[13] The erotic force of love becomes a democratizing force that erodes the traditional boundaries of sex, race, class, family, and propriety and gives rise to alternative forms of social and sexual relations: between a highborn woman and twenty-eight working-class men, between Whitman himself as the "unseen hand" and twenty-eight young men, between a "nearly grown girl" and an American Indian woman of exquisite "beauty," or anonymously between "strangers."

Inseparable from Whitman's democratizing desire to make public love is the Adamic process of naming anew — of finding alternative ways of publicizing and saying what the culture had silenced or banned as sin, sodomy, or onanism. Although critics have tended to treat Whitman's use of the phrenological term "adhesiveness" to describe "manly love" or "the passion of friendship for man" as a term that came into being in the 1860 "Calamus" poems and then disappeared or was sublimated later, Whitman first used the term "adhesiveness" in the 1856 "Poem of the Road" to suggest the sexual and bodily "yearnings" that arouse and draw strangers to each other amid the potentially alienating spaces of the modern world:[14]

Here is adhesiveness — it is not previously fashioned, it is apropos;
Do you know what it is as you pass to be loved by strangers?
Do you know the talk of those turning eye-balls?
. . . .
Why are there men and women that while they are nigh me the
 sun-light expands my blood?
Why when they leave me do my pennants of joy sink flat and lank?
. . . .

What is it I interchange so suddenly with strangers?
What with some driver as I ride on the seat by his side?
What with some fisherman, drawing his seine by the shore, as I walk
by and pause? [15]

Far from being "too literal an application" of "overt, acted-out connectedness," as Kateb argues, adhesiveness is the "not previously fashioned" but
"apropos" term that Whitman uses to describe the very qualities of responsiveness and receptivity that Kateb regards as Whitman's most important contribution to the theory of democracy. "Here is the profound
lesson of reception, neither preference or denial," Whitman writes; "The
black with his wooly head, the felon, the diseased, the illiterate person,
are not denied" (*LG* 1856, 224). Rather than emanating from democratic
individuality, as Kateb proposes, the lesson of reception, equality, and sympathy that grounds "overt, acted-out connectedness" in Whitman's democratic theory emanates from the "fluid and attaching character" of adhesiveness as the erotic and bodily force, or "efflux of the soul" (*LG* 1856,
230), that attracts people — especially men and strangers — to each
other.[16] It is this "shuddering longing ache of contact" (*LG* 1856, 231) that,
to quote Kateb against himself, "gradually build[s] up the overt connectedness of a democratically receptive culture: its tolerance, its hospitable-
ness, and its appetite for movement, novelty, mixture, and impurity" (563).

By using the French term *Allons*, Whitman links his call to the open
road of adhesiveness and comradeship to the democratizing energies of
the French Revolution and the greater bodily openness and fraternity that
he associated with French culture:

Allons! out of the dark confinement!
It is useless to protest — I know all, and expose it!

Behold through you as bad as the rest!
Through the laughter, dancing, dining, supping, of people,
Inside of dresses and ornaments, inside of those washed and
trimmed faces,
Behold a secret silent loathing and despair! (*LG* 1856, 237)

Here again, Whitman's call to the "public road" of democratic freedom
and adhesiveness is inseparable from publication and public expression as
part of an ongoing emancipatory struggle against the oppressive social and

sexual codes of the past — the "limits and imaginary lines" (*LG* 1856, 226) that keep private persons locked in "a secret silent loathing and despair."

This impulse toward public expression of adhesive love received renewed impetus by two events that coalesced in Whitman's personal and political life in the late 1850s: Whitman appears to have had an intense love affair with a man, which he recorded in an unpublished sheaf of twelve poems entitled "Live Oak, with Moss"; and the political union on which he staked his identity as the poet of democracy began to dissolve under the pressure of slavery and other contradictions in the body politic of the American republic. In his unpublished political pamphlet entitled *The Eighteenth Presidency!* and in his journals and notebooks of the time, Whitman was so gloomy about the state of national and party politics, the slavery crisis, and increasing economic hardship that he appears to have contemplated taking his "voice" directly to the people either as a public lecturer or by seeking political office himself.[17] In a notebook entry for April 24, 1857, he imagines himself as a public advocate for the people in Washington or elsewhere, darting "hither and thither, as some great emergency might demand": "*Not* to direct eyes or thoughts to any of the usual avenues, as of official appointment, or to get such anyway. To put all those aside for good. But always to keep up living interest in public questions — and *always to hold the ear of the people*" (*CW* 9:7–8).

In the love poems of "Live Oak, with Moss," which were written between 1858 and 1859, he also appears to have flirted with the idea of taking the path pursued by Emily Dickinson around the same time — of retreating from the public sphere of print and publicity. "I can be your singer of songs no longer," Whitman announces in poem V of the sequence (later "Calamus" 8):

> I have found him who loves me, as I him, in perfect love,
> With the rest I dispense — I sever from all that I thought would suffice
>   me, for it does not — it is now empty and tasteless to me,
> I heed knowledge and the grandeur of The States, and the examples
>   of heroes, no more,
> . . . .
> I am indifferent to my own songs — I am to go with him I love, and
>   he is to go with me,
> It is to be enough for each of us that we are together — We never
>   separate again. —[18]

But Whitman chose against the path of public renunciation. Rather, and in some sense quite extraordinarily, he turned in the 1860 edition of *Leaves of Grass* toward an effort to resolve the political crisis of the Union — the paradox of liberty and union, the one and the many — on the level of the body, sex, and homosexual love.

This effort at personal and national resolution is evident in "Proto-Leaf" (later "Starting from Paumanok"), the long opening poem that would serve as a kind of preface to the 1860 and future editions of *Leaves of Grass*. Rather than allowing himself to be personally consumed by the passion of his love for men, Whitman avows to give open expression to the "burning fires" of this passion as the affective and political force that will hold "These States" together:

> I will sing the song of companionship,
> I will show what alone must compact These,
> I believe These are to found their own ideal of manly love, indicating
>   it in me;
> I will therefore let flame from me the burning fires that were
>   threatening to consume me,
> I will lift what has too long kept down those smouldering fires,
> I will give them complete abandonment,
> I will write the evangel-poem of comrades and of love,
> (For who but I should understand love, with all its sorrow and joy?
> And who but I should be the poet of comrades?) [19]

Believing, as he wrote in the manuscript of "Proto-Leaf," that "the main purport of America is to found a new ideal of manly friendship, more ardent, more general" (Bowers 12), Whitman presents the 1860 *Leaves of Grass* as the "New Bible" of the American republic and himself as the evangel-poet and embodiment of a new democratic gospel of "manly love." He envisions the "burning fires" of "manly" passion as both the affective foundation of political "Union" and a radically democratizing force that will level the distinctions between sexes and classes, "vices" and "virtues":

> O my comrade!
> O you and me at last — and us two only;
> O power, liberty, eternity at last!
> O to be relieved of distinctions! to make as much of vices as virtues!

O to level occupations and the sexes! O to bring all to common
    ground! O adhesiveness!
O the pensive aching to be together — you know not why, and
    I know not why.
. . . .
O hand in hand — O wholesome pleasure — O one more desirer
    and lover,
O haste, firm holding — haste, haste on, with me. (*LG* 1860, 22)

As the preface poem to the 1860 *Leaves*, "Proto-Leaf" reveals a poet newly
articulate about his public role as the evangel-poet of those sexual of-
fenders and social outsiders who were — and still are — among the least
visible and most oppressed within the putatively liberating but in fact het-
eronormatizing structures of the liberal state.[20]

The new role that Whitman conceived for himself as the evangel-poet
of democracy and love receives its fullest articulation in the "Calamus" poems. In the opening poem (later "In Paths Untrodden"), Whitman resolves to publish and give voice to the "not yet published" standard of
manly love as a form of resistance to the traditional "pleasures, profits,
conformities" of public culture and the marketplace:

Escaped from the life that exhibits itself,
From all the standards hitherto published — from the pleasures,
    profits, conformities,
Which too long I was offering to feed to my Soul;
Clear to me now, standards not yet published — clear to me that
    my Soul,
That the Soul of the man I speak for, feeds, rejoices only in comrades;
. . . .
I proceed, for all who are, or have been, young men,
To tell the secret of my nights and days,
To celebrate the need of comrades. (*LG* 1860, 341–342)

Although the "Calamus" poems are frequently treated as Whitman's most
private sequence of poems, they are also his most public and politically engaged. Framed by an appeal to publicity, the "Calamus" sequence seeks to
express, enact, and incite new "types" of "manly attachment" and "athletic
love" as the source and ground of a fully realized democratic culture. This
emphasis on publicity and public exhibition is evident even in the seem-

ingly more "private," separatist, and renunciatory poems of "Live Oak, with Moss": "Publish my name and hang up my picture as that of the tenderest lover," Whitman declares in poem VII (Bowers 84; later "Recorders Ages Hence"). Although Alan Helms, Herschel Parker, and others have argued that Whitman's decision to publish his "Live Oak, with Moss" poems as part of the "Calamus" sequence represents a corruption of some originary purity of homosexual feeling and art, their argument has the effect of reprivatizing both homosexuality and art in a way that is contrary to Whitman's brave homoerotic, democratic, and insistently public and political purpose.[21] Drawing on multiple sources — from Plato's notion of the ethical and political force of erotic love and the erotically charged relation between teacher and pupil in the Greek space of the *Paideia* to the Gospels of Jesus Christ, artisan republicanism, the culture of sentiment, and the radical reform energies of the antebellum United States — Whitman tells "the secret" of his "nights and days" not for sensation or sublimation but as an emancipatory act of sexual, political, and artistic liberation.

Whitman's public and liberatory focus and the relation between sexual "secrets" and political union, manly love and democratic theory, might be effectively illustrated by any one of the "Calamus" poems. In this essay, I want to focus in particular on "Calamus" 5 (later "For You O Democracy"), "Calamus" 15 (later "Trickle Drops"), and "The Base of All Metaphysics," a poem that Whitman added to the "Calamus" sequence after the Civil War.

In "Calamus" 5, Whitman seeks to resolve the paradox of liberty and union and the political crisis of the nation not through an appeal to law, the Constitution, the courts, or "by arms" but through the erotic force of physical love and intimacy between men. How can this be? "Affection shall solve everyone of the problems of freedom," Whitman writes, representing himself and his poems as the embodiment of "a new friendship" that will "twist and intertwist" the "States" in bonds of comradeship and love:

> Those who love each other shall be invincible,
> They shall finally make America completely victorious, in my name.

> One from Massachusetts shall be comrade to a Missourian,
> One from Maine or Vermont, and a Carolinian and an Oregonese,
>   shall be friends triune, more precious to each other than all the
>   riches of the earth.

> . . . .

> The most dauntless and rude shall touch face to face lightly,

Whitman and Political Theory   127

The dependence of Liberty shall be lovers,
The continuance of Equality shall be comrades.

These shall tie and band stronger than hoops of iron.
  (*LG* 1860, 349–351)

Whitman's "new friendship" seeks to intervene in a constitutional imaginary grounded in reason, self-interest, contract, and the marital bond between male and female. His appeal to "manly affection" as the basis of democratic liberty, equality, and union seeks to retrieve the passions of love, sympathy, fraternal feeling, and bodily desire that were, in effect, written out of the Constitution. While Madison subscribed to the "republican theory" that "the people are the only legitimate fountain of power," he feared "the public passions" that would be aroused by referring "constitutional questions" to their power (*Federalist* No. 49, 283–284). "[I]t is the reason, alone, of the public, that ought to control and regulate the government," he wrote in *Federalist* No. 49. "The passions ought to be controlled and regulated by the government" (285). Especially following the French Revolution in 1789 and the Reign of Terror in the 1790s, the Federalists sought to secure the American nation against the effects of passion, sympathy, and fraternal feeling at home and abroad. "No entangling alliances," Washington had warned in his Farewell Address in 1796 in an effort to isolate the United States from the more fraternal, egalitarian, and global forms of sympathy, passion, love, and republican citizenship associated with the French Revolution.[22]

But what exactly does Whitman mean by his assertion that "Affection shall solve everyone of the problems of freedom," and how does it relate to his theory of democracy? Whitman's notion of adhesiveness or erotic attachment — especially between men — redeploys notions of sympathetic attachment, identification, and affection that were regarded as the base of political community by conservative eighteenth-century philosophers such as Edmund Burke and by Scottish moral sense philosophers such as Adam Smith. In Smith's view, human society is held together by moral sympathy, "an internal monitor activated by the sympathetic attachments."[23] It is through the power of sympathetic identification that one can enter into another's body and feel his or her pain. "By the imagination we place ourselves in his situation," Smith writes in *The Theory of Moral Sentiments* (1759); "we conceive ourselves enduring all the same torments, we enter as it were into his body and become in some measure the same person with

Betsy Erkkila

him, and thence form some idea of his sensations."[24] Smith's theory of sympathetic identification adumbrates the fluid interchange of self and other that underwrites Whitman's theory of democracy. Refigured in Whitman's writings as "this never satisfied appetite for sympathy, and this boundless offering of sympathy — this universal democratic comradeship," sympathy, or what Whitman calls "this old, eternal yet ever-new interchange of adhesiveness, so fitly emblematic of America" (1876 preface; *PW* 2:471), creates the fluid conditions for an equitable, just, and democratic society.

Unlike Smith, who excludes erotic love from the moral sentiments, Whitman rewrites eighteenth-century sympathy as "this terrible, irrepressible yearning," a "living, pulsating" desire for "love and friendship" that is at once sexual appetite and democratizing force (1876 preface; *PW* 2:471). The same erotic force that draws the poet to his male lovers also draws him to being in general through sympathetic identification with women, blacks, workers, the poor, the outcast, and the oppressed. "Agonies are one of my changes of garments," Whitman writes as he enters into the body of the "hounded slave": "Hell and despair are upon me . . . . crack and again crack the marksmen, / I clutch the rails of the fence . . . . my gore dribs thinned with the ooze of my skin" (*LG* 1855, 62). This imaginative identification with the feeling of others becomes the affective base for justice, equity, and democratic union and the ground for resistance to injustice and oppression on behalf of oneself and others worldwide.[25]

Whereas the constitutional founders sought to regulate and control passion, Whitman wants to let it "flame out" as the affective basis of political union and the public culture of democracy. He seeks to fill public space with the "new signs" of male passion and love — with men kissing, holding hands, embracing, and touching "face to face." "I will plant companionship thick as trees along all the rivers of America, and along the shores of the great lakes, and all over the prairies, / I will make inseparable cities, with their arms about each other's necks" (*LG* 1860, 351). Beyond the law, the military, and the abstract and disembodied language of democratic rights, Whitman begins to formulate the notion of a public culture of men loving men as a model of the nonstate forms of democratic affection that will unite America and the world in ties "stronger than hoops of iron."

Like the poetic figure of Washington weeping, hugging, and kissing his soldiers, these public displays of physical affection and love between men are also part of Whitman's effort to challenge the male and female marital structures of the Revolutionary and post-Revolutionary imaginary. During the age of the transatlantic revolutions in America and France, transformations in the concept of the subject and citizenship and in the relations between citizens and the state were inseparable from a reconceptualization of men and women and the relations between them. Renouncing models of patriarchal authority associated with the Old World, monarchy, and the feudal past, American patriots represented the affectionate bond of love and friendship between husband and wife as the model of republican relations in family, society, and state. As Jan Lewis argues: "Marriage was the very pattern from which the cloth of republican society was to be cut," and "friendship" was the word most frequently used to describe ideal republican marriage.[26] The extent to which the male and female couple came to dominate not only literature but all aspects of American life in the post-Revolutionary period is suggested by an essay, "From the Genius of Liberty," which appeared in the *Key* on April 14, 1798: "That MAN who resolves to live without WOMAN, or that WOMAN who resolves to live without MAN are ENEMIES TO THE COMMUNITY in which they dwell, INJURIOUS TO THEMSELVES, DESTRUCTIVE TO THE WORLD, APOSTATES TO NATURE, AND REBELS AGAINST HEAVEN AND EARTH."[27] The naturalness of the relation between man and woman that the "Genius of Liberty" encodes is not only a sexuality: it is also a politics and a metaphysics. The "Genius" of American "Liberty," the perpetuation of human community, and the metaphysical order of things come to depend on the naturalness of the union between man and woman.[28]

As early as the 1840s, Whitman challenged this metaphysics of male and female marital love in such tales as "The Child's Champion" and *Franklin Evans* by circulating the countermodel of a real though subaltern culture of male affection and love. In the 1856 *Leaves of Grass*, he avows his intent to write against the forms of male and female love that have dominated the literature and culture of democracy: "This tepid wash, this diluted deferential love, as in songs, fictions, and so forth, is enough to make a man vomit; as to manly friendship, everywhere observed in The States, there is not the first breath of it to be observed in print" (*LG* 1856, 356). In Whitman's view, it was the historically patriarchal and unequal relationship between man and woman that made "manly friendship" a more appropriate, because more egalitarian, model of democracy than the "diluted deferential love" of popular fiction and songs. At the same time, Whitman's com-

Betsy Erkkila

mitment to making both male and female sex public — "that the body is to be expressed, and sex is" (*LG* 1856, 356) — was part of the historical process of achieving political equality between men and women.[29]

As "Calamus" 5 suggests, in the 1860 *Leaves*, and especially in the "Calamus" poems, Whitman's political and democratic project becomes inseparable from his desire to resist both the privatization of sex and the naturalization of male-female marriage as the fundamental means of organizing sexuality and social space: "It shall be customary in all directions, in the houses and streets, to see manly affection, / The departing brother or friend shall salute the remaining brother or friend with a kiss" (*LG* 1860, 350). Whitman infuses his poems and democratic culture with forms of "manly affection" that are neither private nor always sexual and genital but public, erotic, and multiple — a practice of everyday life that is visible and pervasive. Acts of physical affection and love between men not only take place in public: they take place *only* in public.

Whitman fills his poems and the public space of print with forms of manly love that include images of himself as "the new husband" and "comrade," the poet-lover of his readers and teacher of élèves. He is the "suffering" lover who gives voice to the "anguish and passion" of unreturned love between men ("Calamus" 9), and he is the man who joyously sleeps with his lover outdoors "under the same cover in the cool night" ("Calamus" 11). He is the urban cruiser who celebrates Manhattan's "frequent and swift flash of eyes offering me love" ("Calamus" 18). "Lovers, continual lovers, only repay me" ("Calamus" 18), he writes in lines that subvert notions of the couple and monogamy as the only forms of sexual pleasure and love. He is the American comrade who publicly kisses and is kissed by "a Manhattanese" ("And I, in the public room, or on the crossing of the street, or on the ship's deck, kiss him in return") ("Calamus" 19). He is the lover of strangers ("Passing stranger! you do not know how longingly I look upon you") and of "other men in other lands . . . in Germany, Italy, France, Spain — Or far, far away, in China, or in Russia or India — talking other dialects" ("Calamus" 22, 23). He is the "unremarked" person who silently holds hands with "a youth who loves me, and whom I love" amid "a crowd of workmen and drivers in a bar-room" ("Calamus" 29). He is the recorder of "two simple men . . . on the pier, in the midst of the crowd": "The one to remain hung on the other's neck, and passionately kissed him, / While the one to depart, tightly prest the one to remain in his arms" ("Calamus" 32). He is the dreamer who dreams of a city of "robust love":

"It was seen every hour in the actions of the men of that city, / And in all their looks and words" ("Calamus" 34). And he is the poet of a future culture of public love: "Now it is you, compact, visible, realizing my poems, seeking me" ("Calamus" 45).

In *The Structural Transformation of the Public Sphere*, Habermas argues that the appearance of John Stuart Mill's *On Liberty* in 1859 marked a shift away from the revolutionary conceptualization of the public sphere as a site of democratic opinion formation toward a strengthening of the legal and administrative power of the state and an increasing distinction between a private sphere of home, family, and economics and a public sphere of government and politics. Not surprisingly, Mill's *On Liberty* appeared in the same year that Whitman began to theorize the public role of the "secret" culture of male love in securing the future of democracy worldwide. Whereas "Calamus" 5 emphasizes manly love as a force for political union and a practice of everyday life, "Calamus" 15 (later "Trickle Drops") seeks to publicize the private, to make the passions of the heart, the body, and the blood of male love public by bleeding — or more properly, hemorrhaging — into print:

> O drops of me! trickle, slow drops,
> Candid, from me falling — drip, bleeding drops,
> From wounds made to free you whence you were prisoned,
> From my face — from my forehead and lips,
> From my breast — from within where I was concealed — Press forth,
>   red drops — confession drops,
> Stain every page — stain every song I sing, every word I say, bloody
>   drops. (*LG* 1860, 361)

Whitman writes against a disembodied public sphere of reason and print and a nineteenth-century medical discourse that locates nonreproductive sexualities, associated with onanism, intemperance, and other forms of bodily excess, outside the realms of political citizenship and human community.[30] As in "Calamus" 2 (later "Scented Herbage of My Breast"), Whitman resolves to "unbare" his "broad breast" by giving voice to the private or "concealed" as a source of sexual guilt, pain, and repression in an amative order of things. As a nineteenth-century version of "Don't ask, don't tell," privacy is in fact a prison that keeps male and female bodies separate and distinct and nonamative sexualities "secret" and oppressed. The poet's wounds — whether self-inflicted or socially imposed — become a source

Betsy Erkkila

of freedom by bleeding openly into speech, print, and song. The conjunction of tears and blood flowing out of a body without bounds poetically enacts the breakdown of the boundaries between private and public, sex and print, wound and voice, female and male that the poem encodes. Male tears and blood flow into the public sphere in images that associate the poet's body with both the male onanist and the female hysteric as they were being constituted by nineteenth-century medical discourse.[31]

"[A]ll ashamed and wet," Whitman also draws on the medical theory of semen as a form of blood to represent his poems as a kind of masturbatory flow into print and publicity:

> Let them know your scarlet heat — let them glisten,
> Saturate them with yourself, all ashamed and wet,
> Glow upon all I have written or shall write, bleeding drops,
> Let it all be seen in your light, blushing drops. (*LG* 1860, 361)

Saturating a "them" that encompass the printed page, "every song I sing," and the public he addresses with the blood, semen, and tears of homosexual passion, Whitman's poetic act of making the private public is part of a political struggle for freedom and justice. As the political theorist Selya Benhabib observes: "All struggles against oppression in the modern world begin by redefining what had previously been considered private, nonpublic, and nonpolitical issues as matters of public concern, as issues of justice, as sites of power that need discursive legitimation."[32]

Rather than representing a sublimation or retreat from the homoerotic politics of the 1860 *Leaves of Grass*, as some have argued, the Civil War reaffirmed and extended Whitman's democratic vision of the love between men as a force for social, political, and ultimately ethical and religious union. The eroticism of male-male physical contact and love pervades Whitman's Civil War poems, including the more public and political context of "When Lilacs Last in the Dooryard Bloom'd," Whitman's elegy on the death of President Abraham Lincoln in which Lincoln, like Washington, is evoked as comrade and lover. The centrality of physical and public acts of affection between men to Whitman's historical understanding of the Civil War is further suggested by the fact that he later incorporated most of "Calamus" 5 — "The dependence of Liberty shall be lovers, / The continuance of Equality shall be comrades"— into his effort to come to terms with the blood and carnage of the Civil War in his 1865 *Drum-Taps* poem "Over the Carnage Rose Prophetic a Voice."

Whitman envisioned adhesiveness not as a sexual relation only but as a social relation, a politics, and a metaphysics.[33] It is this metaphysics of male-male love that is the subject of "The Base of All Metaphysics," the only poem that Whitman added to the "Calamus" sequence in the post–Civil War period. Rather than sublimating, diluting, or silencing Whitman's celebration of homosexual love, the poem invokes "the new and antique" systems of philosophy — of Plato and Socrates, of Christ and the Christian Church, of Kant, Fichte, Schelling, and Hegel — as the base for alternative forms of male passion and love outside the patriarchal, property-based, and reproduction-centered marriage of man and woman.[34] Perhaps influenced by a recent reading of Plato, "whose whole treatment," Whitman wrote, "assumes the illustration of love" by "the passion inspired in one man by another, more particularly a beautiful youth" ("it is astounding to modern ideas," he added), Whitman represents "The dear love of man for his comrade, / the attraction of friend to friend" as the model of an erotic "attraction" that binds man to man, friend to friend, husband to wife, city to city, and land to land (*NUPM* 5:1882).[35] In "The Base of All Metaphysics," a pervasive and seemingly natural male-female metaphysics of hierarchy and oppression is displaced and denaturalized by an egalitarian and more democratic metaphysics of male-male love.[36]

It was not until after the Civil War in *Democratic Vistas* that Whitman sought to synthesize the relations among individualism, political union, and public love into a major theory of democracy. Written in 1867 as a response to Carlyle's attack on the democratic masses in "Shooting Niagara," Whitman begins by acknowledging the seedy, greedy corruptions of Gilded Age America. "[W]ith unprecedented materialistic advancement — society, in these States, is canker'd, crude, superstitious, and rotten," he writes. "Never was there, perhaps, more hollowness at heart than at present, and here in the United States" (*PW* 2:369):

> The depravity of the business classes of our country is not less than has been supposed, but infinitely greater. The official services of America, national, state, and municipal . . . are saturated in corruption, bribery, falsehood, mal-administration. . . . The great cities reek with respectable as much as non-respectable robbery and scoundrelism. . . . In business, (this all-devouring modern word, business,) the one sole object is, by any means, pecuniary gain. The magician's serpent in the fable ate

up all the other serpents; and money-making is our magician's serpent, remaining to-day sole master of the field. (*PW* 2:370)

Whitman presents the specter of a disunited states — a democratic society disintegrated by the forces of capitalist individualism that were supposed to be its salvation. Democratic individualism had reached a dead end in what Whitman calls "the increasing aggregation of capital in the hands of a few," "the advent of new machinery, dispensing more and more with hand-work," "the growing, alarming spectacle of countless squads of vaga-bond children," "the hideousness and squalor of certain quarters of the cities," and the "advent of late years . . . of these pompous, nauseous, out-side shows of vulgar wealth" (*PW* 2:753). The world of "pride, competi-tion, segregation, vicious willfulness, and license beyond example" (*PW* 2:422) that Whitman describes is, in effect, the world of late capitalism that we know today, only now the serpent's field is corporate and global rather than individual and national.

The question Whitman finally poses in *Democratic Vistas* is whether de-mocracy is possible under the conditions of laissez-faire capitalism. De-mocracy, Whitman argues, cannot be "held together merely by political means": it needs poets to aid in the political creation of a democratic cul-ture that will take "firm and . . . warm . . . hold in men's heart, emotions and belief" (*PW* 2:368). Like the political theorist Hannah Arendt in the twentieth century, Whitman expresses concern that the expansion of the economic sphere will replace the common concern for political com-munity — for the *res publica* — in the hearts and minds of the people.[37] While Whitman believed that "the ulterior object of political and all other government" was "to develop, to open to cultivation, to encourage the possibilities of all beneficent and manly outcroppage, and of that aspira-tion for independence, and the pride and self-respect latent in all charac-ters" (*PW* 2:379), he also feared that unleashed individualism — or what he called "Selfism" — would undermine the common good of the Ameri-can republic. "Must not the virtue of modern Individualism," he asked, "continually enlarging, usurping all, seriously affect, perhaps keep down entirely, in America, the like of the ancient virtue of Patriotism, the fervid and absorbing love of general country?" (*PW* 2:373).[38]

To this "serious problem and paradox in the United States" (*PW* 2:373), Whitman responded with the visionary and utopian force of erotic, or adhesive, love. Countering the revolutionary movement away from the feudal structures of the past toward the sovereign power of the individual, he envisions a universal Hegelian force that binds and fuses humanity: There is "[n]ot that half only, individualism, which isolates. There is another half, which is adhesiveness or love, that fuses, ties and aggregates, making the races comrades, and fraternizing all" (*PW* 2:381). Far from being "too literal" or threatening "to suffocate" "rights based–individualism" in "an all-enfolding merger," as Kateb argues, it is to "the threads of manly friendship" running through the "worldly interests of America" that Whitman looks for the "counterbalance" and "spiritualization" of "our materialistic and vulgar American democracy" (*PW* 2:414): "I say democracy infers such loving comradeship, as its most inevitable twin or counterpart," he writes, "without which it will be incomplete, in vain, and incapable of perpetuating itself" (*PW* 2:415).

Whereas *Democratic Vistas* opens with a tribute to the "lessons" of individual "variety and freedom" affirmed by Mill's *On Liberty*, it closes with a homoerotic rewriting of Hegel's *Introduction to the Philosophy of History*, with what Whitman calls "the Hegelian formulas" or spirit manifesting itself historically in democratic community (*PW* 2:421).[39] In the concluding section of *Democratic Vistas*, as Whitman leaps ahead in "fond fantasy" to imagine what a fully realized democratic culture might look like on the second centennial of the Republic in 1976, the only future he can imagine is one in which "the development, identification, and general prevalence" of homoerotic love, "carried to degrees hitherto unknown," will pervade "individual character" and "general politics": "*Intense and loving comradeship, the personal and passionate attachment of man to man*—which, hard to define, underlies the lessons and ideals of the profound saviours of every land and age, and which seems to promise, when thoroughly develop'd, cultivated and recognized in manners and literature, the most substantial hope and safety of the future of these States, *will then be fully express'd*" (*PW* 2:414; my emphasis). It is in "[i]ntense and loving comradeship, the personal and passionate attachment of man to man" that Whitman finds the affective base for the nonstate forms of political community that will take "hold in men's hearts, emotions and belief" and receive fullest public expression in "the average, the bodily, the concrete, the democratic, the popular, on which all the superstructures of the future are to permanently rest" (*PW* 2:426).

The bonds of loving comradeship that Whitman imagines are the base not only of political union in the United States but of a new metaphysics of democracy worldwide. Although *Democratic Vistas* addresses the problems and contradictions of democracy in the United States in the post–Civil War period, the future — or vistas — it imagines are global and transnational. Like Karl Marx and like C. L. R. James in a later period, Whitman saw the outbreak of the American and French Revolutions and the 1848 revolutions in Europe as part of a broader popular democratic revolution that would eventually spread to the entire world. The empowering of the masses and the structures of law, government, and rights put into place following the American and French Revolutions were only the first stage of a more global revolution. "The great word Solidarity has arisen," Whitman declared in *Democratic Vistas* (*PW* 2:382). Whereas Marx imagines the will of the people becoming the state, like C. L. R. James and recent theorists of what Nancy Fraser has called "subaltern counterpublic" spheres, Whitman imagines a collective popular will that exists apart from the authority of the state. The state is the legal structure of democracy; the people are its base and its future. Beyond a first stage of rights and a second stage of material progress and wealth, Whitman theorizes a future public culture of democracy that will be achieved not by law, government, or the market but by the democratizing force of adhesive, or manly, love, which "alone can bind . . . all nations, all men, of however various and distant lands, into a brotherhood, a family" (*PW* 2:381).[40]

As "Calamus" 23 (later entitled "This Moment Yearning and Thoughtful") suggests, it was through the open road of his feeling for other men — sometimes strangers — that Whitman was able to imagine forms of democratic community outside law and government and beyond the nation-state:

> This moment as I sit alone, yearning and thoughtful, it seems to me
>   there are other men in other lands, yearning and thoughtful;
> It seems to me I can look over and behold them, in Germany, Italy,
>   France, Spain — Or, far, far away, in China, or in Russia or India —
>   talking other dialects;
> And it seems to me if I could know those men better, I should
>   become attached to them, as I do to men in my own lands;
> . . . .
> O I know we should be brethren and lovers,
> I know I should be happy with them. (*LG* 1860, 367)

In Whitman's homoerotic vistas, the love of strangers models the public culture of male love that he imagines as the future of democracy: the stranger exists as an unknown figure, a foreigner in public space, outside the prescribed intimacies of home, marriage, and family. Rather than serving what Kateb calls "the sinister project of nationalism," Whitman's erotic experience of desire for, sympathetic attachment to, and identification with strangers — the swift and fluid exchange of glances, bodies, and love in the streets, bars, buses, theaters, and public spaces of the modern metropolis — enables him to imagine a fully democratic world of strangers loving strangers worldwide.

Returning to Plato's evocation of love between men as a simultaneously erotic, ethical, and political force, Whitman challenges the rhetorics of male and female romance that have ordered sex, society, and politics in the West. Seeking to displace what he calls "the amative love hitherto possessing imaginative literature" (*PW* 2:414), Whitman envisions "adhesive love" as the "base of all metaphysics," the model of alternative forms of social affection and political community, and the erotic base for the future of democracy not only in the United States but worldwide:

> Camerado, I give you my hand!
> I give you my love more precious than money,
> I give you myself before preaching or law;
> Will you give me yourself? will you come travel with me? (*LG* 159)

NOTES

This essay is dedicated to Robert K. Martin with affection and gratitude for his brave and pioneering work in the field of gay studies.

1. Alexander Hamilton, James Madison, and John Jay, *The Federalist Papers*, ed. Clinton Rossiter (New York: New American Library, 1999), No. 37, 194, my emphasis.

2. Samuel H. Beer, "Liberty and Union: Walt Whitman's Idea of the Nation," *Political Theory* 12 (1984), 363.

3. George Kateb, "Walt Whitman and the Culture of Democracy," *Political Theory* 18 (November 1990), 545.

4. Others who have turned to Whitman as a model in contemporary debates about the politics of democracy include the philosophers Richard Rorty and Martha C. Nussbaum. In *Achieving Our Country: Leftist Thought in Twentieth-Century America*

(Cambridge: Harvard University Press, 1998), for example, Rorty urges Americans to return to the nationalist tradition of Whitman and John Dewey as prophets of a "new, quasi-communitarian rhetoric" that "was at the heart of the Progressive Movement and the New Deal" and "set the tone for the American Left during the first six decades of the twentieth century" (8–9); in *Poetic Justice: The Literary Imagination and Public Life* (Boston: Beacon Press, 1995), Nussbaum presents Whitman's democratic poet as a model of the role that the literary imagination and sympathetic identification might play in public rationality, legal judgment, and "political relations among citizens" (xii). See also Wai Chee Dimock, who discusses Whitman's notions of the individual person and justice in relation to the theory of "justice as fairness" set forth by John Rawls in *A Theory of Justice* ("Whitman, Syntax, and Political Theory," in *Breaking Bounds: Whitman and American Cultural Studies*, ed. Betsy Erkkila and Jay Grossman [New York: Oxford University Press, 1996], 62–79).

5. Betsy Erkkila, *Whitman the Political Poet* (New York: Oxford University Press, 1989); "Whitman and the Homosexual Republic," in *Walt Whitman: The Centennial Essays*, ed. Ed Folsom (Iowa City: University of Iowa Press, 1994), 153–171; "Introduction: Breaking Bounds," in Erkkila and Grossman, *Breaking Bounds*, 1–20.

6. Jürgen Habermas, *The Structural Transformation of the Public Sphere: An Inquiry into a Category of Bourgeois Society*, trans. Thomas Burger (1962; rpt., Cambridge: MIT Press, 1989), 49.

7. See, for example, Mary P. Ryan's study of the multiple counterpublics constituted by women in the nineteenth century in *Women in Public: Between Banners and Ballots, 1825–1880* (Baltimore: Johns Hopkins University Press, 1990); see also Nancy Fraser, who uses the term "subaltern counterpublics" to describe the ways "members of subordinated social groups — women, workers, peoples of color, and gays and lesbians — have repeatedly found it advantageous to constitute alternative publics" ("Rethinking the Public Sphere: A Contribution to the Critique of Actually Existing Democracy," in *Habermas and the Public Sphere*, ed. Craig Calhoun [Cambridge: MIT Press, 1992], 123). For a study of the relation between sentimentalism and the Habermassian public sphere, see Bruce Burgett, *Sentimental Bodies: Sex, Gender, and Citizenship in the Early Republic* (Princeton, N.J.: Princeton University Press, 1998). See also Glenn Hendler, *Public Sentiments: Structures of Feeling in Nineteenth-Century American Literature* (Chapel Hill: University of North Carolina Press, 2001); and Peter Coviello, who emphasizes the role of sexual intimacy in congealing American nationality in Whitman's work ("Intimate Nationality: Anonymity and Attachment in Whitman," *American Literature* 73 [March 2001], 85–119).

8. Walter Whitman, *Franklin Evans; or The Inebriate: A Tale of the Times*, ed. Jean Downey (1842; rpt., New Haven, Conn.: College & University Press, 1967), 36.

9. Michael Moon, *Disseminating Whitman* (Cambridge: Harvard University Press, 1991), 53–58; Michael Warner, "Whitman Drunk," in Erkkila and Grossman, *Breaking Bounds*, 30–43.

10. Walt Whitman, *Leaves of Grass: The First (1855) Edition*, ed. Malcolm Cowley (New York: Viking Press, 1959), 28–29; hereafter cited as *LG 1855*.

11. Robert K. Martin, *The Homosexual Tradition in American Poetry* (Austin: University of Texas Press, 1979), 3–89; Gary Schmidgall, *Walt Whitman: A Gay Life* (New York: Dutton, 1997); see also Byrne Fone, *Masculine Landscapes: Walt Whitman and the Homoerotic Text* (Carbondale: Southern Illinois University Press, 1992).

12. The quotation marks around the term "homosexual" are meant to signal the fact that this term did not come into general usage until later in the nineteenth century, and thus it is not an adequate descriptor of Whitman's experience and self-representation as a man who loved other men.

13. For a daring enactment of the influence of the queer working-class voice of Whitman's mother, Louisa Van Velsor Whitman, on Whitman's poetry, see Michael Moon and Eve Sedgwick, "Confusion of Tongues," in Erkkila and Grossman, *Breaking Bounds*, 23–29.

14. Walt Whitman, *The Complete Writings*, ed. Richard Bucke et al., 10 vols. (New York: Putnam, 1902), 10:18; hereafter cited as *CW*.

15. Walt Whitman, *Leaves of Grass: Facsimile of 1856 Edition* (Norwood, Pa.: Norwood Editions, 1976), 229–230; hereafter cited as *LG 1856*.

16. As Rorty writes in *Achieving Our Country*, "Whitman's image of democracy was of lovers embracing" (25).

17. Erkkila, *Whitman the Political Poet*, 129–154; *The Eighteenth Presidency!* in *WPP*, 1307–1325; and *NUPM* 6:2120–2135.

18. *Whitman's Manuscripts: Leaves of Grass (1860)*, ed. Fredson Bowers (Chicago: University of Chicago Press, 1955), 80, 82; hereafter cited as Bowers.

19. Walt Whitman, *Leaves of Grass: Facsimile Edition of the 1860 Text*, ed. Roy Harvey Pearce (Ithaca, N.Y.: Cornell University Press, 1961), 10–11; hereafter cited as *LG 1860*.

20. Not coincidentally, John Stuart Mill's important essay *On Liberty* was published in 1859. Although Whitman was an admirer of Mill (he cites him at the beginning of *Democratic Vistas*), as Habermas notes, Mill's essay marks an increasing distinction between liberal privacy and the public sphere of politics, as the administrative state assumes increasing responsibility.

21. Alan Helms, "Whitman's 'Live Oak with Moss,'" in *The Continuing Presence of Walt Whitman*, ed. Robert K. Martin (Iowa City: University of Iowa Press, 1992), 185–205; and Herschel Parker, "The Real 'Live Oak, with Moss': Straight

Talk about Whitman's Gay Manifesto," *Nineteenth-Century Literature* 51 (September 1996), 145–160. For a contemporary critical attack on Whitman's "public onanism," his "public performance of what most of us would only do in private," see Robert S. Frederickson, "Public Onanism: Whitman's 'Song of Himself,'" *MLQ* 2 (June 1985), 143–160. See also my discussion of the ongoing national policing of Whitman's homosexuality in the introduction to Erkkila and Grossman, *Breaking Bounds*, 5–8.

22. For a discussion of the struggles in the 1790s over the conflicting claims of natal, national, and international family, see Jay Fliegelman, *Prodigals and Pilgrims: The American Revolution against Patriarchal Authority, 1750–1800* (Cambridge: Cambridge University Press, 1982), 227–230.

23. Cited in Ibid., 230–231.

24. Adam Smith, *The Theory of Moral Sentiments*, ed. D. D. Raphael and A. L. Macfie (Indianapolis, Ind.: Liberty Fund, 1984), 9. As Garry Wills writes of Adam Smith and other Scottish moral sense philosophers, including Frances Hutcheson and David Hume: "For them, the heart was often another word for the moral sense (as was benevolence, humanity, or sociability). . . . The moral sense is not only man's *highest* faculty, but the one that is *equal* in all men" (Wills, *Inventing America: Jefferson's Declaration of Independence* [New York: Vintage, 1978], 224–225). See also Edmund Burke, who writes of the new age of reason, self-interest, and law: "Nothing is left which engages the affections on the part of the commonwealth. On the principles of this mechanick philosophy our institutions can never be embodied . . . in persons; so as to create in us love, veneration, admiration or attachment. But that sort of reason which banishes the affections is incapable of filling their place. These publick affections, combined with manners, are required sometimes as supplements, sometimes as correctives, always as aids to law" (*Reflections on the French Revolution*, ed. W. Alison Phillips and Catherine Beatrice Phillips [Cambridge: Cambridge University Press, 1912], 78).

25. For an extended defense of the role that sympathetic identification associated with the literary imagination might play in public reason and democratic life, see Nussbaum.

26. Jan Lewis, "The Republican Wife: Virtue and Seduction in the Early Republic," *William and Mary Quarterly* 44 (October 1987), 689–721.

27. Cited in Jan Lewis, "Motherhood and the Construction of the Male Citizen in the United States, 1750–1850," in *Constructions of the Self*, ed. George Levine (New Brunswick, N.J.: Rutgers University Press, 1992), 147.

28. The ways in which the naturalness of the relation between man and woman gets coded into a contemporary understanding of liberty, public reason, and the

law is suggested by Nussbaum, who notes that in the U.S. Supreme Court's 1986 decision against the right of homosexual privacy in *Bowers v. Hardwick*, the justices determined that "a right to commit homosexual sodomy" had "not been traditionally considered to be implicit in the concept of ordered liberty" (114).

29. "[O]nly when sex is properly treated, talked, avowed, accepted," he wrote in a notebook of the time, "will the woman be equal with the man, and pass where the man passes, and meet his words with her words, and his rights with her rights" (Walt Whitman, *Notes and Fragments*, ed. Richard Maurice Bucke [Ontario, Canada: A. Talbot & Co., 1899], 33n.).

30. See, for example, Drs. Jordan and Beck, who represent onanists as the living dead on the margins of society: "They drivel away their existence on the outskirts of society . . . they are at once a dead weight, a sluggish, inert mass in the paths of this busy, blustering life, having neither the will nor the capacity to take part in the general matters of life" (*Happiness or Misery? Being Four Lectures on the Functions and Disorders of the Nervous System and Reproductive Organs* [N. Y.: Barton & Son, 1861]; cited in Charles E. Rosenberg, "Sexuality, Class and Role in 19th-Century America," *American Quarterly* 25 [May 1973], 146).

31. In *Self Preservation. Manhood, Causes of Its Premature Decline* (1830), R. J. Culverwell writes of the male onanist: "All the intellectual faculties are weakened. The man becomes a coward: sighs and weeps like a hysterical woman. He loses all decision and dignity of character" (cited in Rosenberg, 146).

32. Selya Benhabib, "Models of the Public Space: Hannah Arendt, the Liberal Tradition, and Jürgen Habermas," in Calhoun, *Habermas*, 84.

33. Here the distinction that Lauren Berlant and Michael Warner make between heterosexuality as a way of organizing sexual relations and heteronormativity as a way of ordering the world is useful. Whereas heterosexuality was put in place in the late nineteenth century as a way of organizing sexual relations and male and female identity, heteronormativity is a whole set of relations, structures, and assumptions that pervade every aspect of American life. See Berlant and Warner, "Sex in Public," *Critical Inquiry* 24 (winter 1998), 548.

34. Gay Wilson Allen argues that "The Base of All Metaphysics" moves "toward sublimation and reinterpretation of the original personal confessions" of "Calamus" (*The New Walt Whitman Handbook* [New York: New York University Press, 1975], 133); Martin argues that the poem represents "a descent" from "honest statement" to "increasing vagueness" (*Homosexual Tradition*, 88); and Helms argues that after 1860, Whitman "remained silent on the subject of homosexual love" (197). See also David Oates's reading of "The Base of All Metaphysics" in J. R.

Betsy Erkkila

LeMaster and Donald D. Kummings, eds., *Walt Whitman: An Encyclopedia* (New York: Garland Publishing, 1998), 49–50.

35. Whitman cites Plato's *Phaedrus*, which appeared in volume 1 of Bohn's six-volume edition of Plato, first published in 1854 (*NUPM* 5:1881). Martin suggests that Whitman may also have read Plato's *Symposium* in a text called "The Banquet" in *The Works of Plato: A New and Literal Version*, translated by George Burges. Pausanias uses the term "manly" to refer to men who "are 'the most manly in their disposition' and have 'a manly temper and manly look'" (Martin, *Homosexual Tradition*, 226).

36. Although Whitman's inclusion of "the well-married husband and wife, of children and parents" as part of his vision of comradely love might appear to dilute or silence his emphasis on "manly love" in other "Calamus" poems, it is important to note the slipperiness of the terms "husband," "wife," "child," and "parent" in Whitman's homoerotic metaphysics. Describing himself as "the new husband" to his male lovers in his "Calamus" poems, Whitman fluidly assumes the roles of mother, brother, husband, father, and bride in representing his love relationships with men in his poems. As Ed Folsom has argued, Whitman also left a small cache of "marital" photographs taken with his boyfriends Peter Doyle (in the 1860s), Harry Stafford (in the 1870s), Bill Duckett (in the 1880s), and Warren "Warry" Fritzinger (in the 1890s). These revisionary portraits stage new identities and new versions of the family, marriage, and social relationships that blur the traditional roles of mother, father, husband, wife, brother, lover, friend. See Ed Folsom, "Whitman's Calamus Photographs," in Erkkila and Grossman, *Breaking Bounds*, 193–219.

37. Hannah Arendt, *The Human Condition* (Chicago: University of Chicago Press, 1958).

38. The dialectic between individualism and "the ancient virtue of Patriotism" that Whitman describes anticipates the ongoing liberal versus communitarian debates within democratic theory. Whereas liberals such as John Rawls and Ronald Dworkin emphasize the sanctity of the individual person, communitarians such as Alasdair MacIntyre, Michael Sandel, and Michael Walzer emphasize the need for social virtue and community. Although parts of Whitman's *Democratic Vistas* accord with both liberals and communitarians in equating democracy with America and the American nation-state, in their most visionary dimension, Whitman's democratic vistas — like such poems as "Song of the Open Road" — imagine democracy as an eroticized transnationalism that links "all nations, all men" in an international community of freedom, sympathy, and love.

39. Whitman's main knowledge of Hegel came from Joseph Gostick's *German Literature* (1854) and *Prose Writers of Germany* (1855), edited by Frederick H. Hedge, which Whitman read in the late 1860s and early 1870s or perhaps as early as the 1850s. In addition to his references to Hegel in *Democratic Vistas* and "The Base of All Metaphysics," Whitman referred to Hegel in his 1881 poem "Roaming in Thought. (*After reading* Hegel)." See also the series of notes "Sunday Evening Lectures," in which Whitman declares: "Only Hegel is fit for America — is large enough and free enough" (*NUPM* 6:2011). For a discussion of the importance of Hegelian dialectics to Whitman's effort to resolve the problems and contradictions of democracy in *Democratic Vistas*, see Erkkila, *Whitman the Political Poet*, 246–259.

40. For a recent discussion of the need to distinguish among state apparatuses, economic markets, and democratic associations in democratic theory, see Fraser, 109–142. See also Bonnie Honig's use of the term "democratic cosmopolitanism" to describe nonjuridical forms of citizenship practiced beyond the confines of the nation-state that extend the possibility of "an emerging international civil society" ("Immigrant America? How Foreignness 'Solves' Democracy's Problems," *Social Text* 56 [fall 1998], 19).

Representatives and Revolutionists

The New Urban Politics Revisited

M. WYNN THOMAS

In their introduction to *Walt Whitman and the World,* Gay Wilson Allen and Ed Folsom have noted that "various national cultures have reconstructed Whitman in order to make him fit their native patterns" and how this has resulted in "some radically realigned versions of Whitman, as his writing . . . undertakes a different kind of cultural work than it performs in the United States."[1] Theirs is an important insight into the complex processes of cultural (and not merely linguistic) translation involved in the "globalization" of the work of a poet who may be thought of as holding, in consequence, a kind of dual citizenship — as an American and as a world citizen. Following the practice adopted in postcolonial studies of distinguishing between "English" (the language of England) and "english" (the world language), it might therefore be useful to distinguish, in this connection, between "Whitman" (the American poet) and "whitman" (the world poet).[2]

That "Whitman" becomes "whitman" even in those foreign (that is, non-American) cultures that are anglophone in character and where therefore cultural translation does not entail linguistic translation is neatly illustrated in the case of his greatest English "disciple," Edward Carpenter (1844–1929). Carpenter's "Towards Democracy" (1881), a prose poem of 110 pages and seventy sections, is an English version of "Song of Myself" so uncannily like the "original" in almost all its textual features that if passages from Carpenter's poem were to be introduced at random into "Song of Myself" even the shrewdest of Whitman scholars might be hard-pressed to identify them. Yet in the essay appended to later editions of his collection of poems, *Towards Democracy,* Carpenter insisted on noting the significant difference between his poetry and that of Whitman:

He has the amplitude of the Earth itself, and can no more be *thought away* than a mountain can. He often indeed reminds one of a great quarry on a mountain side — the great shafts of sunlight and the shadows, the primitive face of the rock itself, the power and the daring of the men at work upon it, the tumbled blocks and masses, materials for endless buildings, and the beautiful tufts of weed or flower on inaccessible hedges — a picture most artistic in its very incoherence and formlessness. "Towards Democracy" has a milder radiance, as of the moon compared with the sun — allowing you to glimpse the stars behind. Tender and meditative, less resolute and altogether less massive, it has the quality of the fluid and yielding air rather than of the solid and uncompromising earth.[3]

What Carpenter is implicitly saying, in the language of his day, is that Whitman was an American poet whereas he, Carpenter, is by contrast an English poet — America being, according to Victorian national typology, a young, exhilaratingly crude emergent nation, tending to violent extremes of self-assertion, whereas England is mild, settled, subtle, tolerant, and temperate. For Carpenter to "translate" "Song of Myself" into "Towards Democracy" is therefore, as he recognizes, to turn Whitman into whitman, and our present-day studies of the "global" poet must be principally concerned with precisely such acts of cultural translation as this. But the extraordinary — not to say peculiar — character of this worldwide phenomenon can be fully realized only if we first register the specifically "local" character of the writings of Whitman himself, whatever their universalizing rhetoric, and so this essay will concentrate on relocating them, and him, within the narrow confines of the New York of the 1850s.

The following passage occurs in the open letter to Emerson that Whitman used as a postscript to the 1856 edition of *Leaves of Grass*: "Just so long, in our country or any country, as no revolutionists advance, and are backed by the people, sweeping off the swarm of routine representatives, officers in power, book-makers, teachers, ecclesiastics, politicians, just so long, I perceive, do they that are in power fairly represent that country, and remain of use, probably of very great use. To supersede them, when it is the pleasure of These States, full provision is made; and I say the time has arrived to use it with a strong hand" (*WPP* 1331). In an essay I prepared for publication (in Chinese) under the auspices of Peking University, I suggested that although excellent scholarly work has been done over the last couple of decades placing Whitman in relation to American politics at large, attention might still usefully be paid to the influence on him of his immediate political environment — the distinctive political microclimate of New York City.[4] As a significant example of the overconcentration on macropolitics, I noted the virtual absence, in Whitman criticism, of any mention of Fernando Wood, the controversial Democrat who revolutionized urban politics between 1855 and 1860.[5] Wood's genius was to realize that his mushrooming metropolis was divided, along class and ethnic lines, into new social and economic groups and that new forms of political organization were needed for managing this.[6] Hidden from our modern sight in some of Whitman's most powerful writings of the 1850s, I intimated, may be an argument with Fernando Wood and his kind about what sort of society America should develop. And that argument, so the present essay will go on to suggest, may usefully be understood as being between "representatives" such as Fernando Wood, the populist politician, and "revolutionists" such as Whitman himself.

I took as my starting point in that previous essay a description Whitman wrote for *Life Illustrated* of the Fourth of July parade in New York City in 1856.[7] Implicit in Whitman's article was a critique of Wood as a new-style "city boss," a sort of corrupt dictator who used all his skills — including his skills as orator — to concentrate power in his own hands.[8] Wood's policies were all the more dangerous since, instead of working for social unity, he set natives against immigrants and owners against workers, thus creating the conditions for the kind of violent incident that was reported in a *Brooklyn Daily Times* editorial of July 1857. Following Jerome Loving's important discussion of the issue in his recent biography of Whitman, we must be wary of assuming that Whitman acted as editor of the *Times* from 1857 to 1859, but it remains clear that he did contribute to the paper's editorial columns, and this particular piece, traditionally attributed to him, does seem consistent in political outlook with the *Life Illustrated* article.[9]

Headed "The Dead Rabbit Democracy," it is a scathing editorial comment on the vicious brawl between the brutal street gang ("The Dead Rabbits"), largely composed of fighting Irish, and their rivals, "The Bowery Boys," a clash that brought near anarchy to New York's streets on the Fourth of July, 1857. Clubs, iron bars, stones, and eventually guns were used in a riot engulfing almost a thousand people. Background to the fighting was the power struggle between Wood, the Democratic city mayor, and the Republican state legislature in Albany, several bills enacted by the latter during 1857 having savagely reduced Wood's political powers. Particularly damaging were the Municipal Charter (ostensibly strengthening the mayor's position but in fact denying him control of the key department of finance), the Excise Law (aimed pointedly at the bibulous working-class immigrant culture that was Wood's urban power-base), and the Metropolitan Police Act (replacing the city-controlled force with a completely new unit answerable to a state-appointed board). In response to this last move, Wood formed his own Municipal Police Force (defiantly alternative to the new Metropolitan Force) and dug in, refusing to hand the city's station houses over to the new body, all the while escalating the rhetoric in which he claimed to be the people's representative in their fight against Albany (and upper-class) tyranny.

The "Dead Rabbit Democracy" editorial fulminates against "the most unscrupulous schemers [who] have so far managed as not to give up possession of the party 'station houses'" (*ISLO* 92–93); a year later, another editorial — again possibly by Whitman — represented the future of the Democratic Party (and of America) as being at stake in the struggle against the new urban bosses like Wood, who depended on "the blind following obedience of large masses of adopted citizens" — that is, immigrants (*ISLO* 95). Whitman saw this struggle as centrally involving a contest for the hearts and souls of the masses between himself as "revolutionist" and this new totalitarian breed of political representatives. His obsession with offering the "people" an image of their true (if potential) selves therefore derived from his fear of the alternative (and much more immediately persuasive) images peddled by the charismatic demagogue Wood and his kind.

The tone of the "Dead Rabbit Democracy" article is as prophetic of Whitman's poetry as is the content, in that the tone hovers uneasily between confidence (based on a gradualist, evolutionist reading of the contemporary political scene) and anxiety (based on an intense awareness of the fatefulness of present political choices, decisions, and outcomes). It was this rich, volatile mix of feelings about contemporary democratic America that had helped his imagination ignite in the 1855 edition of *Leaves of Grass*; it is what fills the early editions with unpredictable switches of mood, sudden changes of direction, and baffling somersaults of opinion. When the long-term, gradualist approach is in the ascendancy (as when, for example, Whitman reflects on the Southern slavery question), he tends to favor a rhetoric of conciliation.[10] On the other hand, when his mind is in crisis mode (as it is, for instance, when engaging with

M. Wynn Thomas

the Free Soil issue), he is inclined to employ a rhetoric of apocalyptic confrontation.

The most crudely striking examples of this crisis rhetoric are to be found in *The Eighteenth Presidency!*, the unpublished political pamphlet that was Whitman's highly personal contribution to the presidential campaigns of 1856. This scurrilous squib has long been regarded as a key source for understanding Whitman's political opinions, but it has never been read for what it has to tell us about the complex relationship that, for Whitman, existed between the politics of New York City and the national political scene. It needs, therefore, to be pointed out that in *The Eighteenth Presidency!*, Whitman's opposition to Buchanan's national candidacy may in part reflect his fear and hatred of Wood's Democratic regime in New York — Wood having been one of the very first to declare in favor of Buchanan's presidential campaign. And if this 1856 address is then reread in the light of Wood's control of New York's working class, it becomes clear why the pamphlet is subtitled "Voice of Walt Whitman to each Young Man in the Nation, North, South, East and West." Whitman's pointed directing of his appeal to the working men in every state of his continental nation was an attempt to get the politically corralled workforce of his city to see itself as part of a bigger, wider picture. This was necessary because Wood played on the immediate urgent concerns of the urban proletariat with jobs and wages in order to advocate a pro-Southern policy of appeasement over Kansas and other territorial issues. But Whitman was, of course, convinced that on the outcome of the Free Soil issue depended the whole future of democracy in America, and with it the future of the working people. Therefore, his pamphlet includes an attempt to get the workers to think more globally, to see their place within an enlarged geography of space and time, so that by recognizing their long-term interests they become supporters of the Free Soil cause. If the new politics invented by Wood was the sectional politics of place — Wood had unquestionably made the city of New York his own — then Whitman countered by creating a geopolitics of space. The two presidential candidates, says Whitman, "live in respectable little spots, with respectable little wants. Still their eyes stop at the edges of the tables of committees and cabinets, beholding not the great round world beyond. What has this age to do with them?" (*WPP* 1314). This should help us see that Whitman's poetic panoramas and lists serve an important political purpose — they are in part a "revolutionist's" mind-expanding devices, textual attempts to get New York workers who were being blinkered by Wood's parochial, factional politics to reorientate themselves politically by viewing themselves in a much wider perspective. For Whitman, the new politics of Fernando Wood worked by restricting the people's field of vision, as a passage in *The Eighteenth Presidency!* makes clear: "Workmen! Workwomen! Those immense national American tracts belong to you; they are in trust with you; they are latent with the populous cities, numberless farms, herds, granaries, groves, golden gardens, and inalienable homesteads, of your successors. The base political blowers and kept-editors of the North are raising a fog of prevarications around you" (*WPP* 1316).

Fernando Wood's political genius was manifested in the management culture of the new machine politics he effectively invented to bring his explosively expanding, chaotically unruly metropolis under control. But Whitman raged against the fixers and creatures of this new representative politics — "not one in a thousand has been chosen by any spontaneous movement of the people; all have been nominated and put through by great or small caucuses of the politicians, or appointed as rewards for electioneering" (*WPP* 1309). By deliberate contrast, therefore, Whitman's writing is infused with the spirit of "spontaneity." "Spontaneous me"— "spontaneous" is a prominent word in Whitman's lexicon and a signature term in his poetics, yet the political implications of the spontaneity so deliberately inscribed in the very style of his writing have been overlooked. Even in his prose, he practices a rhetoric of exclamation, of outburst, of calculated indiscretion, in his attempt to enact the arrival of that for which he is pleading — what in *The Eighteenth Presidency!* he suggestively calls "another power," profoundly different in origin and in kind from that "of the nominees that have arisen out of the power of the politicians"(*WPP* 1312). In social and political terms, he professed to place his trust in the "counteraction of a new race of young men" (*WPP* 1312), but for Whitman it was in truth poetic discourse that was the true dwelling place of "another power"; poems were for him enabling instruments, means to the radical empowerment of the people through the potent textualizing of spontaneity. Poetry was the revolutionist's answer to the otherwise irresistible oratory of powerful, new-style "representatives" such as Wood.

"Another power": what kind of power that was and how poetry was uniquely equipped to serve it are made apparent at the very end of *The Eighteenth Presidency!* "The times are full of great portents in These States and in the whole world," Whitman announces in prefacing this grand climactic passage: "What whispers are these running through the eastern

M. Wynn Thomas

continents, and crossing the Atlantic and Pacific? What historic denouements are these we are approaching? On all sides tyrants tremble, crowns are unsteady, the human race restive, on the watch for some better era, some divine war. No man knows what will happen next, but all know that some such things are to happen as mark the greatest moral convulsions of the earth" (*WPP* 1324–1325). This is eschatological writing, the language of revelation. The millenarian strain in Whitman's poetry of the mid-1850s remains to be fully explored and is one of the profoundest manifestations of his stance as a "revolutionist." We need in particular to sensitize ourselves to its presence in his poems, since poetry was for Whitman the native discourse of apocalyptic vision. In "Sun-Down Poem" (later "Crossing Brooklyn Ferry"), for instance, when he looks "at the fine centrifugal spokes of light round the shape of my head in the sun-lit water," what he is seeing is not a trick of light or an optical illusion but a prefigurative vision of an imminent new order, disclosing itself through the sanctification not of kings, nor of saints, but of every ordinary man and woman. And Whitman ends this, one of his greatest poems, by celebrating his newfound power to read the signs of the times, to decipher and thus uncover the secret meanings of the material, temporal order:

> You have waited, you always wait, you dumb, beautiful ministers!
> you novices!
> We receive you with free sense at last, and are insatiate henceforward,
> Not you any more shall be able to foil us, or withhold yourself from
> us. (*LGV* 1:225)

There is an apparent contradiction involved in treating the features of the material world — whose patient, dumb proffering of spiritual significance Whitman humbly recognizes as their ancient, disregarded service to humanity — as if they were young novices. And the peculiar significance of the word "novices" in the 1856 text is underlined by its omission from later editions, published after Whitman's apocalyptic expectations had begun to ebb. In the 1856 text, it appears that he is displacing the new capacity for understanding that has been awakened in him by what he conceives to be his special time and place onto the objects of his transfigured attention. In other words, it is Whitman who is the novice. It is he who is learning to develop an apocalyptic imagination — "*[a]pocalypse* being," as one theologian recently put it, "a Greek word meaning revelation or unveiling, [and] thus that discourse that reveals or makes manifest a vision of ultimate destiny, rendering immediate to human audiences the ultimate End of the cosmos."[11]

"On all sides tyrants tremble," Whitman wrote. In describing himself to Emerson as a "revolutionist," Whitman was identifying with those leaders of the 1848 revolutions in Europe whom he saw as providing further dramatic evidence that he was living in an apocalyptic age. The inclusion in the first edition of *Leaves of Grass* of the poem "Europe, the 72d and 73d Years of These States" has therefore a multiple significance. A defiant boast that though liberty may have been checked (through the crushing of the European revolutionaries) it can never be defeated, the poem also furnishes Whitman with the opportunity of giving indirect expression to his feelings about the threats to freedom in his own country from the new-style tyrants of democracy such as Fernando Wood. The conclusion of the poem is particularly suggestive:

> Is the house shut? Is the master away?
> Nevertheless be ready . . . . be not weary of watching,
> He will soon return . . . . his messengers come anon. (*WPP* 134)

This is, of course, an allusion to the parable of the wise and foolish virgins, which is the classic biblical text of millenarian expectation of a redeemer figure — such as the "Redeemer President" that Whitman prophesied in *The Eighteenth Presidency!* (*WPP* 1321) would inevitably appear in America. And "Song of Myself" is Whitman's ultimate redemption song, to borrow a phrase from the great reggae singer Bob Marley. It is a poem in which Whitman seeks to redeem his people by showing them how, in an egalitarian society, they are all their own redeemers, the only true begetters of their perfected selves. As Emerson put it, "No man, in all the procession of famous men, is reason or illumination, or that essence we were looking for; but is an exhibition, in some quarter, of new possibilities."[12]

Whitman included in the 1855 edition of *Leaves of Grass* a companion piece to his poem about Europe, in the form of his "Boston Ballad." There he produced a savage piece of satire through a kind of reversed and parodic millenarianism. The dead are raised from their graves not for the Last Judgment but to pass judgment themselves on the scene they see enacted before their incredulous eyes in the streets of Boston. And the poem ends not with the fulfillment of time, as promised in the millennium, but with the reversal of time, as American history regresses and the skeleton of George III is recrowned king. But at that point, this reversed millenarian-

M. Wynn Thomas

ism reverses itself, thus reverting to authentic apocalypse, because is it not one of the signs of the coming millennium that King Death shall be given dominion over all the earth during the dark premillennial period? It is this affirmative aspect of Whitman's otherwise dark vision that is highlighted in the 1855 edition by having "A Boston Ballad" followed by "There Was a Child Went Forth Every Day."

As "A Boston Ballad" reminds us, Whitman was periodically afflicted during the 1850s with deep crises of confidence in his America, and in such moods history seemed to him to reverse its flow, turning from progression into regression. Hence, in *The Eighteenth Presidency!*, he pauses at one point to brood on what the future might yet hold:

> Shall the future mechanics of America be serfs?. . . If slaves are not prohibited from all national American territory by law, as prohibited in the beginning, as the organic compacts authorize and require, and if, on the contrary, the entrance and establishment of slave labor through the continent is secured, there will steadily wheel into this Union, for centuries to come, slave state after slave state, the entire surface of the land owned by great proprietors, in plantations of thousands of acres, showing no more sight for free races of farmers and work-people than there is now in any European despotism or aristocracy. (*WPP* 1316)

No wonder that he began one of the poems in the 1855 *Leaves of Grass* with the words "To think of time." Whitman did a lot of that sort of thinking in the 1850s, bringing into play several different models of the temporal order. Thus "Sun-Down Poem," first appearing in the same year as *The Eighteenth Presidency!*, turns on the trope of continuity, invoking a future the character of which can be reliably extrapolated from the familiar features of the speaker's own time:

> It avails not, time nor place — distance avails not,
> I am with you, you men and women of a generation, or ever so many
> generations hence,
> Just as you feel when you look on the river and sky, so I felt. (*LGV* 1:218)

What is now secretly immanent, hidden except to those with redeemed, apocalyptic vision, will become manifest in the fullness of future time. Hence the poem's great concluding benediction on time's process: "Flow on, river! flow with the flood-tide—and ebb with the ebb-tide"(*LGV* 1:223).

Yet when it is read in the light of the passage from *The Eighteenth Presidency!*, this passage of consecration takes on a different complexion. The assured rhetoric of affirmation seems not so much an expression of confidence as an attempt to cast a spell: an attempt to magic the American future into assuming the very image of that freedom that Whitman felt was so profoundly at risk in the year the poem was actually written. He understood, with growing desperation, that the whole future of the United States turned on the *actions* taken in the present. That is why, like so many visionaries before him, Whitman paradoxically produced out of millenarianism a revolutionary rhetoric designed to make certain that actions would be taken to ensure that the millennium would actually happen. In other words, he effectively turned a determinist model of history into an optative and volitive one. In *The Eighteenth Presidency!*, for example, he notes that "to-day, those who are free here, and free in the British islands and elsewhere, are free through deeds that were done, and men that lived, some of them an age or so ago, and some of them many ages ago. The men and deeds of these days also decide for generations ahead, as past men and deeds decided for us" (*WPP* 1315). Consequently, while consoling himself in "Sun-Down Poem" with a vision of a future America in which the freedoms implicit in the New York of 1856 had become fully manifest, Whitman was at the same time marrying present to future in a beguiling way that would make the concept of freedom precious enough for his readers for them to want to act to safeguard it. It is thus worth noticing, for instance, the two lines that appear in the 1856 text but were dropped from later editions, because in these lines Whitman specifically underlines his status as a freedom-loving New Yorker, in defiance of Fernando Wood's political strategy of stressing New York's economic bondage to the slaveholding South. In the first of these lines Whitman announces, "But I was a Manhattanese, free, friendly, and proud!" while in the second he urges his city, and his land, to stand proud on its freedoms: "Stand up, tall masts of Manahatta! — stand up, beautiful hills of Brooklyn! / Bully for you! you proud, friendly, free Manhattanese" (*LGV* 1:224).

The point that has been elaborated throughout this discussion is that, in the mid-1850s, Whitman emerged as a "revolutionist" in his writings partly by defining himself against powerful new "representatives" like Fernando Wood. But Whitman may be followed one step further, to the point in *The Eighteenth Presidency!* where he suddenly, pointedly, and wittily collapses his

M. Wynn Thomas

customary distinction by turning "revolutionist" and "representative" from oppositional terms into cognates, if not equivalents:

> The times are full of great portents in These States and in the whole world. Freedom against slavery is not issuing here alone, but is issuing everywhere. . . . Never were such sharp questions asked as to-day. Never was there more eagerness to know. Never was the representative man more energetic, more like a god, than to-day. He urges on the myriads before him, he crowds them aside, his daring step approaches the arctic and antarctic poles, he colonizes the shores of the Pacific, the Asiatic Indias, the birthplace of languages and of races, the archipelagoes, Australia; he explores Africa . . . he re-states history, he enlarges morality, he speculates anew upon the soul. (*WPP* 1324)

This is Whitman the millenarian reading the signs of the times, and who should appear as an unlikely figure in this apocalyptic landscape, and as a portent of a dynamically emergent new order, but his old adversary, "the representative man." Except, of course, that Whitman the revolutionist is here using the term not in its politically established but in its redeemed sense, the sense given it by Emerson in his book *Representative Men*, when he remarked that "the constituency determines the vote of the representative. He is not only representative but participant" (Emerson 17). The true "representative man," therefore, is the quintessential type, or embodiment, of that which he represents, and as such he makes visible qualities in it that were previously invisible even to itself. Thus whereas the "routine representatives," as Whitman put it in his open letter to Emerson, were so only in the narrow political sense that they had been elected by their "constituencies," the true representative is endowed with apocalyptic power, the power of privileged disclosure, the power to act as a revolutionist. Whitman the revolutionist was, then, in his own eyes, also Whitman the truly representative American, authorized by time itself to read the secret signs of his times and to "divine another's destiny better than the other can," as Emerson had put it. And had not Emerson furthermore asserted that "the pleasure of full expression to that which, in their private experience, is usually cramped and obstructed . . . is the secret of the reader's joy in literary genius"? (Emerson 20). Whitman's writings in the mid-1850s, in response to the politics so balefully represented by Fernando Wood, were therefore imbued with the apocalyptic spirit Emerson had so eloquently celebrated in *Representative Men*: "Justice has already been done to steam, to iron, to wood, to coal, to loadstone, to iodine, to corn, and cotton; but how few materials are yet used by our arts! The mass of creatures and of qualities are still hid and expectant. It would seem as if each waited, like the enchanted princess in fairy tales, for a destined human deliverer. Each must be disenchanted, and walk forth to the day in human shape" (Emerson 15).

But although in Whitman's American dream "representatives" became indistinguishable from "revolutionists," he well knew that in 1850s America those two terms, as he defined them, stood for characters as implacably hostile to each other as Fernando Wood and himself. This is confirmed in a revealing — if fortuitous — juxtaposition of entries Whitman made in 1857 in an unpublished notebook:

> [*Entry One*]: "[Mayor Wood] this forenoon issued an order to the various Captains, directing them to call in the men at 4 o clock this afternoon and have them deliver up the city property." [The reference is to the aftermath of the Fourth of July riots.]
> [*Entry Two*]: "Poem of (my brothers and sisters) artists, singers, musicians." (*NUPM* 1:272)

The first entry records the factional actions of representatives; the second defiantly celebrates the visionary company of revolutionists.

To emphasize, as this essay has done, the specific details of the historical situation that brought Whitman's poetry into being and that are actually inscribed in its textual practices is not to slight the "global" appeal of that poetry. On the contrary, it is to prepare ourselves for the important work that needs to be undertaken by Whitman/whitman scholarship over the coming century; namely, to explore the extraordinary phenomenon of the "global" whitman, always bearing in mind the poet Charles Tomlinson's comment (in his brilliant book *Poetry and Metamorphosis*) on "the sheer degree of imaginative scope and effort it takes to recover a past work in another tongue — or, indeed, at the practical level, a past or *present* work in another tongue."[13] The many ways in which Whitman, the "local" New York poet, became (and continues to become) whitman, a poet of the world — particularly through the remarkable instances of translating "poesie into poesie," as Dryden famously put it — remains a very largely unexplored and untheorized subject. And to examine that subject would mean reflecting on comments such as those made by Edward Carpenter when he tried to explain, to his baffled self as well as to his readers, how the outrageously American Whitman had somehow come to be represented in his own English work: "[I]n 1881 I was finally compelled into the form (if such it can be called) of "Towards Democracy." I did not adopt it *because* it was an approximation to the form of "Leaves of Grass." What ever resemblance there may be between the rhythm, style, thoughts, constructions etc. of the two books, must I think be set down to a deeper similarity of emotional atmosphere and intension in the two authors — even though that similarity may have sprung and no doubt largely did spring out of the personal influence of one upon the other" (Carpenter 518).

NOTES

1. Gay Wilson Allen and Ed Folsom, eds., *Walt Whitman and the World* (Iowa City: University of Iowa Press, 1995), 2.

2. Bill Ashcroft, Gareth Griffiths, and Helen Tiffin, eds., *The Empire Writes Back* (1989; rpt., London: Routledge, 1994), 8.

3. "A Note," in Edward Carpenter, *Towards Democracy* (1883; 17th impression, London: Allen and Unwin, 1931), 518–519.

4. M. Wynn Thomas, "Whitman and the New Urban Politics of New York," *Journal of Peking University (Foreign Languages and Literatures)* (forthcoming).

5. There is, however, an interesting mention of Wood in Paul Benton, "Whitman, Christ, and the Crystal Palace Police: A Manuscript Source Restored," *Walt Whitman Quarterly Review* 17 (Spring 2000), 147–165; and Joann P. Krieg mentions Wood several times in *Whitman and the Irish* (Iowa City: University of Iowa Press, 2000), calling him someone Whitman "heartily despised."

6. For a balanced discussion of Wood's life and political career, see Jerome Mushkat, *Fernando Wood: A Political Biography* (Kent, Ohio: Kent State University Press, 1990). For a survey of the political milieu in which Wood operated, see Michael F. Holt, *The Political Crisis of the 1850s* (London: Norton, 1978).

7. Emory Holloway and Ralph Adimari, eds., *New York Dissected* (New York: Rufus Rockwell Wilson, 1936; rpt., Folcroft Editions, 1972), 80–84.

8. For the new urban politics represented by Wood, see Amy Bridges, *A City in the Republic: Antebellum New York and the Origins of Machine Politics* (Cambridge: Cambridge University Press, 1984).

9. See Jerome Loving, *Walt Whitman: The Song of Himself* (Berkeley: University of California Press, 1999), 227; "The Dead Rabbit Democracy," in *I Sit and Look Out:*

Editorials from the Brooklyn Daily Times, ed. Emory Holloway and Vernolian Schwarz (New York: AMS Press, 1966), 92–94; hereafter cited as *ISLO*.

10. I discuss this in "Whitman and the Dreams of Labor," in *Walt Whitman: The Centennial Essays*, ed. Ed Folsom (Iowa City: University of Iowa Press, 1994), 133–152.

11. Stephen D. O'Leary, *Arguing the Apocalypse* (New York: Oxford University Press, 1994), 5–6.

12. Ralph Waldo Emerson, *Representative Men*, Riverside ed. (London: Routledge, n.d.), 4:36.

13. Charles Tomlinson, *Poetry and Metamorphosis* (Cambridge: Cambridge University Press, 1975), 75.

M. Wynn Thomas

Whitman on Asian Immigration and Nation-Formation

GUIYOU HUANG

Expanding and swift, henceforth,
Elements, breeds, adjustments, turbulent, quick and audacious,
A world primal again, vistas of glory incessant and branching,
A new race dominating previous ones and grander far, with new contests,
New politics, new literatures and religions, new inventions and arts.
  — *Whitman,* "Starting from Paumanok"

In these lines, Whitman envisions a new race rising on the horizon of the Western Hemisphere. In the next section of "Starting from Paumanok," he further enlightens his reader: "See, steamers steaming through my poems, / See, in my poems immigrants continually coming and landing" (*LG* 27). Whitman writes of a nation expanding with economic prosperity and population growth, in part resulting from immigration — a recurrent theme in a number of his major poems, including "Song of Myself," "I Sing the Body Electric," "The Sleepers," "A Song for Occupations," "By Blue Ontario's Shore," "Starting from Paumanok," and "Our Old Feuillage." These poems are largely Euro-American in theme. Other pieces — such as "To Foreign Lands," "This Moment Yearning and Thoughtful," "A Broadway Pageant," "Facing West from California's Shores," "Salut au Monde!" "Passage to India"— are more "Asiatic" in their thematic import.

These Asiatic poems — the focus of my analysis here — offer high praise for Asian civilizations and celebrate their achievements, and his laudatory representations of Asia and Asians have won Whitman admiration from Asian readers, scholars, critics, writers, and politicians, who have demonstrated their appreciation by offering the American bard spiritual friendship, literary discipleship, and generous recognition as America's poetic envoy to the East. These pieces, welcoming Asians and others, provide a venue for analyzing Whitman's evolving definition of America as a new nation and new race. It is obvious that by welcoming immigrants from continents other than just Europe, Whitman remaps the composition of America, acknowledging its changing demographics and anticipating the birth of a new people by embracing and intermingling all world races. In so doing, Whitman casts himself as both an Ameri-centric and internationalist poet. However, he is by no means a racist and is in fact the most racially tolerant of virtually all his contemporaries, writers and otherwise. In Maverick Marvin Harris's words, "Whitman was not patient with prejudiced people."[1] His poetic display of this impatience accounts for his continued popularity with twentieth-century writers of varied ethnic backgrounds, as well as for the widespread admiration he garners outside Euro-American cultural and geographical boundaries.

The 1860 poem "To Foreign Lands" demonstrates Whitman's robust internationalist and egalitarian world outlook and captures the thematic essence of his work:

> I heard that you ask'd for something to prove this puzzle the
>   New World,
> And to define America, her athletic Democracy,
> Therefore I send you my poems that you behold in them what
>   you wanted. (*LG* 3)

This poem, addressed to audiences in foreign countries, sums up three major Whitman themes: America, democracy, and the most effective medium of their expression, his own poetry. Whitman suggests that the answer to the puzzle of America — certainly in his poetic representation of it — can be located in his poems, where America remains the central object of his literary pursuit. This pursuit of America, however, should not be viewed in an isolationist light because other nations and peoples, by virtue of being culturally and racially different and geographically removed, help set Whitman's universalizing views in bold relief. In "This Moment Yearning and Thoughtful," Whitman once again contemplates foreign lands:

> This moment yearning and thoughtful sitting alone,
> It seems to me there are other men in other lands yearning
>   and thoughtful,

It seems to me I can look over and behold them in Germany, Italy,
  France, Spain,
Or far, far away, in China, or in Russia or Japan, talking other dialects,
And it seems to me if I could know those men I should become
  attached to them as I do to men in my own lands,
O I know we should be brethren and lovers,
I know I should be happy with them. (*LG* 128)

One cannot help but notice this piece's thematic similarity to "A Noiseless
Patient Spider": both poems seem to express a concern for the absence of
companionship and a need to deal with loneliness and solitude. But "Spider" is spatially confined to a little promontory while "This Moment" expands the scope of its thought to two hemispheres, with Germany, Italy,
France, and Spain representing Europe, and China, Russia, and Japan
standing in for Asia. The explicit desire to befriend men of other lands
(regardless of whether we hear homoerotic overtones) bespeaks a vision
of world unity and equality.

This vision of unity and equality finds further expression in "A Broadway Pageant" (1860), an occasional poem that celebrates the arrival of
Japanese envoys in Manhattan. The poet praises not just diplomacy between two nations but also "Libertad" (*LG* 242), a key Whitmanian notion
that undergirds his view of American democracy. Calling the Orient "our
Antipodes," "The Originatress," and "the race of eld" (*LG* 243), Whitman
warmly receives Japan as a representative of Asia and as America's comrade. Thus, as Martin Doudna argues, the poem "reflects both the popular nineteenth-century American interest in Asia and the progress in
Whitman's thought toward the idea that receives its fullest expression in
'Passage to India.'"[2] Whitman starts with Japanese envoys in section 1 but
expands the geographical scope in section 2 to encompass the whole of
Asia, with Libertad — representing America — as his standpoint. The
poet's embrace of Asia seems complete and unconditional: Mandarin,
Confucius, Tibet, China, and Malaysia all "show forth to me, and are seiz'd
by me, / And I am seiz'd by them, and friendlily held by them" (*LG* 244).
Referring to Asia as "the all-mother" (*LG* 245), he urges respect for the
old continent, implying that Asia has been treated with less respect than it
deserves; he thus issues a call for renewing nineteenth-century America's
knowledge of Asia.

On the other hand, calling America a "mistress," Whitman chants a "greater supremacy" (*LG* 245), and, noting a westward movement of people, he identifies America as the ultimate destiny of humankind. He chants: "They are justified, they are accomplish'd, they shall now be turn'd the other way also, to travel toward you thence, / They shall now also march obediently eastward for your sake Libertad" (*LG* 246). Whitman sees Asians' westward migration as necessary and beneficial, and at the same time he calls on Americans to travel eastward ("obediently") for Libertad's sake. In the poet's presentation of this relationship between America and Asia, Doudna perceives an inconsistency (79), but if such an inconsistency does exist, it seems to lie between a willingness to recognize an Other as a potential friend and partner and a firm affirmation of the poet's own country as a better and superior body politic and hence a model for other nations — Asian ones included, of course. Whitman observes that Asia, "the long-off mother," is sending "messages over the archipelagoes" to Libertad (*LG* 245), and that the East has been marching westward to America for diplomatic missions and immigration purposes; the West, therefore, needs to reciprocate by journeying eastward for the benefit of liberty. In this exchange of ideas and immigrants, diaspora becomes necessary and even instrumental.

Whitman is convinced that Asia is the original cradle of the human race, an idea that he reinforces in "Facing West from California's Shores" (1860). In the preface to the 1855 *Leaves of Grass*, Whitman had acknowledged "the eastern records" (*LG* 710); even the poet's journey takes the same westward route followed by the earliest human migrants: "When the long Atlantic coast stretches longer and the Pacific coast stretches longer he easily stretches with them north or south. He spans between them also from east to west and reflects what is between them" (*LG* 711). In "Facing West," Whitman calls Asia "home" and "the house of maternity, the land of migrations" (*LG* 111). The speaker, having wandered from place to place for so long, finally feels relieved and pleased to "face home again," with Asia being that home. Standing on California's shores, the poet imagines taking a diasporic tour around the earth:

> For starting westward from Hindustan, from the vales of Kashmere,
> From Asia, from the north, from the God, the sage, and the hero,
> From the south, from the flowery peninsulas and the spice islands,
> Long having wander'd since, round the earth having wander'd,
> Now I face home again, very pleas'd and joyous (*LG* 111)

The speaker, as Adam's descendant who has wandered from Asia to America, now looks back nostalgically at the East as the place of human origin. The poet's quest is a spiritual one, ending with the satisfaction of a revealing discovery that humans of all races are "brethren and lovers" because of a common origin.

The significance of global diasporic movements is made even more clear in "Passage to India" (1871), where Whitman once again searches for a connection to the southern Asian country as well as for a bridge of communication between the two continents:

> Passage to India!
> Lo, soul, seest thou not God's purpose from the first?
> The earth to be spann'd, connected by network,
> The races, neighbors, to marry and be given in marriage,
> The oceans to be cross'd, the distant brought near,
> The lands to be welded together. (*LG* 412)

Whitman sees the separation of lands by oceans and the division of people by races as a temporary impediment to a higher goal: God's purpose is to "weld" them together. The inviolate nature of God's will is thus invoked to help reinforce the poet's vision of human unity, endowed with religious sanctity. The poet, as "the true son of God" (*LG* 416), not only fuses nature and humanity but links all separations and gaps, and most important, unites all continents and peoples. Whitman thus became nineteenth-century American culture's most creative and threatening critic, and as such, the Asian American historian Ronald Takaki asserts, the poet offers a vision of possibility.[3]

However, Whitman's call for unity and equality seems compromised by his insistent and repeated claim that his own America is the superior nation. As Harold Blodgett and Sculley Bradley point out, Whitman "identifies the purpose of his poetry with the aspiration and potentiality of his country" (*LG* 340 n). Calling his country a "nation of nations," the poet writes, "The Americans of all nations at any time upon the earth have probably the fullest poetical nature. The United States themselves are essentially the greatest poem" (*LG* 709). All his life Whitman was writing this epic poem, often equating himself with America and singing its potential. This is clear not only from his poems written about America alone but also from his quick, often unconditional embrace of new immigrants arriving at different ports in American cities. "Salut au Monde!" (1856) — "Whitman's calling card to the world" as Carol Zapata-Whelan terms it — is written in this spirit and is therefore a song of links and sharing, a refusal to divide and separate.[4] Once again, the poet performs the roles of unifier, traveler, world citizen, and equalizer of lands and peoples: "I have look'd for equals and lovers and found them ready for me in all lands, / I think some divine rapport has equalized me with them" (*LG* 148). Critics have generally recognized the contradiction between a cordial nationalism and an imperialist chauvinism in this poem (Zapata-Whelan 604).

Yet Whitman's robust internationalism should not be lost in the zealous overtones of nationalist chauvinism. Whitman in this poem takes on two voices, the national poet and the world lover: he is the former first and the latter second. Such a juxtaposition of the two roles suggests that, for the poet, it is a matter of priority and not one of contradiction. If we can find no reconciliation between the two voices, we still need to remember that the American bard demonstrates a high degree of goodwill and a large spirit of generosity toward people other than himself and nations other than America. Whitman is content to stay in America — that is his anchor and standpoint — but he is also willing to "raise high the perpendicular hand, [to] make the signal" *au monde* (*LG* 148).

Whitman's America, a metaphor for the poet/singer himself, is all-encompassing and all-receiving. This America, throbbing with expansions, movements, inventions, and receptions, needs a poet commensurate with its ambitions and achievements. The nation in Whitman's time was in the process of forming and reforming its national character. As Dana Phillips notes, the country then "had not had time to evolve an identity through some process of natural selection of favorable racial traits," but Whitman probes into this identity and its evolving national traits, as he alludes to in the second section of "A Song for Occupations":[5]

> There is something that comes to one now and perpetually,
> It is not what is printed, preach'd, discussed, it eludes discussion
>   and print,
> It is not to be put in a book, it is not in this book,
> It is for you whoever you are, it is no farther from you than your
>   hearing and sight are from you,
> It is hinted by nearest, commonest, readiest, it is ever provoked
>   by them. (*LG* 213)

To him, "[t]he largeness of nature or the nation were monstrous without a corresponding largeness and generosity of the spirit of the citizen" (*LG* 710). This spirit of the citizen was awaiting discovery and expression; for Whitman, the most qualified discoverer and expresser was the poet.

Whitman believes that "a live nation can always cut a deep mark and can have the best authority the cheapest . . . namely from its own soul" (*LG* 710). The mantle of identifying national traits falls on the shoulders of the American poet who is "to enclose old and new for America is the race of races. Of them a bard is to be commensurate with a people. To him the other continents arrive as contributions . . . he gives them reception for their sake and his own sake. His spirit responds to his country's spirit" (*LG* 711). Such a reception Whitman gives to "the perpetual coming of immigrants" that he first mentions in his 1855 preface (*LG* 712). Though Whitman did not write a single poem focusing on immigration, he was fully aware of the influx of new immigrants into large U.S. cities such as New York and Boston. This awareness is apparent in many poems, and Whitman's references to immigration help show how it contributes to the formation of the American nation.

Whitman's receptive attitude toward immigrants seems to have derived from his belief in political liberty, which, in his mind, was indispensable in the making of great masters. In "Mannahatta," the city not only bustles and booms with business but also receives arriving immigrants "fifteen or twenty thousand in a week" (*LG* 475). The bard loves his city because it epitomizes the nation and represents the freedom that essentially defines the national spirit. Because poets are "the voice and exposition of liberty," their responsibility is "to cheer up slaves and horrify despots" (*LG* 720). Anyone who comes to America to escape despots and seek liberty should be welcomed. Not only should the poet be commensurate with his nation, so should the individual, for "[a]n individual is as superb as a nation when he has the qualities which make a superb nation. The soul of the largest and wealthiest and proudest nation may well go half-way to meet that of its poets" (*LG* 729). Whitman writes in "By Blue Ontario's Shore," "I swear I will have each quality of my race in myself, / (Talk as you like, he only suits these States whose manners favor the audacity and sublime turbulence of the States.)" (*LG* 353). Thus the soul of the poet, the soul of the nation, and the soul of the qualified individual are together the unifying marker of the nation. While such an attitude is at times undercut by Whitman's occasional supremacist, self-indulgent views of his nation, he is willing to give time for new and potential immigrants to "Americanize": to develop or acquire traits commensurate with existing American "standards" that he does not specify. He is reluctant to dismiss the possibilities and potentials in immigrants, and this drives home a key point: while Whitman is impatient with "prejudiced people" as mentioned at the outset of this essay, he *is* patient with people who have the potential to become Americans, regardless of race.

The notion of a superb nation is reiterated in a number of other poems. In "Song of Myself," Whitman explores the newly found relationship between the body and the soul, insisting that in the individual the body and the soul function on absolutely equal terms, thus leveling all possible obstacles that otherwise would hinder the achievement of equality between opposites. The poet himself is "One of the Nation of many nations, the smallest the same and the largest the same" (*LG* 44). Unlike most other writers of his own era, Whitman upholds a more inclusive and receptive attitude toward other races, but only under the condition of domination by the American race. It may be worthwhile to point out here the Darwinian streak of Whitman's thought: America, "the race of races," is established after a selection process — only the fittest of individuals can qualify and survive to become members of the new American race. In this sense, Whitman is not free of the capitalist views and practices of competition in all walks of life in the commercialized, industrialized, and highly materialistic nation of America.

In the 1855 preface, Whitman claims that the American poet responds to the spirit of his or her country; Whitman does just that in "Year of Meteors." The year-long period beginning with John Brown's raid on Harper's Ferry in October 1859 and culminating with Abraham Lincoln's election as president in November 1860 was "all mottled with evil and good — year of forebodings!" (*LG* 239). Writing the poem perhaps in 1865, after Lincoln's assassination, Whitman recalls some significant events that took place during 1859 and 1860: the Lincoln-Douglas electoral contest, the hanging of John Brown, the visit of the Prince of Wales, and the visit of the famous British iron steamship *The Great Eastern*. But even amid these events of a mixed nature, Whitman's optimism allows him to note some more uplifting events: the census returns of the states, the tables of population and products, and "The proud black ships of Manhattan arriving, some fill'd with immigrants, some from the isthmus with cargoes of gold, /

Songs thereof would I sing, so all that hitherward comes would I welcome give" (*LG* 239). Despite the execution of John Brown and the assassination of President Lincoln, the states were reunited after the Civil War and therefore retained an identity as one nation, which continues to grow with the arrival of more immigrants to whom the country (like the poet) opens its arms and receives as its new citizens. Whitman apparently sees no threat to the welfare of America posed by new arrivals, so he joyfully sings of immigration as a contribution rather than a constriction to the expansion of America. In his optimistic song of a prospering country, Whitman portrays himself as America's hopeful critic, the opposite of Melville's critic of despair (Takaki 281).

Whitman's affirmative attitude toward the rapid growth of America finds expression in other poems as well. In "The Sleepers," one of the poet's most imaginative and esoteric pieces, Whitman presents images of death, but images of life seem to prevail. R. W. French argues that the poem describes a dream vision, but it really is a meditative study of the night and its endless possibilities.[6] Much like Dante lost in the woods and threatened by three beasts at the beginning of the *Inferno*, Whitman is "Wandering and confused, lost to myself, ill-assorted, contradictory, / Pausing, gazing, bending, and stopping" (*LG* 424). The dreamer-wanderer seems to suffer some loss or pain that may well be the cause of insomnia, and he wishes to share his suffering with others but cannot because all are asleep. The tone of the poem changes when the vision deepens at line 26, "Now I pierce the darkness, new beings appear," and the speaker assumes several new roles. The meaning of the night also deepens at this point, and the poet probes it:

Elements merge in the night, ships make tacks in the dreams,
The sailor sails, the exile returns home,
The fugitive returns unharm'd, the immigrant is back beyond
    months and years. (*LG* 430)

The night becomes a great healer — it restores peace, dresses wounds, and soothes pain, renewing hopes and projecting possibilities of a new life. The night also conceives, reconciles, and unites, and the resulting dream vision presents a utopian state of unity and oneness:

They [the sleepers] flow hand in hand over the whole earth from
    east to west as they lie unclothed,

> The Asiatic and African are hand in hand, the European and
>   American are hand in hand,
> Learn'd and unlearn'd are hand in hand, and male and female are
>   hand in hand. (*LG* 432)

Herein lies the significance of the dream vision: the unity that night brings to humankind and the reign of peace that only sleep can install. It is important to read the poem as a projection of a utopian state where all wrongs and illnesses vanish and where the world of nations and peoples merges into one nation-people. Such a state is impossible during "the rich running day." As Francis Skipp observes, the poem, like Shelley's "The Witch of Atlas" from which Whitman draws some material, ends with wrongs righted, the oppressed unburdened, and "a restoration of right and harmonious relationships."[7]

Whitman's vision of the nation-state projects a unity of "crowds, equality, diversity, the soul loves," as he proclaims in "By Blue Ontario's Shore" (*LG* 343). The nation is vibrant with the movement of population and is continually constructing itself; Whitman believes that "these States" can be fused into the compact organism of a nation only by poets, and in "these States" "Their Presidents shall not be their common referee so much as their poets shall" (*LG* 347). It is not America that is great but rather the individuals — citizens and immigrants alike — that make up the nation who are great. In "A Song for Occupations," the second of the twelve untitled poems of the first edition, Whitman mentions immigrants as well. He changed the title of this piece several times between 1856 and 1881, and he had revised the poem many times, but the poem's initial and primary concern remains intact: it is a song in praise of work and workers, regardless of their professions or their national origins:

> Offspring of ignorant and poor, boys apprenticed to trades,
> Young fellows working on farms and old fellows working on farms,
> Sailor-men, merchant-men, coasters, immigrants,
> All these I see, but nigher and farther the same I see,
> None shall escape me and none shall wish to escape me. (*LG* 213)

Resonating in these lines is a joyful feeling as well as a hearty acknowledgment of accomplishments made by the subjects of his song, and noteworthy is the poet's willing inclusion of immigrants in his scheme of democracy and his projection of a new nation-state. To the poet, no occupation

Guiyou Huang

is unworthy of his poems. The individual has as much significance as the Union and the Constitution, and the poet embraces them all. This emphatic assertion of individualism underlies Whitman's perception of the strength of the nation, and democracy molds these individuals into a country unlike any other.

While "A Song for Occupations" for the most part focuses on individual members of the nation, "By Blue Ontario's Shore" concerns itself more with the nation itself. This twenty-section poem perhaps represents the best of Whitman's effort to express the aspiration and potentiality of his country that he first describes in the 1855 preface. Whitman is of course conscious of the role of those he calls "The immortal poets of Asia and Europe" (*LG* 343), who have performed their function and are passing into history; now he wants America also to have immortal poets to take the pulse of the new nation. He believes that in any period of human history one nation must lead the rest into the future, and in his view that mantle now fell upon the shoulders of the United States, a country whose national spirit was characterized by liberty, equality, and diversity. In "By Blue Ontario's Shore," he asserts that the American bard reflects all aspects of America, and his spirit surrounds his country's spirit, "tribes of red aborigines," "the immigrants," and "The Union always swarming with blatherers and always sure and impregnable" (*LG* 344). He imagines hearing the voice of demanding bards who possess abilities unmatched by any other: "By them all native and grand, by them alone can these States be fused into the compact organism of a Nation" (*LG* 346). Here Whitman urges other poets to get involved in the building of the nation and be an adhesive force that binds all together. Thus the poet has multiple political offices to execute — arbiter, equalizer, soldier, and leader — in order to achieve one grand idea that he calls "the idea of perfect and free individuals" (*LG* 348). If individual citizens are not free, the country cannot be free, and, for the country to be free, immigrants and slaves must be allowed free-citizen status to prevent the rhetoric of liberty and equality from becoming hollow.

The basic element of the nation is the new man of the Western world, whom Whitman describes in the opening section of "Starting from Paumanok," where he sings of a New World from "an American point of view" (*LG* 19). Whitman again appears very receptive toward incoming immigrants as well as the "red aborigines." He writes what he believes are nation-making poems, like "Our Old Feuillage," where he offers a poetic vision of America in multiple layers, as the French term *"feuillage"* richly suggests. He characterizes American landscapes from Canada down to Cuba, rivers and forests, cities and rural areas, people of all colors from black to white to red, citizens and immigrants, all contributing to the making of one national identity as the poet notes toward the end of the poem: "Singing the song of These, my ever-united lands — my body no more inevitably united, part to part, and made out of a thousand diverse contributions one identity, any more than my lands are inevitably united and made ONE IDENTITY" (*LG* 176). This capitalized identity is what the poet believes his country needs to develop. Once again, Whitman recognizes the diversity that informs such an identity: "Always the free range and diversity — always the continent of Democracy" (*LG* 171); this continent is, metaphorically, a growing tree with a rich foliage comparable to the ubiquitous leaves of grass the poet admires throughout "Song of Myself."

Whitman's view of African Americans is founded on the same principles of diversity and equality, though during the Civil War racial problems diminished to a secondary concern for Whitman as the war threatened to tear apart the Union. The outcome of the war obviously became the predominant concern for the poet, and Whitman eventually recalled the issue this way: "Not the Negro, not the Negro. The Negro was not the chief thing. The chief thing was to stick together. The South was technically right and humanly wrong."[8] This explains Whitman's belief that unity — the American "IDENTITY" — would be achieved only through collaborative efforts of both the South and the North and blacks and whites. In peaceful times, Whitman upheld exceptionally tolerant and inclusive views on immigration and diversity; in war times, he became more concerned with national unity, and racial issues for him faded into the background of national politics. Recent critics have therefore argued that Whitman does not provide an adequate language and conceptual framework for present-day multiculturalism, but that is like asking nineteenth-century technology to launch twentieth-century spacecraft: it is hard to pretend that Whitman's definition of nation is not one of the broadest of his time — or that his perception of other races and immigrants is not tolerant, even by the standards of our time.[9]

Guiyou Huang

NOTES

1. Maverick Marvin Harris, "Immigrants," in *Walt Whitman: An Encyclopedia*, ed. J. R. LeMaster and Donald D. Kummings (New York: Garland, 1998), 299.

2. Martin K. Doudna, "A Broadway Pageant," in LeMaster and Kummings, *Walt Whitman*, 79.

3. Ronald Takaki, *Iron Cages: Race and Culture in 19th-Century America* (New York: Oxford University Press, 1990), 281.

4. Carol M. Zapata-Whelan, "Salut au Monde!" in LeMaster and Kummings, *Walt Whitman*, 604.

5. Dana Phillips, "Nineteenth-Century Racial Thought and Whitman's 'Democratic Ethnology of the Future,'" *Nineteenth-Century Literature* 49 (December 1994), 309.

6. R. W. French, "Whitman's Dream Vision: A Reading of 'The Sleepers,'" *Walt Whitman Quarterly Review* 8 (summer 1990), 1–15.

7. Francis Skipp, "Whitman and Shelley: A Possible Source for 'The Sleepers,'" *Walt Whitman Review* 11 (September 1965), 74.

8. Walt Whitman, *The Correspondence*, ed. Edwin Haviland Miller (New York: New York University Press, 1961), 1:227.

9. Peter Erickson, "Singing America: From Walt Whitman to Adrienne Rich," *Kenyon Review* 17 (winter 1995), 103–119; see especially 107. See also Phillips, 290.

Whitman's Soul in China

Guo Moruo's Poetry in the New Culture Movement

LIU RONGQIANG

Guo Moruo (1892–1978) was a celebrated and well-established Chinese poet, playwright, literary critic, historian, and paleographer. In literature, he was particularly well known for his first poetry collection, *The Goddesses*, published in 1921 and a landmark in the history of modern Chinese poetry. The collection contains a prologue and three main parts: three poetic dramas as part one, thirty poems as part two, and twenty-three poems as part three. All these pieces were written in the years 1916–1921, when Guo Moruo was an overseas student in Japan, and quite a few of the poems, especially the vigorous ones in part two, were written under Walt Whitman's influence. This essay examines Guo Moruo's poetic debt to Whitman during the New Culture Movement in the second decade of the twentieth century. I will discuss the main factors that prompted Guo Moruo to follow Whitman as a poetic guide, his creative use of Whitman's themes and techniques, and the significance of his poetry to the New Culture Movement.

During the New Culture Movement, Guo Moruo was deeply indebted to Whitman. If it were not for Whitman, Guo might not have become a leading poet and might not have written his vigorous and democratic poems at that time. As to Whitman's influence, he frankly admitted: "It was Whitman who made me crazy about writing poems. It was in the year when the May 4th Movement broke out that I first touched his *Leaves of Grass*. Reading his poems, I came to see what to write and how to voice my personal troubles and the nation's sufferings. His poems almost made me mad. . . . Thus, it was possible for me to have the first poetry collection *The Goddesses* published."[1]

A combination of factors prompted Guo Moruo to follow Whitman's poetic example. When Guo was studying in Japan, he became extremely interested in reading and imitating foreign poems written in or translated into Japanese, German, and/or English.[2] In fact, it was in Japan rather than in China that he became an ambitious and radical poet, for there it was possible for him to read foreign poems widely and free himself from the fetters of classical Chinese poetry and traditional Chinese culture that he had been exposed to from his childhood in China. Before reading Whitman, he had already read a great deal of work by other foreign poets. In particular, he had been interested in Rabindranath Tagore's and Heinrich Heine's poems. Following their lead, he wrote some of the earliest Chinese vernacular poems, like "The Crescent Moon and White Clouds," "The Attraction of Death," "Parting," "Venus," "Egret," "The Crescent Moon and the Clean Sea," and "Worry in Spring."[3] He first got to know Whitman by reading the Japanese critic Arijima Buro's book *The Rebels*, in which Whitman is described as a democratic poet. In addition, commemorative activities were held in honor of Whitman's 100th birthday in Japan in 1919 (Dangbo 85–86), and they helped intensify Guo Moruo's interest in the American poet and his poems. He enjoyed reading Whitman and naturally followed him in writing poems.

Because of his strong interest in pantheism, Guo Moruo was especially delighted with *Leaves of Grass*. He had been reading works with pantheistic thoughts from 1915 to 1919, including poems by Tagore and Kabir as well as the *Upanishads*. Meanwhile, he was immersed in *The Complete Works of Wang Yangming*, a Chinese philosopher whose thoughts were typical of traditional Chinese pantheists. While reading Goethe in 1917, he became interested in Spinoza's works (Dangbo 66). Pantheism played an increasingly important role in shaping his own thought. He came to believe that "everything that exists is nothing but a self-expression of God. The ego is nothing but a self-expression of God's nature. Hence, the ego is God and everything that exists is but the self-expression of the ego. . . . Everything that exists will die. That's the nature of the universe."[4] Discovering pantheistic ideas in *Leaves of Grass*, he became more and more interested in Whitman. What attracted him were lines like "all the things of the universe are perfect miracles, each as profound as any" (*LG* 23), or "I believe a leaf of grass is no less than the journey-work of the stars, / And the pismire is equally perfect, and a grain of sand, and the egg of the wren" (*LG* 59). To Guo Moruo, Whitman believed that all things that exist are equally divine, and all are God's self-expressions. Such ideas became significant for Guo Moruo when his concerns turned to China's movement toward becoming a nation building up a democratic system.

Confronted with family hardship and other personal troubles, Guo Moruo saw Whitman's elemental and dynamic poetry as the ideal model for voicing what was in himself. At the end of 1916, he married Satou Tomiko, a Japanese woman whom he renamed Anna, and she gave birth to their first son at the end of 1917. His deep love for Anna inspired some poems written in the styles and tones of Tagore and Heine, poems like "The Crescent Moon and White Clouds," "The Attraction of Death," "Parting," and "Venus," all collected in the third part of *The Goddesses*. However, his happy life with Anna didn't last long, for it was hard for him to support his family on his limited school allowance. In order to make a living, he translated quite a few of Tagore's and Heine's poems into Chinese and hoped to get them published in China. Unfortunately, this plan collapsed because neither Tagore nor Heine was known in China at that time. Depressed over this failure, he became suspicious of the poetically idealized world of Tagore and Heine; writing later about Tagore, he said: "I think he is noble; while I am humble. He lives in a world different from mine" (Dangbo 74). He became less interested in Tagore and more eager to read and follow the poets whose ideas were similar to his. Furthermore, the Chinese government in May 1918 was forced to sign an unequal treaty with the Japanese government, and most Chinese students studying in Japan were deported for demonstrating against the treaty. In the poisonous atmosphere that followed, Chinese students with Japanese wives were regarded as traitors and often forced to divorce. Guo Moruo would not divorce his beloved Anna, so Chinese students discriminated against him. He was saddened and angered by their unfair treatment (Dangbo 78–79), and, finding his situation unbearable, he sought a new kind of poetry that would allow him to howl instead of to whisper, as he had done in his Tagore- or Heine-inspired poems. Fortunately, it was at this time that he encountered Whitman's *Leaves of Grass*. At this critical moment he gained access to Whitman's elemental and dynamic lines, and he realized he had found his model.

Like many other young Chinese people of the time who were inspired by the May 4th Movement, Guo Moruo was enthusiastic about celebrating progressive ideas such as democracy, individual emancipation, and science. He and some Chinese students in Japan formed the so-called Summer Society in the summer of 1919 in an effort to disclose Japan's ambitious plan to invade China. They mailed their own patriotic papers and translated articles to schools and newspaper offices in China. Meanwhile, Guo Moruo became increasingly eager to sing the spirit of the age in his poetry. Reading Whitman's *Leaves of Grass*, he was inspired by Whitman's embrace of democracy, individualism, and science. He found that what Whitman exalted was identical to the ideals in China in his day, and he came to believe that Whitman's poetic techniques were the best way to express those ideals. Soon after reading *Leaves of Grass* in 1919, Guo Moruo wrote two imitative poems, "Bathing at Sea" and "Shouting at the Rim of the World."[5] Without the inspiration of the May 4th Movement, he might have been less eager to accept Whitman.

Guo Moruo devoted himself to writing poems from 1919 to 1920, especially those vigorous ones under Whitman's influence. Of the fifty-six poems in *The Goddesses*, forty-six had first been published in *Study Lamp*, a literary supplement of a Chinese newspaper called *Current News*. Its acting editor-in-chief was Zong Baihua. Like Guo Moruo, Zong Baihua was a poet who was also fond of pantheism. Zong Baihua recognized Guo Moruo's talent and was confident that he would become a top "oriental poet" in the future. Therefore, Zong Baihua became a supportive publisher of Guo Moruo's poems and even encouraged him to write more pantheistic poems (Dangbo 86). With Zong Baihua's encouragement and insightful help, Guo Moruo soon was "crazy about writing poems almost every day during the three or four months at the end of the year 1919 and the beginning of the year 1920."[6] In fact, most of his Whitmanesque poems were written when Zong Baihua was in charge of *Study Lamp*. Guo Moruo even translated Whitman's "Out of the Rolling Ocean the Crowd" into Chinese and had it published in *Study Lamp* on December 3, 1919 (Wang Xunzhao et al. 354). When Zong Baihua left for Germany in May 1920, Guo Moruo became less enthusiastic about writing poems in Whitman's vigorous style, partly because the tide of the May 4th Movement was ebbing and partly because *Study Lamp*'s new editor-in-chief, Li Shicen, didn't appreciate his poetry as much as Zong Baihua did.

Under Whitman's influence, Guo Moruo became a pioneer in writing Chinese vernacular poems in the New Culture Movement. He exalted democracy, individual emancipation, and science in many of his poems, and he also made creative use of Whitman's dynamic techniques, including repetition, parallelism, enumeration, and even foreign words.

Whitman's *Leaves of Grass* is a song of democracy, and Guo Moruo followed Whitman by also celebrating democracy in *The Goddesses*. His democratic ideals especially found expression in "Nirvana of the Phoenixes" through both the male phoenix's bitter curse on the corrupted society and the female phoenix's complaint of her misery living in that society. As the leading voice of the poem, the male phoenix curses in words that have had far-reaching significance in modern Chinese literature:

> Ah!
> Living in such a dirty world,
> Even the granite knife will become rusty!
> Universe, universe,
> I bitterly curse you,
> You are a slaughterhouse full of blood!
> You are a prison full of sorrows!
> You are a tomb full of cries of ghosts!
> You are a hell full of devils!
> Why do you still exist?[7]

The female phoenix echoes the male phoenix's attack on society:

> My five-hundred-year-old tears are flowing out like waterfalls.
> My five-hundred-year-old tears are falling down like water in gutters.
> The unrestrained tears
> Can not wash away the filth,
> Can not quench the passionate fire,
> Can not remove the shame.
> Will our floating illusory life
> Ever end where?

Actually, both voices mirror the nature of the society. Both of them are determined to destroy the corrupt society and build a new one by a kind of rebirth symbolized by burning themselves in the fire. They are eager to welcome the rebirth:

> We are reborn.
> We are reborn.
> All are reborn.

Liu Rongqiang

All of all are reborn.
We are he, and they are we.
We are you, and you are we.
I am you.
You are I.
The fire is the female phoenix.
The male phoenix is the fire.
Flying! Flying!
Singing! Singing!

Whitman worked hard to fulfill his duties as a poet of American democracy, and one of his poetic attributes was his all-embracing patriotism. Likewise, Guo Moruo joined his democratic ideals to his passionate patriotism. In some poems, he dreamed of China as youthful and fresh in the future, and he even compared China to a beautiful young lady in "Coal in the Furnace":

O my young lady!
I'm not unworthy of your hospitality,
You'll not be unworthy of my consideration.
For my beloved,
I'm madly burning!

And in "Good Morning," he exalted his "motherland" again:

Good morning! My youthful motherland!
Good morning! My reborn compatriots!
Good morning! My mighty Yangtse River in the south!
Good morning! My icy Yellow River in the north!

Whitman's democratic ideals were centered on the common people, and he celebrated them, for he believed that the genius of the United States was in the common people. Whitman extolled mechanics, carpenters, masons, boatmen, shoemakers, woodcutters, and so on. In poems like "A Song for Occupations" and "I Sing the Body Electric," he vividly described his heroes as the common people who were both physically and mentally sound. Guo Moruo, too, loved the common people and saw them as the hope of his democratic ideals. In his verse "Earth, My Mother!" he regarded farmers in the rural areas and workers in the coal pits, respectively, as the nurses of humanity and as the modern Prometheus of humankind. In "Records of

My Visit to the West Lake," he expressed the desire to kneel down and call an aged farmer his "benefactor." Like Whitman, who thought highly of great leaders in all fields in history, Guo Moruo expressed his democratic ideals by valuing the great historic figures of other nations, such as Tagore, Leonardo da Vinci, Washington, Lincoln, Whitman, Beethoven, Tolstoy, Lenin, Cromwell, Rizal, Marx, Engels, Copernicus, Darwin, Nietzsche, Rodin, Rousseau, MacSwiney, and others in poems like "Good Morning," "In the Electricity, Fire and Light," "A Lesson from the Cannons," "Ode to the Outlaws," and "Triumphal Death":

> Cromwell, the arch-criminal bold enough to rebel against the king!
> Washington, the bandit establishing a regime and refusing to deliver
>   tax grain and pay tax!
> Rizal, the unyielding guy dying guiltlessly for the ideal of national
>   independence!
> In the west, north, south and east, in the past, at present and in
>   the future,
> All those politically revolutionary outlaws!
> Long live! Long live! Long live! ("Ode to the Outlaws")

Guo Moruo also directly expresses his esteem for Whitman in "Ode to the Outlaws"—"Revolting against all the conventional elegant poetic forms, the rough Whitman!"—and in "Good Morning": "Good Morning! Washington's tomb! Lincoln's tomb! Whitman's tomb! / Ah! Whitman! Whitman! The Pacific-Ocean-like Whitman!"

Like Whitman, Guo Moruo thought highly of individual emancipation and celebrated the self in poems like "Heaven Dog," "A Drunken Song under the Plums," and "I Am an Idolater." He was particularly fond of combining pantheistic thoughts with individual emancipation, as in "Heaven Dog":

> I am a heaven dog!
> I swallowed the moon,
> I swallowed the sun,
> I swallowed all planets,
> I swallowed the whole universe.
> I am myself!
>
> I am the light of the moon,
> I am the light of the sun,

I am the light of all planets,
I am the light of X-ray,
I am the total Energy of the universe!

In "I Am an Idolater," he did the same:

I am an idolater!
I worship the sun, worship the mountains, and worship the oceans,
I worship the water, worship the fire, worship the volcano, and
worship the mighty rivers,
I worship life, worship death, worship the light, and worship
the night,
I worship the Suez Canal, the Panama Canal, the Great Wall, and
the Pyramids,
I worship creativity, worship strength, worship the blood, and worship
the heart,
I worship the bomb, worship the sorrow, and worship the destruction,
I worship the destroyer of idols, and worship myself!
I also am a destroyer of idols!

Whitman embraced science and new technologies in his poems, declaring that "modern science and democracy seem'd to be throwing out their challenge to poetry to put them in its statements in contradistinction to the songs and myths of the past" (*LG* 564). Thus he celebrated science by making use of the new terms representing the scientific development of his day, such as "steamers," "the many-cylinder'd steam printing-press," "electric telegraph," "locomotive," and "factories," and he employed terms like "electric," "element," and "magnetic" to express his emotions and ideas metaphorically. Such scientific terms rarely appeared in the poems of Whitman's contemporaries. Guo Moruo wrote while China was far behind in scientific and technological development, but he nonetheless followed Whitman in welcoming science and introducing scientific terms into his poems. For example, he called the headlight of the motorcycle "Apollo of the twentieth century" in a poem entitled "Sunrise," and he compared the smoke from factory chimneys to "the beautiful black flowers of the twentieth century" in his poem "Overseeing from the Top of Hitsuritsusan." Altogether, he made use of thirty-five new scientific words or terms in *The Goddesses*, including "X-ray," "energy," "vibration frequency," "ignition point," "electricity," "rotation," "revolution," and "nerve." Already in the prologue he begins absorbing these terms:

O *The Goddesses*!
Go to look for those, whose vibration frequency is identical to mine,
Go to look for those, whose ignition point is identical to mine.

And in "Heaven Dog" he continues:

I am the light of X-ray,
I am the total Energy of the universe!
. . . .
I am running as the electricity!
. . . .
I am running on my nerve,
I am running on my spinal cord!

As for poetic technique, Guo Moruo was also much indebted to Whitman, and he made creative use of Whitman's repetition, parallelism, enumeration, and foreign words. First of all, he made frequent use of the technique of repetition: Ou Hong has demonstrated that 36.8 percent of the lines in *The Goddesses* employ anaphora, one of Whitman's favorite techniques.[8] Guo Moruo also learned a lot about parallelism from Whitman and about how to use this structure to enhance thematic and emotional development. According to Ou Hong's statistics, 528 lines in *The Goddesses* (over 30 percent) contain parallel structures. The following lines in "Three Pantheists" are typical:

I like our country's Zhuang-tzu,
Because I like his Pantheism,
Because I like he was a person making a living by making
    straw sandals.

I like the Netherlands' Spinoza,
Because I like his Pantheism,
Because I like he was a person making a living by making lenses.

I like India's Kabir,
Because I like his Pantheism,
Because I like he was a person making a living by knitting fishnets.

Finally, Guo Moruo seems to imitate Whitman by using foreign terms, sometimes (unlike Whitman) by quoting from great authors from many countries (like Goethe and Thomas Campbell) but also (more like Whitman's use of terms like "ma femme" or "enfans d'Adam" or "camerado") using particular foreign words and phrases to add an international edge to the poetry — words like "phoenix," "energy," "pioneer," "pantheism," "open-secret," "hero-poet," "Proletarian poet," "violin," "piano," "soprano," "disillusion," *"unschön."* In his poems, he also used words transliterated from English and German, such as "democracy" and "X-ray." Inspired by *Leaves of Grass,* Guo Moruo liberated himself from formal diction.

For Guo Moruo, Whitman's main poetic significance was his reformation of the conventional forms of poetry. According to Whitman, "The poet sees for a certainty how one not a great artist may be just as sacred and perfect as the greatest artist. . . . . . The power to destroy or remould is freely used by him but never the power of attack. What is past is past. If he does not expose superior models and prove himself by every step he takes he is not what is wanted" (*LG* 713). Whitman goes on: "The poetic quality is not marshalled in rhyme or uniformity or abstract addresses to things nor in melancholy complaints or good precepts, but is the life of these and much else and is in the soul" (*LG* 714). These words were inspiring to Guo Moruo at the start of his poetic career. His writing of Chinese vernacular poems in the form of so-called free verse was a radical act. He always maintained that one should be absolutely free in writing poems and should be able to express emotions and thoughts without any restrictions.[9] Consequently, he tried to throw off the shackles of poetic forms in classical Chinese poetry. Though his poems still retain some conventional features, like a specific number of lines and stanzas, rhymes, and specific rhythmic patterns, they were nonetheless intended to be unconventional. For instance, "Lamp in the Heart" consists of five stanzas, with each stanza made up of four lines; except for the first line in the first stanza and the third line in the fourth stanza, all the other lines are rhymed with the final words. It is a small rebellion, but nevertheless the poem does break conventional metrical patterns. Actually, many of his poems, like "Heaven Dog," "Good Morning," "Shouting at the Rim of the World," "A Drunken Song under the Plums," "I Am an Idolater," "The Pyramids," "A Lesson from the Cannons," and "Triumphal Death," are not regular in terms of the number of lines or stanzas, rhyme, specific rhythmic patterns, or even of Chinese characters in a single line.

For all of his indebtedness to Whitman, however, Guo Moruo did not blindly or uncritically imitate the American's poems. In his letter to Zong Baihua on March 30, 1920, he wrote: "Heine's poems are beautiful but not vigorous; while Whitman's poems are vigorous but not beautiful. I like both of their poems. However I'm not fully satisfied with either of their poems."[10] Due to his personality, experiences, and understanding of the nature and social role of poetry, Guo Moruo's poems were in some aspects different from Whitman's. He sang the ideals of democracy, individual emancipation, and science somewhat differently than Whitman. He was active as a poet when China was a semicolonial and semifeudal society. He was aware that his poetry should serve to enlighten his people and help them imagine and build a better social system. By means of the myth of the the phoenixes in "Nirvana of the Phoenixes," he effectively articulated both his own dreams and those of the whole nation. Even though a student in Japan and relatively immune from political persecution by the Chinese government, Guo Moruo was still careful to express his ideals indirectly through such romantic images as heaven dog, phoenix, and goddess, unlike Whitman, who expressed his ideals in realistic imagery.

Whitman and Guo Moruo were good at illustrating their ardent and profound love of nature as they sang of democracy and individualism. Whitman focused on representing the ordinary things in nature, like leaves, grass, buffalo, bulls, and wild ganders, all based on his own experiences and his observations of life. Though Guo Moruo also depicted ordinary things such as horses, coal, pomegranate trees, birds, sheep, plums, and doves, he seemed more drawn to images of power — the Suez Canal, the Panama Canal, the Great Wall, the Pyramids, the sun, the earth, seas, oceans, and fire. He even used supernatural images in his poems, such as the heaven dog, phoenix, and hell, which are seldom found in Whitman's poems. In fact, Whitman did not think it appropriate to employ such images in poems about America: "the Old World has had the poems of myths . . . but the New World needs the poems of realities and science and of the democratic average and basic equality" (*LG* 568). Guo Moruo, on the other hand, believed that myth comes from both imagination and reality that could contribute to the poet's art, and he therefore employed mythical but powerful images in the hope that they could help express his dreams of democracy and individual emancipation and science.[11]

The Goddesses was so well received when it came out in 1921 that Guo Moruo soon became well known in China during the New Culture Movement. Singing the main political pursuits of Chinese people in the early decades of the twentieth century, Guo Moruo's poems motivated readers, particularly patriotic young people who were longing to free themselves from the sorrows of the times and bring about democracy, individual emancipation, and scientific advancement in China. Like Whitman, Guo Moruo writes as a self-conscious prophet of his people and shows how to build a democratic nation at a critical moment in his nation's development. Guo Moruo's inspiring influence upon his readers was far greater than that of any of his contemporaries. One of those contemporaries, Wen Yiduo, a famous Chinese poet in his own right, points out:

> Only the present-day Chinese young people, those after the "May 4th Movement," are full of sorrow and sadness. They can't see any reason why such a "cruel," "dark" and "dirty" universe should still exist. They dislike this world and even dislike themselves as well. Thus, the impatient ones commit suicide; while the patient ones make efforts to reform. Finding it hard to resist their impulses, the reformers strive to fight, but they fail. Cherishing their life — both its roses and thorns — they neither escape nor give in. However, they feel it hard to bear the sorrow and sadness any longer. All of a sudden, their sorrow and sadness are fully expressed by one person. This very person is Guo Moruo. He expresses their suppressed emotions in *The Goddesses*.[12]

Guo Moruo, then, owes much to Whitman in making a thematic and formal breakthrough and developing Chinese vernacular poetry in the New Culture Movement. But at its first publication, *The Goddesses* made a sensation in the literary circles. As part of the New Culture Movement, before Guo Moruo's original poems appeared, a few pioneer scholars and poets like Hu Shi, Zhou Zuoren, and Shen Yimo had proposed a new kind of vernacular poetry, with the purpose of breaking the fetters of Chinese classical poetry. For instance, Hu Shi published eight vernacular poems in the first Marxist and democratic journal in China, *La Journess*, on February 1, 1917, and then in 1920 had his first collection of vernacular poems, *Attempts*, published. He was the first person to publish vernacular poems. However, Hu Shi and the other pioneers were still largely confined by the traditional culture and by classical poetry, and their early attempts made no real breakthrough in reforming Chinese poetry. It was Guo Moruo who made the historic breakthrough in the development of vernacular poetry by both masterfully voicing the spirit of his age and throwing off the shackles of the forms of classical poetry.[13]

Many of Guo Moruo's contemporaries recognized the radical nature of his achievement. Wen Yiduo said: "Concerning the new vernacular poems, Mr. Guo Moruo's poems are really new! His techniques are far more different from the classical poets' than those of many other contemporary poets. What is more important is that what is written in his poems is entirely the spirit of the age — the spirit of the twentieth century. It's said that literary works are the babies of the age, so *The Goddesses* is worthy of the title of the 'Baby of the Age'" (Wang Jinhou et al. 45). Zhu Ziqing, another famous scholar and writer and also Guo Moruo's contemporary, once said:

> There are two factors in his poems that are original when compared to our traditions and classical poems. One is pantheism and the other the actively rebellious spirit of the twentieth century. China needs poems expressing our deep thoughts. Most of the poets at the moment are humanists, but few of them have attempted to explore the nature of life. As for nature, few of them take care of it at first and later on they would have to deal with it when necessary. However, though enjoying the beauty of nature, they would merely treat nature as a background for their poems. It was Guo Moruo who first felt everything that exists in nature is divine and treated it as a friend of mankind. Besides, in such a stable civilization as that in China, the actively rebellious spirit had not been employed ever before. (Wang Jinhou et al. 245–246)

Hu Shi confessed when talking about his own poetry: "I feel that the poems that I have written over the past five years are like the shoes worn by a lady who unbound her bound feet over the years. Even though they have been becoming bigger and bigger, they still smell of blood."[14] His confession was quite typical in its admission of failure. Most other contemporary poets, like Liu Bannong, Liu Dabai, Shen Yimo, Yu Pingbo, and Kang Baiqing, also remained fettered by classical poetry and traditional culture and could not be as original as Guo Moruo. Even Hu Shi admitted that Guo Moruo's vernacular poems showed inspiring talents, and, according to Kang Baiqing, "Guo Moruo's poems are vigorous. Instead of rigidly adhering to formalities, he really shows the original talents of a qualified poet" (Wang Jinhou et al. 32, 41).

The response to Guo Moruo was not entirely positive, however. While his democratic and even rebellious thoughts generally drew admiration, there was a good deal of criticism about some aspects of his versification.

Wen Yiduo sharply criticized him for using too many foreign words and names:

> When *The Goddesses* came into being, the author was in Japan, a blindly westernized country, and where he lived was an absolutely westernized environment. Besides, the books he read were also those from western countries. Thus, what he heard, read, and thought were all the western things. . . . If I had been Mr. Guo Moruo, I would have been aware of that condition and dealt with it carefully. That is, Mr. Guo should have kept in mind that he is Chinese, and that he should have been writing new vernacular poems, the new Chinese poems, but not those spoken by westerners so that the new poems might not have been misunderstood as the translated ones. Therefore, he should not have written so casually. . . . There is another shortcoming in *The Goddesses*— the unnecessary use of foreign words in the poems. (Wang Jinhou et al. 55)

Even Zong Baihua did not think Guo Moruo's techniques perfect; in a letter to Guo Moruo, he wrote: "Your poems seem a little bit monotonous and need change, so I hope you think it over. You're good at writing powerful poems, so I hope you write more long poems like 'Nirvana of the Phoenixes.' Such poems can hardly be found at home, so you'll be famous for them. Your short poems are good as well, but they are a little bit monotonous in form" (Wang Jinhou et al. 1). Such criticism, however, did not last long and began to disappear when Chinese vernacular poetry became increasingly mature after the May 4th Movement in 1919.

If Guo Moruo had had no access to Whitman's poetry in the years before 1920, he would probably not have become so successful a poet, and he certainly would have become a very different poet. But, again, his poems were never merely mechanical imitations of Whitman's poems; his poetic creation was in many aspects different from Whitman's and original among his contemporary poets. That is why his poems, especially *The Goddesses*, motivated his contemporary poets and ordinary readers and made a significant breakthrough in the development of Chinese vernacular poetry in the second decade of the twentieth century — a breakthrough in which Whitman played no small part.

NOTES

1. Guo Moruo, *Guo Moruo's Works* (Beijing: People's Literature Publishing House, 1961), 13:120–121.

2. Sun Dangbo, *A Critical Biography of Guo Moruo* (Beijing: People's Literature Publishing House, 1987), 61–62.

3. Yan Huandong, ed., *Guo Moruo's Autobiographic Notes* (Taiyuan: Shanxi People's Literature Publishing House, 1986), 99.

4. Quoted in Yan Huandong, *The Phoenixes, the Goddesses and Others — Comments on Guo Moruo's Works* (Beijing: China People's University Publishing House, 1990), 161.

5. Wang Xunzhao, Lu Zhengyan, Shao Hua, Xiao Binru, and Lin Minghua, eds., *Guo Moruo Study Materials* (Beijing: China Social Sciences Publishing House, 1986), 352.

6. Editorial Board of Guo Moruo's Works, *The Complete Works of Guo Moruo — Literature* (Beijing: People's Literature Publishing House, 1992), 12:68.

7. All translations of Guo Moruo's poems in this essay are mine.

8. Ou Hong, "Parallelism: Guo Moruo's *Goddesses* and W. Whitman's *Leaves of Grass*," *Journal of Foreign Languages* 3 (May 1985), 24.

9. Guo Moruo, 10:211.

10. Editorial Board, 15:125.

11. Ibid., 15:284.

12. Wang Jinhou, Qin Chuan, Tang Mingzhong, and Xiao Binru, eds., *Over One Hundred Comments on Guo Moruo* (Chengdu: Chengdu Publishing House, 1992), 50–51.

13. Long Quanming, "The First Poet Making a Breakthrough in Chinese Vernacular Poetry: Guo Moruo's Contribution to Poetry in the May 4th Movement," *Social Science* 4 (1996), 138.

14. Quoted in Yan Huandong, 268.

Pantheistic Ideas in Guo Moruo's
The Goddesses and Whitman's *Leaves of Grass*

OU HONG

The dictionary definition of pantheism is "a doctrine that equates God with the forces and laws of the universe."[1] The twentieth-century Chinese poet Guo Moruo (1892–1978) derived his pantheistic ideas from such a doctrine and wove them into his 1920s collection of poems, *The Goddesses*. Let me begin by examining the pantheistic ideas in Guo's poems.

1. Contempt of and Opposition to Idols and Feudal Authority

Since God is not a personality but a force that is believed to initiate and represent all in the universe, then God is all, and all is God. To say "all is God" can mean, of course, that there is no God. Such a "sacrilegious" point of view was once held by Spinoza, who is usually regarded as the founder of modern pantheism and a brave challenger of seventeenth-century theology and the authority of God. Spinoza spoke for the rising bourgeoisie in his days and rammed the castle of God with the apparatus of pantheism. Guo Moruo expresses, in a similar manner, his contempt for and opposition to all idols and feudal authority in support of the surging emancipation movement initiated by the May 4th Movement. He exclaims:

> I worship iconoclasts, worship myself,
> For I am also an iconoclast! ("I Am an Idolater")[2]

> Every idol has been struck down before me!
> Down! Down! Down!
> I would snap my vocal chords in song!
> ("Drunken Song under a Flowering Plum Tree," *Wenji* 1:62)

In such poems as "Sea of Light" and "Bathing at Sea," we are given intricate descriptions of the joy of a soul freed from idolatry, in sharp contrast to the aversion we feel when idolatry is rampant.

2. Praise of Creative Forces

The pantheist holds that there is only one substance, a basic "stuff" that constitutes the entire universe. Substance is absolutely independent of everything, for it is everything. It is infinite and, what is more, self-caused and self-determined. All the bodies in the universe form a chain of causes. For example, the sea we encounter is caused by something else, which in turn is caused by still another something and so on ad infinitum. That is why Guo Moruo describes the Pacific as "Unending creation, unending effort" and also a "picture of power" ("Shouting at the Rim of the World," *Wenji* 1:62). For him, the universe is an everlasting source of creative forces. He discovers all around him a world full of life, vigor, dynamism, and grandeur, and he holds communion with it — hence the overwhelming affection for nature he expresses in "Shouting at the Rim of the World," "Good Morning," and "Pyramids."

3. Identification of the Poet's Self with Nature

For Spinoza, all the bodies in the universe and all the ideas taken together form a totality, which is God or substance. Every object in the universe — star, tree, animal, water, wind, stone, even humans — is a part of God or is God. While studying in Japan, Guo Moruo was already given to pantheism, considering nature his "Friend, lover and mother."[3] Out of such a belief, Guo Moruo desires his return to nature and wants to be identified with nature, with objects in the universe. For him, every grass-blade or twig is his brother ("Earth, My Mother," *Wenji* 1:69). He sings:

> The one that is all is born again,
> The all that is one is born again.
> We are he, they are I,
> You are in me and I in you:
> I am therefore you,
> You are therefore me.

Fire is you,
Fire is I,
Fire is he,
Fire is fire. ("Nirvana of the Phoenixes," *Wenji* 1:41)

4. Advocacy of the Power of an Expanding Ego and the Emancipation of Individualism

In *The Goddesses*, the poet feels almost as omnipotent as God. He stands on the rim of the world, releasing his overflowing energy in wild shouts. He absorbs all the stars and the whole universe and assumes himself to contain the totality of the universe. The world is too small for him. Time cannot bind him. In a twinkle of an eye, he sweeps over both hemispheres, saying "good morning" to various countries and peoples. "I create the dignified mountains and the majestic oceans," he says, "I create the sun, the moon and the stars and ride the winds, the clouds and the thunderstorms. I may withdraw into just my body, but I may expand and flood the whole universe, too" ("Lianglei," *Wenji* 1:21). This is apparently not an image of the power of the poet but an image of God. Guo Moruo's remarks made one year after the publication of *The Goddesses* confirm this point: "Pantheism is atheism. Everything in nature is just the expression of God. So is one's self. I am God, therefore, nature is the expression of myself."[4]

Guo Moruo recalled in 1959 that Rabindranath Tagore and Goethe were the guides who ushered him into the temple of pantheism when he was young: "At that time, I was not quite clear about the nature of the universe and the life, and believed in pantheism for a certain period of time. I was fond of Tagore, and Goethe as well. As a result, I came into touch with the philosophy of pantheism, or perhaps it was because I myself had a particular slant on pantheism that the poets with the same slant were especially to my liking. My early works, I must say, were heavily tinged with pantheism."[5] On another occasion, Guo Moruo admitted that, after reading Tagore, he became interested in ancient Indian pantheism and that it was Goethe who led him to read Spinoza ("Chuangzao Shinian," *Wenji* 7:58). This sufficiently accounts for the Spinoza-oriented ideas in *The Goddesses*.

Although Whitman's name does not turn up on the list of Guo Moruo's initiators into pantheism, the part the American poet played in shaping Guo Moruo's pantheistic thinking should not be underestimated. Unlike Tagore and Goethe, Whitman exercises his pantheistic influence on Guo Moruo through an intermediary, the Chinese philosopher Chuang-tzu (who died around 300 B.C.), whose writing Guo Moruo counted among his favorite books during his adolescence (*Wenji* 7:58). In other words, when Guo Moruo began reading and translating Whitman's work just before 1920, *Leaves of Grass* elicited and energized Guo's latent, vague comprehension of Chuang-tzu's pantheistic ideas. Guo Moruo was well aware of this process. He said, "While getting to know overseas pantheism, I rediscovered *Chuang-Tzu*, which I liked so much in my young days" (*Wenji* 7:58). As a schoolboy, he was carried away by the charming and witty style of *Chuang-Tzu* (as Chuang-tzu's book is called), though the essence was lost on him. Only after a comparative study of overseas and Chinese pantheism did he "suddenly see the whole thing in a clear light" (*Wenji* 7:58).

But how could Whitman wake up Chuang-tzu's pantheistic ideas lying dormant in Guo Moruo's mind? Do *Leaves of Grass* and *Chuang-Tzu* share a common wavelength? The answer is "yes." At this point, I must mention another Chinese literary work, *Lao-Tzu*, commonly known as *Tao Te Ching*. Both *Lao-Tzu* and *Chuang-Tzu* are considered the oldest and most important writings of Taoism, and together they form the Lao-Chuang philosophy. Since these two classical works are ideologically inseparable, we must not omit mentioning *Lao-Tzu* in the comparative study of Whitman and Chuang-tzu.

Our attention in the following discussion will focus on "Song of Myself," which, it might be said somewhat disparagingly, makes up at least half of Whitman's best poetry. Nineteenth-century America witnessed an undeclared movement toward Orientalism — Emerson's gnomic wisdom and transcendental insight, Thoreau's pastoral ideals and practical individualism, and, last but not least, Whitman's democratic chant and cosmic vision. Tagore once commented, "No American has caught the Oriental spirit so well as Whitman."[6] Yet Whitman himself denied that he had read any Orientals.[7] Certainly Whitman read neither *Lao-Tzu* nor *Chuang-Tzu* — at least he had not done so before the 1855 edition of *Leaves of Grass* was published.[8] Therefore, to trace Whitman's pantheistic influence on Guo Moruo, we have to go deeper than merely finding apparently similar passages and philosophical ideas between Whitman and the intermediary

Lao-Chuang. First, we must make clear the meaning of Taoism as a basis for any further discussion. The underlying principle in Taoism is Tao (we are dealing here with the Taoist philosophy, not the later version of the Taoist religion). But what is Tao? To try to define it is to contradict the opening words of *Lao-Tzu*:

> The Tao that can be comprised in words is not the eternal Tao;
> The name that can be named is not the abiding name.
> The unnamable is the beginning of Heaven and Earth;
> The namable is the mother of all things.[9]

Tao is unnamable; at the same time, it is a "same" with which all things in the universe are identified. It is like Whitman's "untranslatable" self:

> There is that in me — I do not know it is — but I know it is in me.
> . . . .
> I do not know it — it is without name — it is a word unsaid,
> It is not in any dictionary, utterance, symbol.

> Something it swings on more than the earth I swing on,
> To it the creation is the friend whose embracing awakes me. (*LG* 88)

Since it is unnamable and yet since we wish to speak about it, we have to give it some kind of designation, so we call it Tao, which is not a name at all. It stands for the totality of all things. It flows everywhere: "The myriad things derive their life from it, and it does not deny them."[10] Like Whitman's fluid principle of life, it is an omnipresent clue to the mystery of the universe metaphysically and the basic stuff out of which all things are made.

Tao is the invariable law underlying the ever-changing phenomena of the universe, inexhaustible and all pervading:

> Out of Tao, one is born;
> Out of One, Two;
> Out of Two, three;
> Out of three, the myriad things.
> The myriad things bear the Male and embrace the Female,
> And attain harmony through the union of immaterial breaths.[11]

Who are the Taoists, then, who believe in the natural laws of the universe rather than in the artificial laws of humans? Ironically enough, no better answer is ever made than the one given by the Taoists' rival, Confucius:

These men travel beyond the rule of life; they consider themselves as one with God, recognizing no distinction between human and divine. They look on life as a huge tumor from which death sets them free. All the same they know not where they were before birth, nor where they will be after death. Though admitting different elements, they take their stand upon the unity of all things backward and forward through all eternity; they do not admit a beginning or end. They stroll beyond the dust and dirt of mortality, to wander in the realms of inaction. How should such men trouble themselves with the conventionalities of the world, or care what people may think of them?[12]

This passage may also be taken as a picture of Whitman, who similarly does not speak of the beginning or the end, for in temperament, personality, and spirit, he is congenial to both Lao-tzu and Chuang-tzu, and perhaps much more so to the latter.

In Chuang-tzu, Whitman could easily have found his ideal comrade. Both are individualistic, democratic, and sympathetic. The works of both are tinged with unconventionality and humor. They have a dislike of authority and a great concern for the freedom of the individual. For Chuang-tzu, Tao is the only authority in life, and a person's sense of it is his or her only priest and prophet. Seldom resorting to argument or moralization as his strategy, Chuang-tzu is in agreement with Whitman when the American poet says: "I have no mockings or arguments, I witness and wait," and "Logic and sermons never convince" (*LG* 32, 58).

When we examine some of Whitman's basic concepts, we should not be surprised to find that they echo those of Lao-Chuang. The first that comes to mind is the principle of identity, or "the Identity of Contraries." In many philosophies, the dichotomies of contraries — that is, good and evil, right and wrong, beauty and ugliness, light and dark, body and soul, male and female, life and death, and so on — are in constant conflict, whereas in Whitman and Lao-Chuang they are in eternal harmony. That is why Whitman seldom uses antithetical parallel structures, in which the second part contradicts or denies the first. To Whitman, all contraries blend indistinguishably into one; all things are one: "Lack one lacks both, and the unseen is proved by the seen, / Till that becomes unseen and receives proof in its turn" (*LG* 31). Likewise, Chuang-tzu says, "A beam and a pillar are identical." To him, separation is the same as construction: construction is the same as destruction, "only the truly intelligent understand this principle of identity of all things."[13]

Whitman speaks of the progress of time, of the idea of movement in transition, with focus on change. All terms and conditions are relative:

Urge and urge and urge,
Always the procreant urge of the world.

Out of the dimness opposite equals advance, always substance and
    increase, always sex,
Always a knit of identity, always distinction, always a breed of life.
    (*LG* 31)

The first chapter of *Chuang-Tzu* also points out that both time and space are relative, just as great and small are relative. This emphasis upon relativity and the identification of humans with nature runs through the thought of *Chuang-Tzu*. The gigantic roc at the height of 30,000 miles is a mere mote in the sunbeam, for size is relative. The cicada, which can fly only from tree to tree, laughs with the dove at the roc's high flight, for space is relative. Compared with ephemeral puffballs, Peng Tsu's 800 years on earth is longevity indeed; but what is his age to that of the legendary tree whose spring and autumn span 16,000 years? Time, then, is also relative.

Whitman, like Lao-Chuang, believes that good and evil, right and wrong, beauty and ugliness should be seen from a relative point of view, for they vary with individuals and environments:

I am of old and young, of the foolish as much as the wise,
Regardless of others, ever regardful of others,
Maternal as well as paternal, a child as well as a man,
Stuff'd with the stuff that is coarse and stuff'd with the stuff that
    is fine,
One of the Nation of many nations, the smallest the same and the
    largest the same. (*LG* 44)

Whitman believes that beauty and other values are functions of relationship and that truth and beauty are attributes of the whole experience of humans, not isolated items, so in the 1855 preface he says that "nothing out of its place is good and nothing in its place is bad" (*LG* 712), which agrees with *Lao-Tzu*'s statement: "It is because every one under Heaven recognizes beauty as beauty that the idea of ugliness exists. / And equally if every one recognized virtue as virtue, this would create fresh conceptions of wickedness."[14]

In terms of life and death, Whitman's opinion is that "It is just as lucky to die" (*LG* 35) as to be born. He believes that both death and birth are merely stages in the never-ending transmutation of body and soul, parts of the great process of evolution like the alternation of day and night or the succession of spring and autumn. Death is not to be feared since it opens the door of our confined world to infinity. It is important to note that death as a stage of the life-death-rebirth pattern also forms one of the most significant themes of Guo Moruo's poetry. Similarly, Chuang-tzu observes, "When we come into this world, it is because we have the occasion to be born; when we go, we simply follow what is natural."[15] Bearing this principle in mind, he refrained from wailing over his wife's death. When he himself was to die, he refused a splendid funeral offered by his disciple. Whitman and Chuang-tzu never depart from the universe, even after their deaths:

> The last scud of day holds back for me,
> It flings my likeness after the rest and true as any on the
>   shadow'd wilds,
> It coaxes me to vapor and the dusk.
>
> I depart as air, I shake my white locks at the runaway sun,
> I effuse my flesh in eddies, and drift it in lacy jags.
>
> I bequeath myself to the dirt to grow from the grass I love,
> If you want me again look for me under your boot-soles. (*LG* 89)

It is in the sense that nothing is ever lost from the universe that both Whitman and Chuang-tzu find pleasure in identifying themselves with the vast cosmic process, just as Guo Moruo does. Exalted by the beauty of nature, then lulled by its harmony, the poets are able to comprehend truths beyond ordinary perceptions and to lapse into mystical reverie and revelation. Once Chuang-tzu dreamed that he was a butterfly. After he awoke, he did not know whether it was the man's dream or the butterfly's. Whitman had the same experience: "I cannot be awake, for nothing looks to me as it did before, / Or else I am awake for the first time, and all before has been a mean sleep" (*LG* 652). This perhaps can help to explain how Whitman's "I" in "Song of Myself," while loafing and inviting his robust soul, can turn out to become the earth, or the grass, or nature itself speaking "without check with original energy" (*LG* 29).

According to Justin Kaplan, Whitman also considers the butterfly as "symbol of the soul, resurrection, metamorphosis, and eternal life."[16] On the first of the emblematical decorations of the third edition (1860) of *Leaves of Grass*, probably designed by Whitman himself, is a pointing hand with a butterfly poised on the forefinger. Kaplan goes on to note: "The same symbolic butterfly appears on the back strip of *Leaves of Grass* in 1884, a year after Whitman sat for a studio photograph (used as frontispiece in 1889) that showed him with a butterfly apparently perched on his index finger" (Kaplan 250 n).

The parallels between Whitman and Lao-Chuang reveal a kinship in insight and experience greatly conducive to the study of Whitman's poetry and help explain the way that Whitman's pantheistic ideas influenced Guo Moruo through *Chuang-Tzu*. The poetic souls of Whitman and Guo Moruo converge on pantheism, and the parallel structure used by both poets, which always maintains harmony and admits no subordination, is one manifestation of these poets' pantheistic natures.

NOTES

1. *Merriam-Webster's Collegiate Dictionary*, 10th ed. (Springfield, Mass.: Merriam-Webster, 1995), 840.

2. "I Am an Idolator," *Moruo Wenji* (Beijing: People's Literature Publishing House, 1958), 1:86; hereafter cited as *Wenji*.

3. Guo Moruo, "My Life in Japan," cited in Wang Zhinhou and Wu Jialun, "How Guo Moruo Became a Writer," in *An Anthology of Guo Moruo Criticism* (Chengdu: Sichuan People's Publishing House, 1980), 106.

4. "Introduction to the Chinese Translation of *Die Leiden des jungen Werthers,*" *Chuangzao Jikan* (1922), 1.

5. "Reply to Some Young People," *Wenxue Zhishi* (May 1959).

6. Frederick Ives Carpenter, *Emerson and Asia* (Cambridge: Harvard University Press, 1930), 250.

7. During his visit to Brooklyn in 1856, Thoreau remarked on the oriental qualities of Whitman's poetry and asked him if he had ever read any Orientals. Whitman answered, "No: Tell me about them." See Henry David Thoreau, "A Letter to Harrison Blake, December 7, 1856," in *Literature in America: An Anthology of Literary Criticism*, ed. Philip Rahv (New York: Meridian Books, 1973), 149.

8. Whitman, of course, could not read Chinese. He never traveled outside North America and perhaps never came in direct contact with Chinese scholars in the United States, the first of whom graduated from Yale in 1854. See Wing Yung,

My Life in China and America (New York: Henry Holt, 1909). The first English translation of *Chuang-Tzu* appeared in 1881, and a second, more accurate version was published in 1889 by Herbert A. Giles. In Gay Wilson Allen's *Walt Whitman Handbook* (Chicago: Packard, 1946) and *A Reader's Guide to Walt Whitman* (New York: Farrar, Straus & Giroux, 1970), which deal with Whitman's ideas, there is no evidence presented of Whitman reading *Lao-Tzu.*

9. *Tao Te Ching. Sibu Congkan Chubian* (Shanghai: Commercial Press, 1919), chapter 1.

10. Ibid., chapter 34.

11. Ibid., chapter 42.

12. Chuang-tzu, *Chuang-Tzu. Sibu Congkan Chubian* (Shanghai: Commercial Press, 1919), chapter 6.

13. Ibid., chapter 2.

14. *Tao Te Ching*, chapter 2.

15. Chuang-tzu, chapter 32.

16. Justin Kaplan, *Walt Whitman: A Life* (New York: Simon and Schuster, 1980), 250.

Modernity and Whitman's Reception in Chinese Literature

WANG NING

The present era is usually defined as the era of globalization, but while economic globalization, cultural globalization, and mass media globalization are booming, cultural and literary markets are depressed, and the global influence of literature and other forms of elite culture is shrinking. So why are we still discussing Walt Whitman, who should certainly be regarded as a representative of elite culture and literature, albeit with a strong avant-garde sense? It is my view that Whitman's significance today lies not only in the role he has played in the era of globalization but also in his aesthetics, which encouraged the manufacture of works of art without elaboration and without traditional artistic flourish. Whitman was a literary explorer and adventurer and had one of the most powerful imaginations of the last half of the nineteenth century. He and his poetry played a unique role in the development of Western and Chinese postmodernity and the avant-garde. His poetry anticipated the experimental poetry in the high time of Western modernist literature and in the May 4th period in China, and the latter was strongly influenced by the former. Since modernity is still a heatedly discussed and debated topic in the era of globalization, it is necessary first to place Whitman and his poetry within the framework of modernity before discussing him in a comparative context as a link between Western and Chinese literature.

Modernizing Whitman: The West and China

Whitman has long been regarded as a romantic poet or as a historically significant proponent of American democracy. But in this essay, I would like to view him in the context of modernity by looking at his poetry from today's point of view. It is true that literary modernism is a sort of outgrowth of romanticism, and various writers of the nineteenth century contributed a great deal to modernist writers. In speaking of the pioneers of modernism, we usually include Edgar Allan Poe in poetry, Henrik Ibsen in drama, and Gustave Flaubert in the novel. But many twentieth-century literary scholars, in part because they tend to overlook the rise of American literature in the latter part of the nineteenth century and in part because they are stubbornly Eurocentric, seem to have forgotten Whitman, another important figure from the United States, where American literature was at that time still under the shadow of English literature. With poetry as his trumpet, Whitman sounded the strong note of democracy, both in politics and in aesthetics. The basic tone of Whitman's poetry was romantic, but his was a late version of romanticism whose aesthetic exploration developed a sort of premodern code. Malcolm Bradbury and James McFarlane are among the few insightful scholars who have observed the pioneering role played by Whitman in the process of European modernism. They state, "When the German writers of the late 1880s thought of 'modern' literature, of whom did *they* think? Of Ibsen, of Zola and Tolstoy, Daudet, Bret Harte, and Whitman."[1] These writers either gave inspiration to the modernists or were themselves pioneers of modernist literature.

In Western academic circles, scholars of different critical orientations have appreciated Whitman's artistic achievements and worldwide impact. Some scholars regard him as "one of the pioneering figures in modern poetry" or the "innovator of modern free verse," simply because his works helped cast a sort of American national and cultural identity, uttering a strong American voice in world literary circles. Critics have also found him relevant to the historic avant-garde of twentieth-century literature because of his democratic spirit and his endless search for the true identity of the American nation.[2] If we read Whitman's poetry next to some contemporary American experimentalist poets, we can undoubtedly find the inherent connections between him and postmodernism.[3] That is perhaps one of the reasons why he is still read and discussed today not only in the West but in China.

Another obvious reason why Chinese scholars discuss Whitman in regard to modern Chinese literature is the unique role he played in the process of China's political and cultural modernity as well as in the Chinese literary modernist movement. It is well known that during the May 4th period

Whitman was one of the very few American poets who had a strong influence on such revolutionary Chinese poets as Guo Moruo, Hu Shi, Tian Han, Xu Zhimo, Wen Yiduo, Liu Bannong, and Ai Qing, all of whom either translated his poems into Chinese or consciously drew upon his writings.[4] Because the critical and creative reception of Whitman's poetry was absolutely relevant to the Chinese social revolution and to Chinese literary innovation, he was for a long time classified in the tradition of nineteenth-century romanticism. With the recent advances made in Western academic circles, however, Whitman is now viewed more as a pioneering figure of literary modernism than merely as a romantic poet, for his appearance in the nineteenth century actually anticipated the rise of modernist poetry in the twentieth century, and many of his prophetic and insightful ideas paved the way for the process of modernity in Western culture and Western thought. Inspired by these recent discussions, I would like to undertake a new exploration of Whitman and his poetic writing from the perspective of modernity, with special attention to his critical and creative reception in China.

To study Whitman and his poetry from the perspective of modernist theory is by no means a recent event in Western academic circles. To my mind, however, the reason Whitman and his works are still appreciated and studied by scholars is largely due to the fact that his poetry includes many different cultural and aesthetic codes. That is, apart from the romantic and realistic codes, there are several other literary and cultural codes, and, among them, modernism or modernity might well be the most important code that continues to make Whitman's writings relevant to the current theoretical debate about modernity and postmodernity. In speaking of the characteristics of contemporary postmodernist literature, Douwe Fokkema states, "In Postmodernism, the most 'democratic' of all literary codes, the role of the reader is emphasized even more than in Modernism."[5] Since Whitman's poetry has more than one code, the reader can find significance far beyond romanticism. His poetic writing not only inspired modernist writers but also postmodernist writers. We could easily trace T. S. Eliot's symbolic parody of the theme of sex in *The Waste Land* to his encounter with the sexual imagery in *Leaves of Grass*. The two writers certainly represent different times and speak in different tones — Whitman's tone is highly enthusiastic and sublime, while the major tone in Eliot's work is profound and sad, putting the reader deep in meditation. We can also find Whitman's influence and hear him echoed in Allen

Ginsberg's beat poems in the postwar years, poems that focus on the destruction of all the old assumptions.

Whether or not these writers of later generations explicitly identified Whitman as an influence, they could not help but regard him as one of the possible sources of creative inspiration. Many of the issues Whitman touched upon over a century ago are still dealt with in the present age, whether people perceive this age as late modernism or postmodernism. Like Ibsen, Whitman wrote for a rising people and society, celebrating an aggressive and ambitious nation, the identity of which is very distinctive. He wrote not only for his own age but also for the future. It is not surprising, therefore, that during his lifetime his work was out of favor in most critical circles and even severely attacked by many short-sighted critics. Those who attacked Whitman are now forgotten, but he and his poems are still discussed by scholars and literary critics both in the West and in China.

When we discuss Whitman in terms of modernity, we need first to recognize that different scholars have different definitions of the concept of modernity. It is a literary and aesthetic movement as well as a cultural project of enlightenment in its broadest political and intellectual sense. So I want to distinguish between modernity and modernism: the former refers to a cultural and intellectual state or a project, and the latter refers to a literary and artistic movement or an aesthetic spirit and principle that represent a dominant cultural and aesthetic trend in a particular historical time. Different scholars may define modernism differently, but many of them view it chiefly as a European cultural and literary movement.[6] Thus it is not strange that Whitman is regarded as one of the pioneering figures of modernist literature both for his intellectual and artistic innovation. Whitman's role in the process of Western modernity manifests itself in the field of cultural and intellectual enlightenment as well as in the field of literary innovation: his symbolic description of erotic love certainly offers Freudian psychoanalytic critics precious texts; his breakthrough with unconventional poetic diction opens broad possibilities of writing modern poetry; and his celebration of nature is assigned great importance even by contemporary ecocritics. As long as modernity remains a stimulating and fascinating theoretical topic for contemporary scholars, Whitman and his poetry cannot be ignored because he has played such an important role in shaping Euro-American and Chinese modernity.

Like any great writer, Whitman is unique both in his literary goals and in the artistic devices he uses to attain them. His aim, in his own well-known words, is "mainly . . . to put a *Person*, a human being (myself, in the latter half of the Nineteenth Century, in America,) freely, fully and truly on record" (*PW* 731). He was therefore "the bard of personality" (*LG* 22), speaking for all Americans (and for all humankind), since he believed that all other human beings were essentially the same as himself. That is why his poetry not only helped form an American national spirit and identity but is also filled with a humanistic sense in general, one that goes beyond national bounds. His legacy belongs not just to America but rather to the whole world. All his sympathetic feelings for human beings went into the first edition of *Leaves of Grass*. In his 1855 preface to *Leaves of Grass*, Whitman declares that "of all mankind the great poet is the equable man" (*LG* 712). The same phrasing recurs in "By Blue Ontario's Shore," and it is the word "equable" that best sums up Whitman's peculiar temper. Democracy and freedom are symbolized by the humblest of natural growths — the grass which grows freely. To him, the idea that life is a precise structure like classical architecture is a fiction. It is, rather, like an object in nature, with an organic form that is unexpected, asymmetrical, even willful: he finds he conceals "his rhythm and uniformity . . . in the roots of his verse, not to be seen of themselves, but to break forth loosely as lilacs on a bush, and take shapes compact, as the shapes of melons, or chestnuts, or pears."[7] Whitman's view of the poet, then, is as one who "judges not as the judge judges but as the sun falling round a helpless thing" (*LG* 347). Obviously, like any other poet's theory of the poet's function, this is a personal testament. Whitman himself is close not only to human beings but also to nature itself, as is indicated both in the manifest meaning of grass itself and its latent significance. He wrote about humankind and sang about nature, and he loved them both. For him, if the poet cannot speak *to* humankind, he or she can at least speak *for* humankind. This is how Whitman's poetry represents the very spirit of the era when the American nation was rising and developing energetically like the wildly growing grass. Even in the early twentieth century, when romanticism had already been replaced by modernism in literature, the American nation was still in an emergent state, awaiting its full flourishing, and American literature was seldom filled with a sense of fin de siècle. Whitman expressed the spirit of the time.

Whitman and Modern Chinese Literature Revisited

In dealing with Whitman's significance in American literature, James E. Miller Jr. correctly regards him as an Adamic singer and his *Leaves of Grass* an Adamic song, for his poetry voices the very pulse of the spirit of the time, both culturally and aesthetically.[8] It should also be pointed out that Whitman, among many other Western writers, has indeed had considerable influence on quite a few modern Chinese writers and intellectuals, especially through his experimentation with free verse, which even helped the rise of China's New Poetry movement. Since these writers, such as Guo Moruo and Hu Shi, were major figures of modern Chinese literature, this influence has actually helped rewrite modern Chinese literary history, especially in terms of poetry.

Compared with what has been achieved in the Western academic circles, Whitman studies in China have a very different orientation: in China, he has always been introduced and studied as merely a romanticist or, more precisely, as a revolutionary romanticist with his poems of social change highlighted and his symbolic poems virtually neglected. Although the mysterious and symbolic elements in his poems are sometimes mentioned, they are usually dealt with in a cursory way. This is probably because of the cultural and intellectual atmosphere at the time Whitman was first introduced in China, a period instrumental to China's modernity and its new literary movement. This was the period around the significant May 4th Movement, which marked not only the beginning of new Chinese literature but also the very beginning of Chinese modernity. During that time, China needed something or someone from abroad to help promote its cultural and literary revolution. Since some of the major revolutionary writers or intellectuals, such as Guo Moruo and Hu Shi, loved Whitman's poetry and writing style and appreciated his democratic spirit and enthusiastic attitude toward new things, Whitman was one of the very few Western writers who became regarded as Chinese cultural intellectual idols.

I need here to describe Chinese modernity, since its characteristics differ from what appeared in the Western cultural context. Chinese intellectuals are famous for "grabism," that is, grabbing everything from abroad for our own use. This finds particular embodiment in the May 4th period, when almost all the Western trends of culture and literary thought were introduced into and metamorphosed by the Chinese context. Thus to deal with modern Chinese literature from the comparative perspective of influence-reception study is an important strategy for rewriting modern Chinese literary history.[9] First of all, we should admit that even if there is such a thing as so-called Chinese modernity, it is still something introduced from the West, even though, to a large extent, it does represent the internal logic of the development of modern Chinese culture and thinking. Like modernity in other regions, Chinese modernity, as part of the global project of modernity, is characterized by its totality and enlightenment function. Since Chinese intellectuals in the May 4th period attached great importance to science and democracy with which they hoped to enlighten ordinary people, they enthusiastically welcomed Whitman's powerful and democratic poetics as well as his poetry. Poe and Whitman were two of the most frequently translated and most often discussed American poets at the time, and, according to research data, Whitman's poetry ranked seventh among the most popular foreign literature in China, only behind the King James Bible and the works of Shakespeare, Dryden, Goethe, Milton, and Hugo.[10]

I will not try in this essay to trace the origin of the translation and introduction of Whitman into modern China in detail (since this job has already been done by many others), but I do need to mention a few important facts before exploring Whitman's inherent connection with and significance to Chinese modernity and China's literary modernism. During the May 4th period, along with the enthusiastic translation and introduction of Western literary thought and creative writing, Whitman was one of the very few American authors who attracted attention in China's translation circles and literary world, as well as in its critical circles. In July 1919, just three months after the important May 4th Movement, the appearance of the avant-garde journal *Shaonian Zhongguo* (Young China) marked the beginning of translating extensively Western poetry in modern China. In the first issue of that journal, Tian Han, author of China's national anthem, published a long article entitled "Pingmin Shiren Huiteman De Bainian Ji" (Centennial commemoration of Whitman as the common people's poet). In this article, Tian not only introduces Whitman's life and work but places particular emphasis on his democratic thought and aesthetic ideas (Fan and Zhu 405–406). Obviously, for Tian and other Chinese intellectuals and writers at the time, the greatest significance of Whitman to modern China as well as its literature lies not merely in his formal innovations, necessary as they are, but, more important, in the democratic thought inherent in his poetry, which becomes one of the two most stimulating factors — "Mr. De" (Chinese transliteration of democracy) and "Mr. Sai" (Chinese transliteration of science) — speeding up the process of China's cultural and intellectual modernity. In another literary journal, *Shi* (Poetry), Whitman, along with the imagist poets, were deemed the Western poets who most deserved to be translated and introduced to the Chinese audience.

Previous scholarship and my own investigations demonstrate that Guo Moruo was the Chinese writer most profoundly influenced by Whitman and the poet who got the most inspiration from his American master. Like Whitman, Guo hated all those who would limit his creative imagination, and he wanted absolute freedom to express his individuality. Thus "he received influences from Tagore, Shelley, Heine, Goethe and Whitman, especially Whitman's 'wild and violent' poetry. Through drawing upon foreign poetry and his own creative transmutation, he formed a new poetic form characterized by both originality and traditional Chinese style" (Fan and Zhu 405–406). Because of Guo's dominant position and wide influence in China's literary circles during the May 4th period and later, Whitman's reputation and influence in China are far greater than those of many of his contemporaries. What should be particularly noted here is that Guo himself is even regarded as "China's Whitman," a characterization he has never rejected. Guo, in fact, has frankly expressed his indebtedness to Whitman: "When I approached Whitman's *Leaves of Grass*, that was the year of the May 4th Movement. The repression of my feeling and that of the whole nation now found the outlet and the way of release. At the time I was almost paranoiac."[11] Guo's indebtedness to Whitman and admiration for him find particular embodiment in his great work *Nushen* (The goddesses), generally recognized as one of the modern classics in Chinese literature. *Nushen* highlights Whitmanian freedom and democracy by celebrating the self and nature. Guo candidly admits Whitman's impact on his work: "Whitman's poetic style, characterized by getting rid of all the conventions, coincides with the spirit of *Sturm und Drang* of the May 4th period. I was totally shocked by his grand and eloquent tone. Influenced by him . . . I wrote all these poems full of masculine violence: 'Trumpet Standing on the Edge of the Earth,' 'Earth, My Mother,' 'Song of the Bandits,' 'Good Morning,' 'Nirvana of the Phoenixes,' 'Heavenly Dog,' 'Heart-lamp,' 'Coal in the Stove' and 'Lesson of the Huge Gun.'"[12] It is true that Guo Moruo is one of the very few modern Chinese poets who contributed to China's cultural and intellectual modernity as well as to Chinese modernist literature. Since he got much of his inspiration from Whitman, the latter's contribution to China's modernity is obvious.

If we regard Guo Moruo chiefly as a poet who contributed to modernism primarily through his literary work, then we should not neglect Hu Shi's wide influence among Chinese intellectuals who felt strongly that China should be engaged in the process of modernity. Guo and Hu both contributed a great deal to the origin and development of China's New Poetry up until the contemporary era.

During the period of the 1930s to 1940s, and then during the seventeen years before the Cultural Revolution, Whitman was still influential and favorably received among Chinese writers. Even after the Cultural Revolution, when modernism was largely introduced (and sometimes reintroduced) into the Chinese context, the younger generation of writers enthusiastically read and talked about such high modernist writers as Joyce, Proust, Faulkner, Woolf, and O'Neill, but they did not forget the pioneering role played by Walt Whitman. Among the young Chinese "misty poets," Gu Cheng was the most frank in admitting his indebtedness to Whitman.[13] Even in poets after the misty period, we can still discover the influence of Whitman both in aesthetic spirit and in poetic diction. Along with the publication of the two versions of Whitman's *Leaves of Grass* and the deepening of Whitman studies in China, Chinese scholars and intellectuals have fully recognized Whitman's anticipation of literary modernism in the West and his potential anticipation of China's modernity project and modernist literary movement.[14] Today, when we reread Whitman from the modernist perspective in regard to his reception in China, we cannot help but think that further reflection on Whitman's significance might well lead to the rewriting of modern Chinese literary history from a new perspective.

Toward a New Understanding of Whitman in a Global Context

Reading Whitman in the age of globalization leads us to consider the significance of Whitman and his work in a global context. It is true that Whitman uttered a distinctly American voice emerging from an American national and cultural identity. It is also true that Whitman produced all his poems in the nineteenth century when romanticism and then realism dominated writers' creative consciousness. But it is significant that many of Whitman's contemporaries have long been out fashion and are seldom mentioned in the modern and postmodern periods, while Whitman is still discussed not only in the English-speaking world but recently, and especially with increased cultural communications between the East and West, is analyzed more and more in a global context. Whitman now belongs to the whole world; he crosses the artificial boundary between East and West, and he leaps the aesthetic gap between different literary movements. Since the beginning of the twentieth century, a large number of Western cultural trends, literary currents, and representative figures and works have been brought into China, often exerting strong influences on Chinese literary creation and on China's process of modernity. But few American writers or thinkers have affected China's cultural modernity and literary modernist movement like Whitman. Hemingway, Faulkner, and Eliot in the twentieth century have been important influences, but Whitman is the only nineteenth-century American poet whose significance has helped form China's cultural project of modernity and has helped rewrite modern Chinese literary history. Only recently has Whitman been recognized in this global context, so there is much theoretical and comparative work for future Chinese scholars to do.

NOTES

1. Malcom Bradbury and James McFarlane, eds., *Modernism: 1890–1930* (New York: Penguin Books, 1976), 43.

2. Bradbury and McFarlane, 243.

3. Gerald Graff, *Literature against Itself: Literary Ideas in Modern Society* (Chicago: University of Chicago Press, 1979), 58. See also Ihab Hassan, *The Dismemberment of Orpheus: Toward a Postmodern Literature* (New York: Oxford University Press, 1971), especially 7, 8, and 252.

4. For the critical and creative reception of Whitman in China, see Fan Boqun and Zhu Donglin, eds., *1898–1949 Zhongwai wenxue bijiao shi* (A comparative history of Chinese and foreign literatures: 1898–1949) (Nanjing: Jiangsu Education Press, 1993), 420–428; one section, "China's Whitman," deals with Guo Moruo's reception of Whitman.

5. Douwe Fokkema, *Literary History, Modernism, and Postmodernism* (Amsterdam/Philadelphia: John Benjamins, 1984), 48.

6. Douwe Fokkema and Elrud Ibsch, *Modernist Conjectures: A Mainstream in European Literature 1910–1940* (London: Hurst, 1987), 1–47.

7. Walt Whitman, "Walt Whitman and His Poems," *United States Review* (September 1855), in Kenneth M. Price, *Walt Whitman: The Contemporary Reviews* (Cambridge: Cambridge University Press, 1996), 10.

8. James E. Miller Jr., *A Critical Guide to Leaves of Grass* (Chicago: University of Chicago Press, 1957), especially 36–51.

9. For the study of modern Chinese literature from a comparative perspective of influence and reception, see Yue Daiyun and Wang Ning, eds., *Xifang wenyisichao yu ershishiji zhongguowenxue* (Western trends of literary thought and twentieth-century Chinese literature), (Beijing: China Social Sciences Publishing House, 1990).

10. See Jin Siyan, "Xinshi de qidai shiye" (The horizon of expectation for new Chinese poetry), in Yue and Wang, *Xifang wenyisichao*, 362.

11. Guo Moruo, "Xu wode shi" (Preface to my poetry), in *Moruo Wenji* (Collected works of Guo Moruo) (Beijing: People's Literature Press, 1959), vol. 13.

12. Guo Moruo, "Wode zuoshi de jingguo"(The process of my writing of poetry), in *Moruo Wenji*, 11:143.

13. For Whitman's influence on Gu Cheng, see Liu Shusen's "Gu Cheng and Whitman: In Search of New Poetics," elsewhere in this volume.

14. The two complete Chinese versions of *Leaves of Grass* are by Chu Tunan and Li Yeguang (Beijing: People's Literature Press, 1987) and Zhao Luorui (Shanghai: Translation Press, 1991).

Gu Cheng and Walt Whitman

In Search of New Poetics

LIU SHUSEN

None of the foreign poets introduced into China in the twentieth century is comparable to Walt Whitman with regard to his enthusiastic reception and far-reaching influence on the reading public, literary scholars, and writers, poets in particular. On the eve of the May 4th Movement in 1919, a nationwide campaign against Western political and economic aggression that called for a new democratic and antifeudal revolution, Whitman was introduced into China by Tian Han (1898–1968) and a few young poets who were among the earliest Marxist-influenced Chinese intellectuals. Tian Han is well known as the author of China's national anthem, which he composed in 1935 after the Japanese invasion of the three northeast provinces of China in the early 1930s. While there are other possible sources of inspiration, Tian's anthem seems to echo *Leaves of Grass* in its call for the united forces of an invaded people against foreign aggression and for a struggle to defend a nation's identity and sovereignty.

But long before Tian Han's composition of the Chinese anthem, the Chinese poet Guo Moruo (1892–1978) was a pioneer in adopting Whitman as a model for writing so-called new vernacular verse or Chinese free verse in the 1910s and the 1920s. As one of the leading Chinese intellectuals in the first half of the twentieth century, Guo Moruo created innovative poems with patriotic and political themes, some of which were ardently received as a culturally domesticated Chinese version of *Leaves of Grass*. It is commonly recognized in China's critical circles that Guo Moruo contributes most to Whitman's reception among Chinese readers, or, in other words, Whitman's reception and influence in China in the first half of the twentieth century result from Guo Moruo's Whitman-mediated poems. As for Chinese translated texts of *Leaves of Grass*, Chu Tunan's *Selected*

Poems from "Leaves of Grass" is undoubtedly the most popular. First published in 1949, by the 1990s nearly half a million copies in ten printings had appeared. A quick search of the title catalogs of the six main libraries in China shows that there are more than sixteen Chinese versions of Whitman's poetry published from 1949 to 2000, of which two are complete versions of *Leaves of Grass*. Such facts may help us visualize a history of Whitman's general reception in China in the last century and set the stage for my examination of Whitman's impact on a more recent poet.

Any discussion of Whitman's influence in China in the second half of the twentieth century would be incomplete without including the poet Gu Cheng (1956–1993). Judged by his own comments on his work, Gu Cheng is undoubtedly the poet whose indebtedness to Whitman is the greatest among his Chinese peers. Gu Cheng traces his first reading of Whitman to his adolescence in the 1960s, but he claimed that the dynamic impact of *Leaves of Grass* never really hit him until 1983, when he was in search of a new poetics. While Whitman influenced Guo Moruo and other influential Chinese poets before the 1950s in stylistic and political ways, he inspired Gu Cheng in ways that demanded him to restructure the political, economic, and cultural contexts within which he worked.

Whitman's lifelong dream was to embrace the entire world, make it his home, and recruit all people as his readers, although his unremitting efforts to achieve this dream were in vain. Gu Cheng, on the other hand, seems to be a nonchalant witness to all social ups and downs of his time — a detached poet dedicated to writing nature poems. His poetry appears to reveal someone disengaged from the life of other people and the progress of society, but his poetics, like Whitman's, are characterized by the mission of a prophet/poet, and his "misty poetry" had considerable influence in China through the last quarter of the twentieth century. Thus it is important to see how Gu Cheng reads Whitman and builds up his own theory of poetry as one of the leading poetic voices in China after the Cultural Revolution (1966–1976). However, just as Whitman is wont to voice his thoughts in prefaces and poems, with an aversion to conventionally systematized theory, Gu Cheng is disinclined to express his theory of poetry in a traditional way. His ideas are scattered throughout his poems, interviews, essays, and correspondence with his relations and friends. To study Gu Cheng's poetics requires a familiarity with his life, his poems, and abundant other published material.

Gu Cheng is a self-taught but well-established poet. According to the complete collection of his poems edited by his poet-father, Gu Gong, Gu Cheng wrote his first poem in 1964, when he was eight years old. He remained active in writing what is generally called "misty poetry" from the late 1970s to 1993, when he suddenly put an end to his wife's life and then committed suicide in New Zealand as a result of his inability to deal with their dilemma of love. His wife, Xie Ye (1958–1993), was also a poet. Just before their untimely deaths, the two poets extended their joint creativity in fiction and coauthored *Ying-er*, an autobiographical novel of a triangular love story, with Gu Cheng as its romantic but love-stricken protagonist. The swan song of their literary career, this novel was posthumously published in 1993, and its subject matter anticipates the deaths of Gu Cheng and Xie Ye.

While his tragic death at a young age differentiates him from Whitman, Gu Cheng nonetheless resembles Whitman in his personal experiences as a teenager and in his way of growing up as a poet. Like Whitman, he had little schooling. During the Cultural Revolution, he went to live in a rustic area along with his parents. Many intellectuals were ordered to dwell in the remote countryside, where they were to be reeducated through field labor, and Gu Gong, a well-known poet and a military serviceman, was no exception. Life was thorny. At the age of thirteen, Gu Cheng began to make a living as a swineherd. It was during the days of his rural life that Gu Cheng had his first encounter with Whitman's *Leaves of Grass* in Chinese. In a poem entitled "Eupatorium," Gu Cheng gives a brief but picturesque account of how he incidentally began reading Whitman:

> A lass
> In a dream
> Sent me a letter
> With a twig of flower
> Called eupatorium.
> . . . .
> Eager to unveil the page of heart,
> But I happened to open
> *Selected Poems from Leaves of Grass*
> With the shadow of the eupatorium
> Shading "a live-oak."[1]

Gu Cheng's footnote to the last line of the poem reads: "In *Leaves of Grass* there is a poem entitled 'I Saw in Louisiana a Live-Oak Growing'" (*Poems*

378). He had only an adolescent knowledge of *Leaves of Grass* at this point, but this poem cleverly suggests that the foreign "live-oak" could not grow in "the shadow of the eupatorium" in the Chinese countryside in the 1960s. However, the central images of the poem, the "eupatorium" and the "live-oak," are clearly redolent of Gu Cheng's juvenile affection for nature. Away from an urban environment, relatively unschooled, Gu Cheng followed a rural life that led him directly to his attachment to nature. Besides, during the Cultural Revolution, nearly all books in the humanities and social sciences, except revolutionary ones, were unavailable, but books in natural sciences were less forbidden. In his interview with Suizi Zhang-Kubin in 1992, a year before his death, Gu Cheng confessed that at the age of ten he happened to read a popular book on insects by the French entomologist Jean Henri Fabre (1823–1915) and that this book profoundly inspired him and drew his attention to nature when he first felt the poetic impulse.[2] He emphasizes that Fabre's book had a lifelong impact on him. Fabre is renowned for his research into the behavior of insects, the relationships of insects to other aspects of nature, and the relationship between human and insect social patterns. In reading Fabre, Gu Cheng came to see how the world of the insect could mirror the world of humankind. In view of this historical and cultural background, it is reasonable to assume that such favorite Whitman images as the "live-oak," and in fact all of his nature poems, intensified Gu Cheng's interest in nature and in singing of the natural world instead of humans and the social world.

Gu Gong, who edited *Gu Cheng: Selected Poems*, estimates that Gu Cheng wrote about a hundred poems from 1964 to 1976, and none of them touches upon politically fervent and changeable urbanism. During the time when revolutionary poems with anti-imperialist, antirevisionist, and anticapitalist themes were fashionable in the four corners of the country, Gu Cheng was like "a noiseless patient spider," ceaselessly writing what he later labeled as experimental poems about natural landscapes and containing visual impressions of trees, flowers, land, seas, rivers, sky, stars, changes of seasons, and the simple bucolic life. But none of the poems he wrote in these years was published until the early 1980s. In his representative poems in this period, like "Life Fantasia" and "I Celebrate the World," his adolescent impulses inspired him to express the freshness and vitality of nature. He was eager to identify the self with nature because he believed he and nature were one; by conversing with trees, birds, flowers, streams, winds, and so on, he not only identified with them but also experienced the harmony of life and nature: he approached the spiritual ideals of a utopian vision. In "Life Fantasia," he began to sing as ambitiously as Whitman did in the 1855 " Song of Myself":

I insert my illusion and dream
Into a slender shell.
The roofing of the boat is woven with willow twigs,
Overhead steeps the chirping of the summer cicadas.
Pulling the mast cord,
With the breeze filling the sails in the morning fog,
I set sail.
. . . .
The sun is baking the earth,
As if it were a piece of bread.
I am walking
With my feet bare.
I am stamping my footprint
As my seal all over the world;
Then the entire world will be dissolved
Into my life.

I want to sing
A song of humankind,
Through thousands of years
That shall resound in the universe. (*Poems* 41–44)

While singing the landscape and life of nature and identifying with nature in the 1960s and the 1970s, however, Gu Cheng had little idea of ecology. His attachment to nature was simply a part of his strategy as a poetically original but psychologically standoffish writer.

Both Whitman and Gu Cheng assume they are the prophetic poet of humankind, but Gu Cheng is even more ambitious than his American predecessor: "In the world of the mind the poet is God. What he builds up is a road of hope, and what he constructs is a garden in heaven."[3] Gu Cheng is distinct from Whitman, however, in his stance toward his readership. Whitman always has his readers in mind in order to initiate an interactive, ongoing communication. He proudly sounds his "barbaric yawp over the roofs of the world" (*LG* 89) because he wants to awaken all people as if they were slumbering. Whitman's strategically and rhetorically anticipated reader — the "you" of *Leaves of Grass* — remains an inseparable companion of the "I," the lyrical protagonist, and one is always identified with the other. Thus "Song of Myself" begins and concludes with the "I"/"you" relation:

> I celebrate myself, and sing myself,
> And what I assume you shall assume,
> For every atom belonging to me as good belongs to you.
> . . . .
> You will hardly know who I am or what I mean,
> But I shall be good health to you nevertheless,
> And filter and fibre your blood.
>
> Failing to fetch me at first keep encouraged,
> Missing me one place search another,
> I stop somewhere waiting for you. (*LG* 28, 89)

This relationship between "I" and "you" contributes much to dramatizing the tension and thematic profundity of *Leaves of Grass*, typifying Whitman's reader-oriented theory of poetic mediation and communication.

In contrast, the lyrical self in Gu Cheng's poetry, his "I," is principally solo. His intended readers seem always invisible in his poems before 1985, though not indiscernible, as the poet positions himself as their soothsayer and therefore stands in need of their presence and involvement for his poetry to have meaning. But despite Gu Cheng's claim to be the people's seer, the "I" in his poems seems to communicate with no one except himself, as if he were alone on a spiritual odyssey in nature. What essentially accounts for this stance is Gu Cheng's conscious alienation from the political and cultural mainstream, his belief in nature, and the solitude he searches for and finds, even in a social context. In "Far and Near," he visualizes the social and psychological alienation between human beings and captures their close and fearless attachment to nature:

> You
> Look at me now
> And then at the clouds.
>
> I feel
> You are far away while looking at me
> But when looking at the clouds we are near and dear.
>   (*Poems* 899–900)

As a result of absorbing Taoism, Gu Cheng supposes that the poet does not need to persuade readers directly because poetry can, subtly and on its own, assimilate the readers' minds and hearts. Therefore, unlike Whitman, who urges his readers to take action, Gu Cheng enjoys singing alone and avoids any explicit request for his readers' cooperative action. Gu Cheng believes the best poems are characterized by a free flow of the vitality of life, an unrestricted gush of imagination, a cordial kind of love for nature, and especially a free expression of one's self. To illustrate his mid-1970s view of poetry, Gu Cheng (in a later interview with Suizi Zhang-Kubin) retold a story of a talented Chinese poet in the second or third century A.D. This poet, Liu Ling, is celebrated for his love of nature, his unfettered imagination as a poet, and his Taoist concept of discipline involving the commission of no act against nature. At a party in his house, Liu Ling got drunk on wine and stripped himself naked, running around in the presence of his guests and relations. One of the guests was deeply offended and confronted Liu Ling: "It is a shame. How dare you keep running naked in the presence of your friends and guests? You behave offensively and discourteously." At this, Liu Ling became irritated and cried out to his guest: "The heaven is my immense house. This hall is my garment. Then why do you intrude yourself into my trousers?" (*Poems* 3).

Gu Cheng interprets Liu Ling's impromptu intoxicated retort as vividly epitomizing the key aspects of the best poetry. Gu Cheng is in no way advocating the theory of art for art's sake, however; rather, he highlights the freedom of poetic creation as an open expression of one's innermost being, a striking belief in the mid-1970s when China was still afflicted with the Cultural Revolution. His faith is that, given due respect and freedom, the socially responsible poet and his or her poetry might revamp the topsy-turvy social order and return it, at least somewhat, to normality. He demands an unrestricted expression of self because he despises the way the popular literature and art of his time eradicate or exterminate one's self, encouraging the "mechanical" expression of all that is "non-self" (*Essays* 16). A person is not seen as a unique thinking individual but as a common social appendage or, metaphorically, as an indistinguishable grain of sand on a vast beach or a small gear in a gigantic social machine. In writing lyrics on nature, Gu Cheng finds the freedom and an open expression of self that a poet needs for his or her creation, but he makes no effort to relate his poetry to society. In this respect, Gu Cheng bears more of a resemblance to the reclusive Emily Dickinson than to Whitman. Dickinson and Gu Cheng both wrote innovative poems with unique values and qualities, but their poetic voice was barely heard by their contemporaries because the publication of their work was much delayed.

Gu Cheng's theory of poetry evolves and undergoes some conspicuous transformations, as does Whitman's, and those transformations closely track his changing views of Whitman in different periods. When retrospectively looking at his poetic career in 1987, Gu Cheng roughly divided his career into two stages. The first stage extends from 1964 to the early 1980s, when he consciously learned from nature and focused his efforts on articulating in his lyrics his emotional connection with nature. During this period, he deliberately avoided any direct representation of social realities in his poems and gleefully experimented with translating the sound and imagery of nature into poetic language. But, in fact, even in these years he was not completely unconcerned with social reality, and he voiced his thoughts in fables and fairy tales. From 1973 to 1978 he wrote a total of twenty-eight poems, mostly poetic fables and fairy tales, including "The Great Life of Small Birds," "The Proposal of the Vice God," "A King of Masterful Leadership," "Ivan's Judgment," "The Speech of a Fox," "A Big Mosquito and a Child," "The Marriage of a Cockroach Couple," and "Poems on Insects and Crabs." His fables in verse anticipate a major turning point in the evolution of his theory and poetry.

The second stage of Gu Cheng's career began in the early 1980s, when he turned his attention to exploring the realm of the spirit and to voicing the self. But compared with Whitman's stance about the poet's active involvement in social transformation, Gu Cheng's attitude was still marked by a relatively circuitous involvement in social issues. Whitman urges his readers to take action and shows the way, but Gu Cheng seems content with searching the unknown and seeking inspiration, perhaps in the interest of the people, but only indirectly. Such is the chief discrepancy between Gu Cheng and Whitman. Discussing the social value of poetry, he emphasizes: "Writing poems is not merely meant to reflect something, it also should show the origin of things, the mind, and the luminosity of heaven. When the light appears, the dark will fade away, as when the morning comes, the nightmare flies away" (*Poems* 928). One of his emblematic poems, "Our Generation," vividly portrays his search for this inspiring ideal: "The dark night gives me a pair of dark eyes, / Yet I use them in search of light" (*Poems* 121).

It is in the second phase of his career that Gu Cheng finds himself reawakened by Whitman. In his interview with a Hong Kong poet in 1984, Gu Cheng narrates in detail how he was mystically reenlightened by Whitman one morning in 1983:

> Whitman is transcendental; he manages to have straight access to the ontological being. . . . I first read Whitman's poems at an early age but got reawakened much later. I was a curbed person. It was not until one morning in 1983 that the electricity of my anguish dissolved my skin, which had been as stiff as lead, and as a result I came to perceive the great ontological being — Whitman. His sound came down vertically from the air, blowing on me and shaking my every hour and minute. The century between us no longer exists; nor does the Pacific Ocean, leaving Whitman himself — the visible but untouchable "I" and himself only — the eternity that was getting nearer and clearer. I was stunned, almost desirous to throw myself away and give up my work grinding flowers on the glass of images. I was shaken again and again, lying there and feeling like a wooden piece in a piano. From morning to evening I was just listening to the sound of the falling raindrops. On that day I ate nothing. (*Essays* 14)

In this second inspiration from Whitman, Gu Cheng comes to see that the profoundly moving power of *Leaves of Grass* lies in its original presentation of the depths of one's identity while showing readers the "path between reality and their souls" (*Essays* 911; *LG* 714). As he echoes Whitman, Gu Cheng turns increasingly toward investigating the sphere of the spirit: "With its illusionary nature, poetry is destined to keep exploring new realms forever and build up fresh worlds of the spirit" (*Essays* 904).

In addition to absorbing Whitman's impact, Gu Cheng consciously opened himself to and embraced a great variety of modern foreign poetry. In terms of fables, he gained inspiration from Hans Christian Andersen. For Gu Cheng, Andersen's fairy tales embody the true wisdom of poetic nature. To express his indebtedness to Andersen, Gu Cheng wrote the poem "To My Respected Master Andersen," celebrating Andersen's ability to carry "a paradise with the balloons of flowers and dreams" in his tales: "All the hearts of pure childishness are his harbors" (*Essays* 151).

As he reconstructed his theory of poetry in the early 1980s, Gu Cheng maintained a sense of literary globalization that allowed him to begin thinking of Chinese poetry in a transnational context. In his eyes, the time had come when "[w]e must give up prejudice" and "[t]he poetry of the world should enter into China. Chinese poetry should go abroad" (*Essays* 74). Gu Cheng thus announced an opportunity to accelerate the modernization of Chinese poetry and align it to the needs of social reform. Gu Cheng's ambition finds exquisite expression in such poems as "The World and I," a sequence of eighty-five poems that marks a turn from searching for what the spirit needs in nature to solving contemporary social problems. Subtitled "Politics," the following poem from this sequence articulates Gu Cheng's new aspiration:

> The compass of the crow draws
> The border between the sky and the earth.
>
> The sky
> Looks perfect as it is;
> But the earth
> Still bears its scars and wounds.
>
> My tremulous pen shall guide
> The anguish of the earth
> Up into the sky. (*Poems* 210)

Although he is as ambitious as Whitman in wanting to remove "The anguish of the earth," Gu Cheng is not interested in working out any pragmatic approach other than showing the passageway between reality and the soul. In one of his lectures on poetry, he appreciatively emphasizes Whitman's viewpoint in the 1855 preface to *Leaves of Grass*: "the readers want the author to indicate the path between reality and their souls so that they may have access to the infinite world that life can't reach" (*Poems* 911). However, as Betsy Erkkila demonstrates, particularly from the perspective of "the relation of writing and history, politics and art," Whitman consciously makes himself a political poet who looks for practical solutions.[4] In an attempt to subvert his mainstream contemporaries' neglect of and contempt for America's political and cultural identities, Whitman characterizes himself as a model of "the Modern Man" in *Leaves of Grass* (*LG* 1) and tries to cogently persuade all his intended readers to accept this model and remold themselves in its impression, in the hope that one day America and its people — and even all the people of the world — could be modernized that way. Gu Cheng is by no means a political poet with the same kind of practical wisdom as Whitman, but he nonetheless is involved in a painful search for an alternative way to modernize people and society.

Gu Cheng makes clear his view on the social function of poetry in a published letter about "misty poetry":

> The connotation of poetry may be miscellaneous, so I think the social function of poetry can be diverse as well. I agree that there should be some poetry of political discussion that directly reflects social issues, but I like better the lyric that originally shows the soul and the beauty of nature. I think all genuinely beautiful poems are endowed with their own progressive meaning in a social context. Rose and sword don't stand in opposition. Struggle is justified not for its own purpose but as a way of improving the world for a better status. Thus in this respect, sword exists for rose. (*Poems* 905)

When Whitman assumed the title and mission of America's bard, he endeavored to make *Leaves of Grass* all-embracing, absorbing politics, power struggles, science, technology, sex, and many other subjects that his lyrical peers saw as poetic taboos. From this Whitman, Gu Cheng seems to learn little, because the subject matter and themes of his poetry are comparatively constricted. He responds negatively to the practical and political Whitman not only because he never dreams of himself as China's all-representing bard but also because he holds some different philosophical, ethical, and psychological notions from Whitman. As early as the mid-1970s, he seems to have shaped his subject matter and themes, and these included avoiding a direct presentation of political issues, modern science, technology, and sex. Unlike Whitman, who celebrates as a major driving force the progress of the world for men and women in their personal and social lives, Gu Cheng is so much influenced by Taoism that he always tends to think of men and women as separate, socially and mentally interrelated but not physically associated. Traditionally, corporality is debased in Chinese culture. Though Gu Cheng always thinks highly of science and technology and writes a number of poems on scientists such as Benjamin Franklin, James Watt, and A. B. Nobel, he attaches more importance to aestheticism in literature and art, poetry in particular: "Politics cannot act instead of all other things; nor does materiality. The progress of a race needs not only electronic technologies and scientific management but also highly advanced spiritual civilization, including the making of new-fangled modern aestheticism. Beauty shall no longer be imprisoned or enslaved. It shall show its radiance as the sun and the moon do. . . . It shall illuminate the awakened or still slumbering souls of mankind through the window of art and poetry" (*Essays* 325).

Whitman thinks of himself, his theory, and his poetry as interrelated, one organic being, believing that a national bard's devotion to building up his poetics and poetic textures must be unshakable as long as he can breathe. Thus, notwithstanding his paralysis and several untreatable diseases in his last years and despite his unsatisfactory reception among his contemporary readers, he went on editing the "deathbed" edition of *Leaves of Grass* and writing hopeful poems until his final days. As to the future of his poetic ideals in America and other parts of the world, he generally remained confident and optimistic from the beginning of his career to his death. Only a few months before his death he wrote "Good-bye My Fancy!" and made it the concluding poem in *Leaves of Grass*. In singing his intense love and pride in his career as poet, he bids final farewell: "Farewell dear mate, dear love! . . . Good-bye — and hail! my Fancy" (*LG* 557–558). Whitman the poet, his theory, and his poetry are one, mutually dependent in their makeup, existence, and influence.

Gu Cheng seems, in this way, different from Whitman. In spite of his popularity since the late 1970s, he followed a circuitous route in constructing his theory and poems. His long-term quest for a harmonious beauty in poetry and reality fails to match his personal life. From 1990 to 1993, Gu Cheng's interest in writing poems dramatically dwindled. In 1992 he wrote only two poetic works, including "The Ghost Comes into the City," a short sequence of eight fabulous poems, and he turned to writing fiction in collaboration with his wife in an attempt to keep his literary creativity from dwindling and to try to save his family from a tragic end. His obvious pessimism toward art and life is manifest in his last letter to his parents, written a number of days before his final tragedy occurred. He confesses, in a dejected mood: "There is no way to take hope as reality. In fact, hope is by and large illusionary" (*Poems* 905). Their very different attitudes at the ends of their lives explain some of the principal disparities between Gu Cheng's and Whitman's poetics and poetry.

It seems paradoxical that Gu Cheng, who began his career in the mid-1960s writing nature poems, terminated it in 1993 with "The City," a sequence of reminiscent poems on the fifty-one well-known sights and architectural landmarks in downtown Beijing. These poems reveal his fond memory of the urban life of his hometown and perhaps indicate one final association with Whitman, who expressed such fondness for New York City. In his preface to "The City," Gu Cheng writes: "I often dream of a revisit to Beijing. Although it has nothing to do with my present life, it is a must place I should go to."[5] His life ended in New Zealand, where he was dreaming of revisiting his homeland.

NOTES

1. Gu Cheng, *Gu Cheng: Selected Poems*, ed. Gu Gong (Shanghai: Shanghai San-lian Bookstore, 1995), 377–378; hereafter cited as *Poems*. The edition of *Leaves of Grass* referred to here is Chu Tunan's Chinese translation, a selected version first published in 1949. A revised edition appeared in 1955 (Beijing: People's Literature Press) and remained the most popular Chinese translation of *Leaves of Grass* until the early 1990s. All the English translations of Gu Cheng's poems in this essay are my own.

2. The original German version of this interview, "Suizi Zhang-Kubin: Das ziellose Ich: Das Ich: Gesprach mit Gu Cheng," appeared in *Minima Sinica* 1 (1993), 18–26. The Chinese translation of the interview is included in *Gu Cheng: Selected Poems* as a general preface to the book.

3. Gu Cheng, *Gu Cheng: Selected Essays* (Tianjin: Baihua Literature and Art Press, 1993), 8; hereafter cited as *Essays*.

4. Betsy Erkkila, *Whitman the Political Poet* (New York: Oxford University Press, 1989), v.

5. Gu Cheng, *Gu Cheng: Selected Essays*, 856.

Liu Shusen

Grass and Liquid Trees

The Cosmic Vision of Walt Whitman

ROGER ASSELINEAU

Walt Whitman thought of other titles (or subtitles) for *Leaves of Grass*: "What name? *Religious Canticles. These perhaps* ought to be the *brain*, the *living spirit* (elusive, indescribable, indefinite) of all the 'Leaves of Grass'" (*NUPM* 4:1357). Had he chosen *Religious Canticles* as his title, it would certainly have underscored the religious character of his book, and it is precisely this quality that I want to examine in my essay.

In July 1855 there suddenly occurred a "big bang" in American poetry. It was caused by the appearance of *Leaves of Grass*. Except for Emerson, few people realized it, but from then on, American poetry was not and could not be the same. The thick battalions of lines of more or less equal length were broken up and ceased to be the order of the day. It became possible to write sprawling lines of indefinite length. As Whitman himself said later: "The hawk, the seagull, have far more possess'd me than the canary or mocking-bird, / I have not felt to warble or trill, however sweetly" (*LG* 576).

Besides, in 1855 the reader also discovered that, for Whitman, there was no line of demarcation between traditional "poetic diction," as it was called, and everyday vocabulary and even the most technical terminology of modern industry. Whitman saw no reason either for limiting himself to descriptions of nature and ignoring the "Shapes of turbulent manly cities," as he was to call them the following year in "Song of the Broad-Axe" (*LG* 195).

Leaves of Grass was indeed an extraordinary and outlandish production. Was it prose? Was is poetry? There was not even an author's name on the title page, only a portrait. And he wore no poet's garb. He was dressed like an ordinary worker. The twelve pieces that composed the book bore no titles. It looked like a flow of lava after an eruption. The very title, *Leaves of Grass*, was unexpected. What was grass doing there? It is a most unpoetical subject, something banal, common, uninteresting, meant to be trodden upon, and yet it was the central subject of this strange book. We are told so at the beginning — these poems are an attempt to answer a child's impossible and baffling question: "*What is the grass?*" (*LG* 33), and grass grows all over the poems. The word occupies a full column in Edwin Harold Eby's *Concordance*.[1]

Whitman did not ask himself if grass was beautiful. That was not what counted. He conceived beauty as a mystic rather than a plastic quality. Beauty to him did not come from physical qualities but from the fact that "anything is but a part" of the great whole and consequently suggests the infinity of space and time and so is wonderful and a miracle. What counts is the spiritual quality behind and beyond material appearances.

What is grass? Whitman owns he does not know, and yet it is an important and unavoidable question, since grass grows all over the world, in all latitudes, and in the most unpromising places, even between the paving stones of the central yard of the Tombs, the sinister New York state jail. Whitman did not know it, but Melville did and made it grow under the nose of his dying hero Bartleby the Scrivener. It is a sort of living hieroglyph, meaning *ankh*, eternal life and hope, Melville suggests.[2] And this is indeed the meaning that Whitman also gives to grass: it is the materialization (the incarnation, to use a theological term) of the irresistible flow of life that circulates in all things throughout the world, a phenomenon which Henri Bergson described as "l'élan vital" in *L'Evolution créatrice*.[3] Whitman saw this impulse in the form of water (and sometimes of electricity). He felt its presence not only in grass but also inside trees, and he thus refers to "liquid trees," a most surprising phrase: "Earth of the slumbering and liquid trees!" he says in "Song of Myself," for the earth for him is both "solid and liquid" (*LG* 49, 222).

So Whitman could speak of the liquidity of *Leaves of Grass*. Liquidity is its quiddity, so to speak. I wish this liquidity had been analyzed by a compatriot of mine who was both a philosopher who specialized in the study of scientific methods and a very perceptive literary critic. His name was Gaston Bachelard. He was what Wordsworth called "a silent poet." He never wrote a line of poetry, but he read poems of all kinds with great gusto and enthusiasm. To him, a poet's imagination is not haunted by phalluses, as psychoanalysts would like us to believe. He thought that a poet's interior universe consists of images of air, fire, water, and earth,

Roger Asselineau

and they keep moving like a kaleidoscope. It is what he called the "material or dynamic imagination." The study of the methods of the proto-science called alchemy brought him into contact with prerational modes of thought and pre-Socratic systems, with Thales in particular, who believed that water was the primary stuff of which everything is made; with Heraclitus, who preferred to think it was fire; and with Empedocles, for whom the world resulted from a combination of these two elements plus earth. Whitman, of course, did not know the theories of these Greek philosophers, but he instinctively thought along the same lines. Unlike Empedocles and Bachelard, he did have a favorite element, and, as we have seen, it was water.

Grass, grows, green. The alliteration of these three words indicates an obscure existential kinship of the three things in the mind of the original speakers of the language, for grass inevitably and irrepressibly grows. It is synonymous with constant changes, movement, progress — in short, life. Whitman's poems reflect this restless hidden life. They are, he says, "subterranean sea-rills making for the sea" (*LG* 356). They are "Overtures sent to the solid out of the liquid," "from the sea of Time . . . eternity's music faint and far" (*LG* 357). All these images of water, ocean, time, and eternity were not consciously called up by the poet. They were not literary reminiscences either. They were not supplied by his fancy or his memory, but rather they sprang from the very depths of his imagination. They corresponded to lifelong obsessions, and this explains their recurrence.

Water in tangible form as rivers, seas, and oceans naturally occupies an important place in *Leaves of Grass*. After all, Whitman spent his childhood and youth on an island, Long Island, never far from the sea and, later, in Manhattan (he preferred the aboriginal name, Mannahatta, which means, according to him, "*shores where ever gayly dash the coming, going, hurrying sea waves*" [*LG* 507]). In Manhattan, he was also on an island, surrounded by two mighty tidal rivers, the Hudson and the East Rivers. All streets led to them, and he thus found water everywhere. It is no wonder that he guessed and felt the presence of water even when it was invisible in grass and trees. He was, as it were, a natural dowser, a water-diviner.

He lived in water both spiritually and physically. To be in more intimate contact with it, he often swam in the sea. He was no athletic swimmer, however, like the "beautiful gigantic swimmer swimming naked through the eddies of the sea," whose death he described in "The Sleepers" (*LG* 428).

He preferred to hug the shore and float lazily rather than swim. He surrendered to the caresses of the water, being, as he said, "the caresser of life," with "instant conductors" all over his body (*LG* 40, 57). He experienced voluptuous sensations:

> You sea! I resign myself to you also — I guess what you mean,
> I behold from the beach your crooked inviting fingers.
> . . . .
> Cushion me soft, rock me in billowy drowse,
> Dash me with amorous wet, I can repay you. (*LG* 49)

The sea thus "bath[ed] him in bliss," to use his own expression in "Proud Music of the Storm" (*LG* 407). The sea is love and life to him. It flows and runs and rushes perpetually.

Whereas he calls the land "my father" (a rather unflattering identification when one knows how negatively he usually rated his father), he again and again treats the sea as a universal mother: "the old mother sways her to and fro," "the fierce old mother incessantly moaning" (*LG* 260, 251). Sometimes she is even "the savage old mother" (*LG* 251), a rather sinister and ominous figure, but the sea is for him a kind of *Janus Bifrons* (a double-faced presence). One of its faces expresses love, while the other frowns and threatens, for the sea is both love and death. Whitman's thought about it follows a curious Hegelian dialectic. Thesis: the sea is life; antithesis: the sea is death; synthesis: death is not the cold and implacable male God of tradition but a *"lovely and soothing"* goddess (*LG* 335). The poet feels *"Lost in the loving floating ocean,"* he says in "When Lilacs Last in the Dooryard Bloom'd," *"Laved in the flood of thy bliss O death"* (*LG* 335). He aspired to sail on this ocean in his old age, thus spending all his life among "liquid" or "fluid" things, flying "those flights of a fluid and swallowing soul," as he said in "Song of Myself" (*LG* 65). The French poet Paul Claudel, who incidentally spent a number of years as a diplomat in China, used the same kind of water imagery and referred in particular to "l'âme soluble dans l'âme" (the soul soluble in the soul).

Though Whitman did not ignore the other elements, he made water triumph over them, because it was both material and fluid. It enabled him to keep his promise to write "the most spiritual poems" by making "the poems of materials" (*LG* 18). He was attracted to it as a child (see "There Was a Child Went Forth"), and it became the very substance of his dreams.

He lived in air, trod on the earth, but dreamed of water. It was the medium of his internal life, and it became a source of vital and ever-present images — images with a core of sensuous experience, for in a way, he could still hear through them the actual ripple of Long Island Sound or the howling storms that sometimes beat on the shores of Paumanok, both the melody and the strong rhythm of the ocean: "*The tones of unseen mystery, the vague and vast suggestion of the briny world, and the liquid-flowing syllables, . . . the melancholy rhythm*" (*LG* 3).

Water tends to become in *Leaves of Grass* an immaterial substance, a spirit. *Leaves of Grass* celebrates the apotheosis of water. The world is liquefied, so to speak. Everything flows toward the mystic ocean: "All, all toward the mystic ocean tending" (*LG* 357). His soul, as he points out in "Passage to India," is full of "Thoughts, silent thoughts, of Time and Space and Death, like waters flowing," and God is the "reservoir," the "fountain" from which they flow (*LG* 418, 419).

Ultimately, even God is liquid. Whitman could have entitled his book *Liquid Leaves of Grass* as early as 1855 since there were already "liquid trees" in the poem that was to become "Song of Myself," and he assigned an aquatic origin to all things, which, according to him, had cohered from a nebulous "float," as he called it — in other words, a sort of vapor floating in space. The world to him was essentially an "eternal float of solution" suspended "here and everywhere" (*LG* 164). He could have answered this to the child, but the child would probably have been little enlightened.

What is the grass? I have tried to bring together the main elements of Whitman's answer to the child, but this is not the end of the story, for we must not forget that Whitman is universally considered "the bard of democracy." It is surprising that he did not make the child also ask: what is democracy? But the child apparently was not interested. Yet even if Whitman gave religion priority over politics, he did not, even in 1855, neglect this other aspect of the world he lived in. After all, he was a journalist and a loyal supporter of the Democratic Party (until the Free Soil controversy of the 1850s), and he could not ignore and turn his back on what occupied such an important place in his everyday life. So the theme of democracy is hardly absent from the 1855 *Leaves of Grass*. In Eby's *Concordance*, the words "democracy" and "democratic" fill only half a column, but Whitman nonetheless already "utter[ed] the word Democratic, the word En-Masse" (he used this French word because revolutions were then a kind of French specialty)

(*LG* 1). He spoke, he also said, "the pass-word primeval" and gave "the sign of democracy" (*LG* 52). He even dared to rank democracy with religion, and he celebrated in "Starting from Paumanok," "The greatness of Love and Democracy, and the greatness of Religion" (*LG* 21).

But in 1855, for all his love of democracy, *Leaves of Grass* was above all the quiet affirmation of the existence of the "self" in the middle of a world teeming with multiple forms of life. It was, as a recent biographer of Whitman put it, the "Song of Himself."[4] He thus placed the individual above all. He was not interested in a leveling of all individuals and in their enforced equality. To avoid this, he exalted liberty to the point of anarchy. *"Resist much, obey little"* (*LG* 9), he recommended, for each individual, "a simple, separate person" (*LG* 525), is "not contain'd between [his] hat and boots" (*LG* 35), and he is not an empty entity, but a thing full of vital energy, like grass. A contemporary poet, Irving Feldman, taking up Whitman's image of grass, has rightly emphasized this vitality:

> and grass comes up
> singulars out of the earth
> lifting their spears and shouting *Ahhhh!*[5]

Each individual is part of the central energy of the world. He or she is an end in himself or herself, not a means to an end. Every individual must be respected. Whitman later developed this political principle in prose in *Democratic Vistas* under the name of "personalism" (prose is for politics and poetry for religion). To the end, Whitman made his reader aware of "the joyous, electric all" of the "Electric life forever at the centre" (*LG* 501, 483). He thus made *Leaves of Grass* a vibrant proclamation both of his pantheism and of his democratic faith.

Leaves of Grass was his *carte de visite*, his visiting card to posterity, as he said of the work of Champollion, the French Egyptologist who cracked the secret of the Egyptian hieroglyphs. For his part, Whitman cracked the secret of the hieroglyphs of the physical world that surrounded him and more particularly the hieroglyph of "grass," which was the key to all the others, and for this we remain grateful.

NOTES

1. Edwin Harold Eby, ed., *A Concordance of Walt Whitman's Leaves of Grass and Selected Prose Writings* (Seattle: University of Washington Press, 1955).

Roger Asselineau

2. Roger Asselineau, *The Transcendentalist Constant in American Literature* (New York: New York University Press, 1980), 3.

3. Henri Bergson, *L'Evolution créatrice* (Paris: F. Alcan, 1907).

4. Jerome Loving, *Walt Whitman: The Song of Himself* (Berkeley: University of California Press, 1999).

5. Irving Feldman, *Leaping Clear and Other Poems* (New York: Viking Press, 1976), 10.

Contributors

Roger Asselineau was professor emeritus at the University of Paris–Sorbonne at the time of his death on July 8, 2002. He served for nearly fifty years on the advisory editorial board of *The Collected Writings of Walt Whitman*, and his classic study of Whitman, *L'Evolution de Walt Whitman*, was published in France in 1954 and in a two-volume English translation as *The Evolution of Walt Whitman* (1960, 1962). An expanded edition of this work was published in one volume in 1999. He is the author of *The Transcendentalist Constant in American Literature* (1980) and the editor or author of numerous other books on American writers.

Sherry Ceniza is associate professor of English at Texas Tech University and the author of *Walt Whitman and Nineteenth-Century Women Reformers* (1998) as well as essays on Whitman in *Approaches to Teaching Whitman's Leaves of Grass* (1990), *The Cambridge Companion to Walt Whitman* (1995), and elsewhere.

Betsy Erkkila is the Henry S. Noyes Professor of English at Northwestern University and the author of *Walt Whitman among the French* (1980) and *Whitman the Political Poet* (1989) and the co-editor of *Breaking Bounds: Whitman and American Cultural Studies* (1996). She has published widely on American poets, literary history, and literary theory.

Ed Folsom is the F. Wendell Miller Distinguished Professor of English at the University of Iowa, where he edits the *Walt Whitman Quarterly Review*, edits the Iowa Whitman Series for the University of Iowa Press, and codirects the *Walt Whitman Archive*, an online research and teaching resource. He is the author of *Walt Whitman's Native Representations* (1994), the editor of *Walt Whitman: The Centennial Essays* (1994), and the co-editor of *Walt Whitman and the World* (1995), *Walt Whitman: The Measure of His Song* (1981, 1998), and *Major Authors on CD-ROM: Walt Whitman* (1997). He has published widely on nineteenth- and twentieth-century American poets, and he directed the "Whitman 2000" international conference.

Walter Grünzweig is professor and chair of American studies at Universität Dortmund in Germany. He is the author of many essays on Whitman and other American writers, and he wrote the definitive studies of Whitman's influence in German-speaking countries: *Walt Whitmann: Die deutschsprachige Rezeption als interkulturelles Phänomen* (1991) and *Constructing the German Walt Whitman* (1995).

Guiyou Huang is associate professor of English at Kutztown University and the author of *Whitmanism, Imagism, and Modernism in China and America* (1997). He wrote the chapter, "Whitman in China," in *Walt Whitman and the World* (1996), and he is the author or editor of books and essays on Asian American literature as well as the translator of numerous Chinese texts into English and English texts into Chinese.

M. Jimmie Killingsworth is professor of English at Texas A&M University and the author of *Whitman's Poetry of the Body* (1989) and *The Growth of Leaves of Grass: The Organic Tradition in Whitman Studies* (1993) and the coauthor of books on communication and ecocriticism. His many essays on Whitman have appeared in numerous journals and books, including *A Historical Guide to Walt Whitman* (2000).

Liu Rongqiang is associate professor of English at Hebei Normal University in China. He has published books and essays on American literature and English-language teaching and is currently completing a book on the use of English in international diplomacy.

Liu Shusen is professor of English at Peking University in China and was associate director of the "Whitman 2000" international conference. He has published books and essays on American literature, comparative literature, and translation studies and is currently completing a book on the Chinese translation of foreign literature from 1840 to 1919.

Robert K. Martin is professor of English at the University of Montreal. His classic study, *The Homosexual Tradition in American Literature* (1979), was published in an expanded edition in 1998. He is the editor of *The Continuing Presence of Walt Whitman* (1992) and the author or editor of books on Melville, American Gothic, and other subjects.

James E. Miller Jr. is the Helen A. Regenstein Professor of Literature Emeritus at the University of Chicago and the author of *A Critical Guide to Leaves of Grass* (1957), *Walt Whitman* (1962; updated edition, 1990), *The American Quest for a Supreme Fiction: Whitman's Legacy in the Personal Epic* (1979), and *Leaves of Grass: America's Lyric-Epic of Self and Democracy* (1992); the editor of *Whitman's "Song of Myself": Origin, Growth, and Meaning* (1964) and the Riverside edition of Whitman's *Complete Poetry and Selected Prose* (1959); and the co-editor of *Start with the Sun: Studies in the Whitman Tradition* (1960). He has published books and articles on a wide range of American authors.

Joel Myerson is Carolina Distinguished Professor of American Literature at the University of South Carolina and the author or editor of many works on American nineteenth-century writers. He has compiled the definitive bibliography of Whitman's work, *Walt Whitman: A Descriptive Bibliography* (1993), and has edited *The Walt Whitman Archive* (1993) and *Whitman in His Own Time* (1991), published in an expanded edition in 2000. His essays on Whitman have appeared in numerous journals and books, including *Walt Whitman: The Centennial Essays* (1994).

Ou Hong is professor of English at Zhongshan University in China. He has published essays on Whitman and Chinese literature, has done research on Gary Snyder and Chinese culture, and is currently working on a book entitled *The Double-Faced Muse: Literature in the Transitional Periods.*

Kenneth M. Price is the Hillegas Professor of English at the University of Nebraska, Lincoln, where he codirects the *Walt Whitman Archive*, an online research and teaching resource. He is the author of *Whitman and Tradition* (1990), the editor of *Walt Whitman: The Contemporary Reviews* (1996), and the co-editor of *Dear Brother Walt: The Letters of Thomas Jefferson Whitman* (1984) and *Major Authors on CD-ROM: Walt Whitman* (1997). He has published widely on American periodicals and American writers and is currently completing a book on Whitman and popular culture.

M. Wynn Thomas is professor of English at the University of Wales, College at Swansea. The author of several books on Welsh writers and many essays on Whitman in journals and books, including *Walt Whitman and the World* (1996), he is the author of *The Lunar Light of Whitman's Poetry* (1987) and the editor of *Wrenching Times: A Selection of Whitman's Wartime Poetry* (1992), as well as the translator of a selection of Whitman's poetry into Welsh, *Dail Glaswellt* (1995).

Wang Ning, professor of English and comparative literature at Tsinghua University in China, is secretary-general of the International Association for Literary Theory and Criticism and director of the Research Institute for Postmodern Studies. His publications include books and essays on American literature, Chinese literature, and translation studies.

Index

Whitman's works appear in a separate section at the end of the regular index entries. Numbers in italics indicate illustrations.

velopment of film technology, 36–40; and early films, 40–46; and Free Soil, 149, 225; and global diaspora, 162–163; and globalization, 20, 197, 205–206; and Gu Cheng, xx–xxi, 208–220; and Guo Moruo, xix–xx, 172–185, 190–195, 199, 204–205, 208; and hieroglyphics, 65n; and homosexuality, xvi–xvii, 51–62, 73, 97–104, 105–109, 119–121, 125–128, 132–134, 137–138; and illustrated texts of his work, 71–95; and the imagery of grass, xxii, 201, 221–222, 225–226; and the imagery of water and fluidity, xxii, 222–225; and immigration, 148, 160–162, 165–168, 170; influence on Chinese poetry, xix–xxi, 172–220; internationalism in tension with his chauvinism, 163–166; and Japan, 161, 173; and laissez-faire capitalism, 135; and late twentieth-century films, 50–63; and F. O. Matthiessen, 97–104; and Mark Merlis's *American Studies*, 97–104; and mid twentieth-century films, 46–50; and millenarianism, 151–155; and modernity, 197–206; and nineteenth-century New York City politics, 147–157; and the "normal," xv, 28–34; and personification, 14–17, 22–23; and photography, 37–40, 71; and postcolonial studies, xiv, 145; and postmodernism, 198, 199, 200; and Ezra Pound, 9–10; and public love, 118–119, 121–122, 131–134; and the public sphere, xvii, 105, 118–120, 132–133, 139n; and the relationship between democracy, sexuality, and love, 115–138; and religion, viii, 27–28, 29, 221, 225–226; as "revolutionist," 149–156; and

romanticism, 198, 199, 201, 202, 205; and sexuality, xvi–xvii, xix, 1, 29–30, 51–63, 73–74, 83–84, 89–95, 97–104, 105–114, 218; and slavery, 84, 85, 87, 89; and statistics, 28–32; and technology, 179; views on African Americans, 84, 170; views on Asia, 159; views on China, vii–viii. *See also* titles of individual works at the end of this index.

Whitman's Men, 73
Whittier, John Greenleaf, 17
Widmann, J. V., 34n
Wiebe, Robert H., 110–111; *Self-Rule*, 110–111
Williams, Francis Howard, vii
Williams, Robin, 50, 54
Williams, William Carlos, 9
Wills, Garry, 141n
Wilt, Napier, 3, 7
With Honors, 50
Wood, Fernando, xvii, 147–156
Woolf, Virginia, 205
Wordsworth, William, 222
World War II, 9
Wyne, Kevin, viii

Xie Ye, 210
Xin Qiji, viii
Xu Zhimo, xix, 199

Young, Robert, 49
Youth's Companion, 72
Yu Pingbo, 184

Zabel, Morton D., 3
Zapata-Whelen, Carol, 164
Zhang-Kubin, Suizi, 211, 214
Zhao Luorui, xii, xiii, xxi, 2–13; translation of Whitman's *Leaves of Grass*, xii, 2, 4–8, 13
Zhou Zuoren, 183

Zhu Donglin, 206n
Zhu Ziqing, 184
Zhuang-tzu, 180

Zola, Émile, 198
Zong Baihua, xix, 175, 181, 185

WORKS BY WHITMAN

The Iowa Whitman Series